RUPERT MURDOCH

ALSO BY JEROME TUCCILLE

Wall Street Blues

Trump

Kingdom

How to Profit from the Wall Street Mergers

Inside the Underground Economy

The New Tax Law and You

Dynamic Investing

Mind Over Money

The Optimist's Guide to Making Money in the 1980's

*Everything the Beginner Needs to Know
to Invest Shrewdly*

Who's Afraid of 1984?

Here Comes Immortality

It Usually Begins with Ayn Rand

Radical Libertarianism

RUPERT MURDOCH

by
Jerome Tuccille

DONALD I. FINE, INC.
New York

Copyright © 1989, 1990 by Jerome Tuccille

Library of Congress Cataloging-in-Publication Data

Tuccille, Jerome.
Rupert Murdoch / by Jerome Tuccille.
p.   cm.
Includes index.
ISBN 1-55611-224-6 (pbk.)
1. Murdoch, Rupert, 1931–   . 2. Publishers and publishing—
Australia—Biography.   3. Newspaper publishing—History—20th
century.   4. Publishers and publishing—Biography.   5. Broadcasting—
Biography.   I. Title.
Z533.3.M87T8 1991
070.5'092—dc20
[B]   90-55021
                                                              CIP

Manufactured in the United States of America
10 9 8 7 6 5 4 3 2 1

DESIGNED BY IRVING PERKINS ASSOCIATES

TO
MARIE,
JERRY
AND
CHRISTINE
WITH LOVE

Contents

Acknowledgments

THANKS FIRST and foremost to Rupert Murdoch, who spent time with the author discussing his values and goals despite a busy schedule, while he was in the midst of reorganizing the financial structure of his empire. His legendary life and accomplishments on three continents inspired me to take on this project.

Thanks also to those close associates of Murdoch and others familiar with his personal life and business dealings who spoke to me either on or off the record. Where I could, I have quoted them and identified them by name. Those who requested anonymity are identified simply as "a friend of Murdoch" or "an associate of Murdoch."

I would like to thank my research associate, Geri Shapiro, who contributed a great deal of her time and labor to this effort. Geri was particularly successful in establishing lines

ACKNOWLEDGMENTS

of communication to the Murdoch organization independent of my own sources.

I would also like to thank all those who contributed in any way to my research for the book. Some supplied anecdotes and information, others in the financial field discussed fairly arcane accounting rules and tax regulations that are important for anyone looking to understand why Rupert Murdoch is so successful.

In addition to the dozens of interviews conducted by the author, the following books were helpful in supplying background material on Murdoch, especially for his earlier years: *Citizen Murdoch,* by Thomas Kiernan (Dodd, Mead & Company, 1986); *Good Times, Bad Times,* by Harold Evans (Atheneum, 1984); *The Life and Death of the Press Barons,* by Piers Brendon (Atheneum, 1983); and *Arrogant Aussie,* by Michael Leapman (Lyle Stuart, 1985).

A number of newspaper and magazine articles were also extremely valuable. They included: "Murdoch's Global Power Play," by William H. Meyers, The New York Times Magazine (June 12, 1988); "Anna, the Other Murdoch," by Cynthia Cotts, The Illustrated London News (August 1988); "A Fistful of Dollars," by Gail Sheehy, Rolling Stone (July 14, 1977); "Crocodile Povich," by Maura Sheehy, Manhattan, Inc. (April 1989); "The Magnate from Down Under: an Interview with Rupert Murdoch," Gannett Center Journal (Winter 1989); " 'Monster' Entrepreneurs and 'Builder' Entrepreneurs," by Richard J. MacDonald, Gannett Center Journal (Winter 1989); "Out-'Fox'-ing the Nets: Barry Diller Stalks His Prey," by Betsey Sharkey, Adweek (April 24, 1989); and "Rae Has Ambitious Plans for Fox News," by Adam Buckman, Electronic Media (January 23, 1989).

ACKNOWLEDGMENTS

SPECIAL NOTE: Unless otherwise indicated, all quotes were obtained in interviews conducted by the author.

All figures mentioned are in U.S. dollars unless stated otherwise.

Introduction

MY PURPOSE in writing this book was to shed light on the changes now occurring in the field of media and communications—as well as on the individual most instrumental in bringing them about, Rupert Murdoch. More than anyone else, he has set the pace others are following.

This book covers his entire life and times, from his start as a young boy in Australia to the present day. I have managed to uncover details of his early life not included in previous biographies, but the bulk of the story concentrates on the past few years since the last Murdoch biography appeared. During this period Murdoch has succeeded in increasing the value of his empire sixfold. He has taken unprecedented risks and accomplished more in terms of financial expansion than he did in the first thirty years of his career.

Rupert Murdoch has been called many things, some good,

some bad. Above all, however, he is the Citizen Kane of our time. And much more.

Citizen Kane, portrayed by Orson Welles in the movie of the same name, was based on the life of William Randolph Hearst, the leading press lord of his day. Rupert Murdoch's empire extends beyond newspapers into the worlds of magazine and book publishing, network and satellite cable television, and includes an airline, a hotel reservations service, as well as a sheep farm in the Australian outback. It engulfs much of the globe—his native Australia, the United States, Great Britain and continental Europe, and the Orient.

Murdoch's communications empire was estimated at about $12 billion as this book went to press. By comparison, Hearst's empire, adjusted for inflation, would have been worth about $660 million in 1989; Joseph Pulitzer, the press lord who died in 1911, left an estate with combined assets totaling approximately $280 million in today's dollars. No single individual has ever wielded as much power over the media as Rupert Murdoch does today.

The United States contributed 42 percent of the revenue for Murdoch's treasury in 1988, Australia and the Pacific Basin 30 percent and Great Britain 28 percent. Among the various companies Murdoch controls, his newspapers brought in 43 percent of his total revenue, filmed entertainment 20 percent, magazines 10 percent, television 9 percent, commercial printing 4 percent, and 14 percent was derived from other operations, including his airline, a computer service firm, a wool export company and a record business.

In the United States Rupert Murdoch owns the 20th Century Fox Film Corporation, Fox Broadcasting, the Boston *Herald,* the San Antonio *Express-News,* New York magazine, the Star, New Woman, TV Guide, major television stations across the country, book publishers such as Harper & Row, Salem House and Zondervan, and scores of other publications. His interests in Great Britain include the *Times*, the *News of the World*, the *Sun*, Times Books and William Collins & Sons, Sky Channel, Reuters and Pearson P.L.C. And in the country of his birth Murdoch controls some 60 percent of the total newspaper circulation, plus television stations and Ansett, the nation's second-largest airline.

As the driving force behind the most far-reaching communications empire in existence, Murdoch can claim to be one of the most powerful men on earth. Certainly, no one is in a better position than he to influence public opinion throughout the globe—a fact his critics have been complaining about for some time now. The fact that he has accomplished this largely on his own, after starting out with a modest inheritance from his father, is a testament to his shrewd business and negotiating skills.

The story of Rupert Murdoch is more than the saga of a single individual. He stands at the center of a communications revolution that is reshaping the way we receive our information. Data is now transmitted from one corner of the earth to the other with lightning speed. Financial trading is linked globally, with markets in Tokyo and Hong Kong tied inextricably to those in London, New York and Sydney. All this is made possible by modern technology—a technology that connects the worlds of computers, satellites, telecommunications and print journalism as they never have been before.

Whether Murdoch is a force for good or evil in this revolution is something you will decide for yourself by the time you finish this book.

INTRODUCTION

But no one will deny that a genuine media revolution is taking place. And that Rupert Murdoch is a true revolutionary in the strictest sense of the word: He is the primary mover behind the most far-reaching changes affecting all our lives today.

To a great extent, the most exciting part of the Rupert Murdoch story has only recently begun.

Part One

PRESS
BARON

Chapter
One

FIFTH AVENUE in the Eighties is home to some of the richest and most powerful families in New York City. Solid old buildings sit like granite fortresses across the street from Central Park. Trees line both sides of the avenue, limousines and town cars occupy the parking spaces in front of the buildings, many with their engines idling and their drivers at the ready.

Rupert Murdoch's triplex apartment, where he lives with his novelist wife Anna and their three children, commands an enviable view of the reservoir in Central Park, as well as the towering West Side skyline. The Murdochs moved here at the end of 1983 after selling their Fifth Avenue duplex twenty blocks to the south.

Murdoch was not in the best of moods at the beginning of 1988. He had just returned from the West Coast after visiting one of his companies, 20th Century Fox, and he was preoccupied with legislation introduced apparently at the urging of Senator Edward M. Kennedy of Massachusetts that Murdoch felt was directed primarily at him.

The legislation was actually originated by Senator Ernest F. Hollings of South Carolina, who was then the chairman of the Senate Commerce Committee. After consulting with Kennedy, Hollings attached a measure to a catchall appropriations bill banning cross-ownership of newspapers and television stations in the same city. Since Murdoch owned the Boston *Herald* and WFXT-TV in Boston, and the New York *Post* and WNYW-TV in New York, he was perhaps more affected by the bill than anyone else. If he failed to find a suitable buyer, he would be forced either to sell or shut down one of his holdings in each city.

"The process was an outrage," Murdoch said to William H. Meyers, a reporter for the New York *Times*. It was an exercise, according to Murdoch, in "liberal totalitarianism."

"I was glad to do it," Hollings said, according to the New York *Times* of January 1, 1988. The same article quoted him as saying that his legislation was "aimed directly" at Murdoch. However, on January 9, 1989, Jenny Holiday, Senator Kennedy's press deputy, denied that Kennedy had targeted Murdoch exclusively. Hollings later amended his own statement by saying that he opposed cross-ownership "on principle."

There had been bad blood between Murdoch and the senior senator from Massachusetts ever since 1980 when Murdoch endorsed Jimmy Carter in the New York Democratic presidential primary. The Boston *Herald,* which is owned by the politically conservative media lord, had been bashing both Massachusetts senators—Kennedy and John F. Kerry—for their liberal voting records. Kennedy's press deputy told the author that the attacks had nothing to do with Kennedy's

4

support of the Hollings bill; he simply felt that banning cross-ownership was in "the best interests of Boston and the best interest of the First Amendment."

Not surprisingly, New York Senators Alfonse M. D'Amato and Daniel Patrick Moynihan felt differently about the matter. D'Amato was particularly vocal, stating at the time that he was "absolutely outraged that this was not brought up in committee . . . a matter of this importance should have been brought to the table." Moynihan agreed, saying, "They should have told us—they damned well should." During the ensuing weeks, both senators tried unsuccessfully to reverse the legislation.

On January 10, 1989, Zenia Mucha, D'Amato's press secretary, claimed the matter was still of concern to the senator, "although it's not the big issue today it was then. If it comes up again the senator will fight to change it." Brian Connolly, Senator Moynihan's press deputy, was a bit more vague. "Senator Moynihan's main concern was keeping the *Post* from closing," he said. Since the New York *Post* remained open after Murdoch sold it in the spring of 1988, Moynihan apparently lost interest in the issue.

Ironically enough, the unions at the New York *Post* found themselves lining up on the side of the conservative Murdoch.

"I feel outraged about the action of the Congress," said George E. McDonald, president of the Allied Printing Trades Council, which includes all the newspaper's unions, according to the New York *Times* of January 1, 1988. "They're supposed to be trying to preserve jobs and newspapers, not destroy them."

The issue was still very much alive a year later. Barbara Yuncker, administrator of the New York *Post*'s Guild Insurance Fund, said, "It wasn't a matter of Murdoch's merit, but a matter of fair is fair. He was the only one to whom the law applied. The Constitution . . . forbids special legislation of that sort . . . Other publishers in his two markets did have cross-ownership which was protected by being grandfathered. This was putting him at special disadvantage vis-à-vis his competitors, when in fact the provision of the original law was meant to encourage competition."

To comply with the cross-ownership ban, Murdoch placed his Boston television station in an independent trust, and he sold the New York *Post* to New York real estate developer Peter S. Kalikow. He won a moral victory of sorts on March 29, 1988, when a federal appeals court ruled that Congress had unconstitutionally singled him out in the legislation. "The Hollings amendment strikes at Mr. Murdoch with the precision of a laser beam," read the opinion, which was written by Judge Stephen F. Williams.

The ruling came too late to affect the sale of the *Post*, but it did cast a cloud of doubt over the future of the legislation.

The struggle was a bitter one for Murdoch, who, according to a New York *Times* report, said later, "I feel depressed. This will be the first time I've lived in a city with no newspaper going on around me."

Unwelcome as the battle was, Murdoch is no stranger to controversy; it has followed him, in one form or another, most of his life. This was only the latest skirmish in a continuing battle with political figures in Australia, Great Britain and the United States.

In 1980, Murdoch testified before the Senate Banking Committee on the propriety of a low-cost loan he received on the same day he had lunch with President Jimmy Carter to help finance the purchase of jetliners from Boeing.

In 1975 his newspapers' attacks on Gough Whitlam, the left-wing prime minister of Australia, were instrumental in toppling the Labor Party government from power.

In 1969 he incited a storm of controversy in Great Britain by publishing the memoirs of Christine Keeler, the call girl whose liaison with defense minister John Profumo six years earlier had brought the Conservative government of Harold Macmillan near ruin.

Rupert Murdoch was absolved of any wrongdoing in the 1980 loan controversy, and he eventually emerged unscathed from his other contretemps, but these episodes and more like them have created strong feelings among his enemies and most ardent supporters alike.

"Basically I like the man," said one of his aides, who requested anonymity. "He's not the smoothest man in the world. At times he's gruff, but he's also honest and charming when he wants to be. You either like him or not. There's no in-between with Rupert."

No in-between. Politically, emotionally, journalistically, Rupert Murdoch has always been a man of extremes. From the time he was a youth, he was determined not to trod the middle ground.

Chapter
Two

WINSTON CHURCHILL reportedly once said, "Whoever is not a socialist at twenty has no heart; whoever is not a conservative at forty has no brain."

The American poet Robert Frost had a different perspective on the subject. In his poem "Precaution" he writes:

> *I never dared be radical when young*
> *For fear it would make me conservative when old.*

Both the English statesman and the American poet could well have had Murdoch in mind when they bequeathed those sentiments to posterity. The young Australian was so far to the left politically that he was known alternately as Red Rupert and Rupert the Red at Oxford University in the early fifties, but twenty years later he had metamorphosed into a supporter of Richard Nixon, Margaret Thatcher and Ronald Reagan.

Born Keith Rupert Murdoch on March 11, 1931, on a farm thirty miles south of Melbourne, Australia, he was the second child and the only boy in a line of four children. The family property was called Cruden Farm after the Scottish village from which both parents' families had emigrated. Keith Rupert Murdoch was the namesake of both his father, Keith Murdoch, and his maternal grandfather, Rupert Greene, who was only slightly older than his son-in-law. Keith Murdoch married Rupert Greene's daughter Elisabeth in 1928 when he was nearly forty-two and she was only nineteen. Their only son was known by his middle name shortly after he was born.

"I think it was a very normal childhood," his mother was quoted in a February 9, 1981, New York *Times* interview. "not in any way elaborate or an overindulged one. I suppose he was lucky to be brought up in attractive—you could say esthetic—surroundings."

The same article described the house at Cruden Farm as an imposing stone building faced with colonial-style pillars. It stands at the end of a long drive of ghost gum trees. Dame Elisabeth was interviewed in the drawing room. A sheet of music by Bach was open on the grand piano, an Augustus John painting hung on the opposite wall, books on ornithology adorned the coffee table. The Murdochs were Presbyterians, and his grandfather was moderator of the church in Australia. Among other skills, Rupert learned to ride horses at the age of five.

Young Rupert graduated from Geelong Grammar, an Australian boarding school, in 1949, then was admitted to Worcester College at Oxford University, where he is said to have installed a bust of his political hero, Lenin, on the windowsill of his room. According to Thomas Kiernan, one of Murdoch's earlier biographers, Rupert (or Rupe as his close friends called him) considered himself to be "a normal, red-blooded college student who had many friends, chased girls, went on the usual drinking binges, engaged in slapdash horseplay, tried at sports, and never had enough money, no doubt due to his gambling."

The gambling part of his nature was apparently inherited from his grandfather Rupert Greene, who was reputed to have been something of a gambler and sportsman himself. Rupert's own father was quite the opposite—conservative, frugal, a compulsive worker devoted to his business. By the time his son was off in England pursuing his studies at Oxford, Keith Murdoch was an established newspaperman in his own land, the owner of a string of dailies that included the *Herald* in Melbourne, the *Courier-Mail* in Brisbane and the *News* and *Sunday Mail* in Adelaide.

The death of Keith Murdoch following a heart attack in the fall of 1952, at the age of sixty-six, imposed a mantle of responsibility prematurely on his only son's shoulders. Rupert returned to Australia to find his father's estate, unexpectedly, in a state of some confusion. Though he was considered well-off by those who knew him, the bulk of Keith Murdoch's wealth was tied up in his Adelaide and Brisbane newspapers, which were still struggling financially. Despite the extent of his holdings, he owned little stock in the extremely successful *Herald*, from which he had all but retired just before his death. The administrators of the estate suggested selling the struggling newspapers to raise money for estate taxes that threatened to wipe out what was left of his wealth.

The matter was eventually resolved when Keith's widow found a buyer for the Brisbane paper, and agreed at her son's urging to hang on to the two in Adelaide. Rupert served a brief apprenticeship on Lord Beaverbrook's *Daily Express* in London, then returned home to take over as publisher of the Adelaide *News* and *Sunday Mail.* The year was 1953, and he had just turned twenty-two.

"Rupert was determined not to repeat his father's mistakes," a friend of Murdoch said, speaking off the record. "No one would ever gain control over his business, and he's followed that practice right along."

In an interview published in the Winter 1989 issue of the Gannett Center Journal, Murdoch was asked about his allegedly "stormy" relationship with his father, and whether he would have pursued the newspaper business if his father had not been in that business.

"I never had a stormy relationship with my father at all," Murdoch said. "He died when I was only twenty-one and away in Europe at college, and I had enormous respect for him. He was a great journalist who started as a reporter and finally became the chief executive of a company that he built, but was not a large shareholder of. He was able to buy a little paper in Adelaide which he left to my sisters and me. But I was brought up in a publishing home, a newspaper man's home, and was excited by that, I suppose. I saw that life at close range, and after the age of ten or twelve never really considered any other. Because if you're in the media, particularly newspapers, you are in the thick of all the interesting things that are going on in a community . . . I can't imagine any other life that one would want to dedicate oneself to."

Murdoch expressed similar sentiments to me in 1989. "I sensed the excitement and the power," he said. "Not raw power, but the ability to influence at least the agenda of what was going on. I think it led me to grow up being very idealistic, and I've always been much more interested in the content of our newspapers, political positions day to day, the thrill of communicating with people through words than I am in the pure business aspects. So, the idea of communicating news and ideas, and of transmitting other people's ideas is still the fascination. It's a lot more fun than distributing popular entertainment.

"But, you've got to understand," Murdoch continued, "that my father—who was a great journalist—was not really an owner, and I started out all over again. Just a tiny paper in Adelaide that he started. And I guess I was always reaching up to be bigger than just a little paper in Adelaide, to have enough financial muscle to be able to buy your own writers and your own cartoonists, and that led us to buying or starting newspapers beyond Adelaide. And when you get on that, it's a bit of a treadmill."

At the time, Adelaide boasted a population of nearly half a million, and it was Australia's third-largest city after Sydney and Melbourne. When Rupert arrived on the scene the *News,* an afternoon daily, was barely profitable. The young publisher immersed himself in the daily operations of the newspaper business, doing everything from writing headlines and rearranging the layout to dirtying his fingers in the typesetting and printing rooms.

"Rupe was doing everything in those days," one of my sources continued. "You Americans have an expression for it—a one-armed paperhanger. Well, that could have been invented to describe Murdoch."

According to the same person, Murdoch worked feverishly, writing stories, headlines, designing the layout, setting type. There wasn't an aspect of the business he overlooked. Despite objections from other board members, as well as the nominal editor of the *News,* Murdoch insisted on doing things his own way, and the formula worked. Within a few years he merged the *Sunday Mail* with its biggest rival, the *Advertiser,* and managed to turn the *News* into a huge success. Many observers criticized his style of journalism and his manner of reporting the news, but no one could argue with the results.

His success in Adelaide gave him the confidence he needed to entertain notions of expansion. Again, fighting resistance from more cautious board members of News Limited, the parent corporation, he initiated a search for new acquisitions. The only paper available at a suitable price was the *Sunday Times* of Perth, a city of only 350,000, situated on the west coast of Australia, six hours by air from Adelaide. The *Sunday Times* was hemorrhaging money, but the ambitious young Australian was determined to have a go at it.

"As I recall," said a long-time friend of Murdoch, who has worked for him both in the United States and Australia, "he borrowed heavily against the assets of News Limited to raise the purchase price—$400,000 I think it was. He has always and always will, I think, operate with OPM—other people's money."

Murdoch bought the *Sunday Times* in 1956 and flew to Perth every Friday to oversee production. The existing newspaper, he decided, was too tame, too tepid. Its readers would respond more favorably to a publication that put them in closer touch with the outside world. He sacked most of the staff and replaced them with others who agreed with his approach to successful journalism.

"Rupert's a tremendous sacker," Maxwell Newton, a syndicated financial columnist who has known Murdoch for over twenty-five years, said in a 1989 interview. "He sacked me in 1965 and it did me a very great turn. It also did me a very great turn when he rehired me and brought me up to the States."

Murdoch tore the *Sunday Times* apart, rewrote headlines, changed the layout and presented the citizens of Perth with a bolder, more colorful newspaper than they had known. Again his formula worked. In short order, circulation increased and losses turned into profits. Rupert Murdoch, still barely twenty-five years old, had vindicated himself with the more cautious board members of News Limited and was beginning to win their grudging approval.

"He married Patricia that year," another associate of Murdoch said, "but he won't talk about it with anyone, you know." He was referring to Murdoch's first wife, Patricia Booker. His only child from the marriage, a daughter named Prudence, was born three years later, but from all accounts the marriage was an unhappy one and it ended in divorce in 1965.

So far, the young newspaperman's successes had occurred in the minor leagues of Adelaide and Perth. Murdoch felt he was ready for the more challenging, rough-and-tumble newspaper world of Sydney, as well as the intensely competitive field of television. Television licensing in Australia is regulated by the Australian Broadcasting Board, which is a rough equivalent of the FCC in the United States. After a good deal of political infighting, he managed to acquire TV-9—a station in Adelaide—in 1958. Within a year it was generating handsome profits and advertising revenues for the coffers of News Limited.

But his greatest challenge was Sydney, and it was there that most of his critics expected him to fail. Three powerful dynasties—the Fairfax, Packer and Norton families—dominated the newspaper market in Australia's premier city. The major papers were the *Morning Herald* and *Evening Sun* owned by The Fairfax Company; the *Daily Telegraph* and *Sunday Telegraph* owned by the Packers; and a tabloid called the *Mirror*, a competitor of the *Sun*, which was owned by Ezra Norton who, alone among the major players, was looking to sell.

Competitive with one another as the three Sydney dynasties were, they had established a truce of sorts by this time, with each maintaining a comfortable niche within the overall market. Their common concern was preventing the young upstart from the hinterlands from establishing a toehold on their turf. Norton sold the *Mirror* to the Fairfax family, his closest rival, which was anxious to keep it out of Packer's hands and avoid upsetting the balance of power. But by 1960 the *Mirror* was such a drain on Fairfax resources that the family put out feelers for a new buyer—anyone but Packer, whose *Daily Telegraph* already competed with the *Morning Herald*.

Enter Rupert Murdoch. The Fairfax organization sold the *Mirror* to him, the lesser of two evils in its eyes, for $4,000,-000, a princely sum at the time to the twenty-nine-year-old Murdoch. There was a touch of irony in his purchase of the *Mirror* since his favorite newspaper when he was a student in England was the *Daily Mirror* of London, and he entertained schoolboy dreams of buying it one day.

Murdoch worked harder than ever before, remodeling his Sydney tabloid along the lines of London's *Daily Mirror*, the biggest-selling newspaper in the world, in an effort to turn it around. His hard work started to pay off slowly, and his incipient success put him in direct conflict with Frank Packer, the fiery leader of the Packer family.

"Packer was a tough old bastard," according to Frank Devine, the editor of one of Murdoch's newspapers, the *Australian*.

Indeed he was. I happened to be living in Sydney in the early 1960s, and I remember Frank Packer as a colorful figure around town, an ex-boxer with an earthy sense of humor to say the least. Packer declared a circulation war on Murdoch's revamped *Mirror* and vowed, according to Murdoch biographer Thomas Kiernan, to send the young interloper "back to Adelaide with his fookin' tail between his fookin' legs."

Young Rupert accepted the challenge and went head to head against the powerful, politically conservative Packer. It was the greatest gamble of his life so far, and the ensuing battle was observed closely by the entire city which, itself, was still struggling for an identity of its own. At the time, Sydney was a city of two million people in a country of scarcely more than ten million. The famous Sydney Opera House was not yet completed, and there was more than a touch of small-town provincialism beneath its metropolitan veneer. (I had moved there for a stay of six months after a stint at the Wall Street *Journal,* and was writing occasional articles for the *Morning Herald*—reflections of an American visitor, a novelty in 1961.)

In the end, neither man lost. Murdoch held his own against the combative Packer, increasing the *Mirror*'s circulation and eventually putting it into the black. (Murdoch's memory was long, however, and a decade later he would have his revenge when he outmaneuvered the Fairfax organization and acquired the *Telegraph* from the aging Frank Packer. By then, the *Mirror* had evolved into Sydney's best-selling afternoon newspaper.)

Despite their political differences—Murdoch was still on the left—Murdoch and Packer were more alike in style and temperament than either wanted to admit. They were able to find common ground when Packer sold Murdoch a 25 percent interest in his television stations in Sydney and Melbourne, enabling his young challenger to break into the tightly regulated and highly lucrative big-city markets. Murdoch would later remember the older man with some touch of fondness as "an amusing rascal," according to Kiernan.

With the success of the *Mirror* firmly established, Murdoch grew restless for new conquests. His operations in Sydney, Adelaide and Perth gave him something no other newspaperman in Australia had: printing capability throughout the length and breadth of the entire country. Until this time, Australia had very little of a national identity, and most publishers considered the creation of a successful national newspaper to be little more than an idealistic dream, all but impossible to achieve.

Murdoch disagreed. He saw he had the geographical presence to bring it off. He was evolving politically and wanted to have a stronger influence on the policies of his country. The right kind of national newspaper could succeed, he reasoned. Perhaps a cross between the New York *Times* and the Wall Street *Journal.* And so the *Australian* was born.

Chapter
Three

IN 1965 Maxwell Newton was the managing editor of a Fairfax publication, the Financial Review of Sydney. Murdoch hired the thirty-five-year-old editor to run his national daily newspaper, commencing an on-again, off-again relationship with Newton that has survived until this day. Max Newton is now based in Boca Raton, Florida, where he moved in 1988. His financial column is syndicated throughout the Murdoch system and elsewhere, appearing in the New York *Post*, Boston *Herald*, Chicago *Sun-Times*, Melbourne *Herald*, the *Australian*, South China *Morning Post* and other newspapers.

He was also president of MaxNews Financial Network, a financial consulting and publishing firm he established in 1982. He described his relationship with Murdoch to me as a rewarding one, though not without its hazards.

"He can be gruff," he said. "If you get on the wrong side of him, all he has to do is put a cross next to your name and you cease to exist."

According to Newton, the name of the national daily originated with Murdoch. Such names as the National *Inquirer,* Canberra *Star,* and National *Chronicle* were considered until Rupert finally said, "What about calling it the *Australian?"*

And so the *Australian* it was, and remains today. The newspaper has been described as "the other side of Rupert Murdoch"—a tony journal of financial and political affairs that stands in marked contrast to his hugely popular tabloids on the other end of the spectrum. Despite the fact that it lost a considerable amount of money, to his credit Murdoch kept the newspaper running until it finally showed a profit some fifteen years later, and today it flourishes under the editorial guidance of long-time Murdoch associate, Frank Devine.

It was around this time that a young cub reporter—a cadet in Australian parlance—named Anna Torv was assigned to the staff of the *Australian.* Rupert first met her in 1961 when she was seventeen and working for the *Mirror* in Sydney. She interviewed her boss for the newspaper, and Rupert and Anna hit it off at once.

"I had probably seen him around the office," Anna told Cynthia Cotts, who did an article on her for the August 1988 issue of The Illustrated London News, "but, as you know yourself, a lowly cadet sees very little—you're lucky if you see the editor. You're usually being sent out by the finance editor to buy iced buns with extra butter on the side."

Murdoch's marriage was foundering badly at this time, and he and Anna began dating in earnest. In 1989 Anna was a striking woman in her midforties with a mane of lush blonde hair. When I spoke to her she had already published two novels and was finishing a third.

But, in 1965, her literary ambitions were still a distant

dream. She was born in Scotland, the daughter of an Estonian who had fled to Scotland during World War II, and a Scottish mother. The Torvs emigrated to Australia when Anna was nine. After attending a Roman Catholic convent school, she studied acting, then gave that up for her job on the *Mirror*. She and Rupert, who is thirteen years her senior, continued their courtship for five years until they married in April 1967, two years after his divorce from Patricia.

The launching of the *Australian* took up much of Murdoch's time between 1965 and 1968. But even though he failed to turn it into a financial success during this period, his other operations were generating more than enough money to make him a wealthy man. He acquired a yacht, a sheep and cattle farm fifty miles from Canberra and other publishing interests in New Zealand. More and more he was beginning to think about expanding his horizons beyond the South Pacific. On his periodic visits to the United States to buy programs for his television stations, he struck up a friendship with Leonard Goldenson, the head of the American Broadcasting Company. Goldenson, twenty years older than Rupert, was something of an underdog himself in his own battles with the larger CBS and NBC networks. But he was making inroads on their dominance of American television, and he took a liking to the young Australian who was fighting similar odds Down Under.

"Goldenson was Rupert's first major contact in the United States," an associate of the Australian said. "Rupert was flying up a lot, looking for some programs he could buy on the cheap for his little stations in Adelaide and Wollongong. Goldenson showed him around, treated him like a son. It was he who taught Rupert how to get things done in the States."

Goldenson was an ardent supporter of Israel, as well as other Jewish interests in the United States. Murdoch, himself a product of a Christian-dominated society, had always felt like an outsider in his own country—a scrapper from the boondocks trying to get a foothold in an industry dominated by a handful of rich and powerful men. Despite their religious and cultural differences, Murdoch identified with the older Goldenson, whom he regarded as more of a mentor and father figure than a mere business acquaintance, and he came to admire Israel's struggle for survival in a hostile environment while surrounded by a largely indifferent world beyond.

To a great degree, Murdoch saw some parallels between Israel's emergence as an economic and political presence in the world and Australia's need to shed its image of an indolent colossus, a provincial backwater whose fate was largely determined by richer and more powerful nations. On a personal level he identified with Jews as outsiders fighting for survival, and on a geopolitical scale with Israel as an underdog nation that was clawing its way to a position of strength. Increasingly, Murdoch's newspapers began to take on an unreservedly pro-Israel tone. His defense of Israel and his support of Jewish charities continues unabated to this day. In April 1982 he was honored by the American Jewish Congress as "Communications Man of the Year," in recognition of his continuing support of Israel and Jewish interests in the United States.

Howard Squadron, Murdoch's friend and attorney, told my research associate Geri Shapiro that Murdoch has "always been pro-Israel. He admires Israel's fighting spirit in creating a new country." He considers Murdoch to be a "gracious and charming social companion" who has gotten a "bad rap" in some quarters over the years.

On the eve of his assault on England (for that's how it was viewed by much of the London media), Murdoch was well armed for combat. His burgeoning empire was valued at an estimated $50,000,000 in 1968, and at the age of thirty-seven he had developed a management style that was decidedly hands-on. Max Newton was just one of many editors sacked by Murdoch when they contested his interference.

"The first four or five months," Newton told Murdoch biographer Michael Leapman, "up until the time I left the organization, Rupert would quite often be seen down on the stone making up the paper . . . Very unnerving. This is the sort of work that should be done . . . by a subeditor earning about twenty-five pounds a week."

He had a reputation for ruling by telephone when he was not in a particular office. Impatient with chains of command and with face-to-face meetings with subordinates, he would pick up the telephone and call whoever was in charge of an operation across the country (later, around the world) when something bothered him. Yelling and screaming was not his style. Those on the other end of the phone would often have to listen carefully to his unusually low voice asking questions, demanding answers.

Those close to Murdoch claim they can read his moods on his face, despite his attempts to hide emotion. Of medium height, slim, with dark eyes and dark thinning hair, he has a naturally jowly, rubbery face and bears a slight resemblance to the American actor Walter Matthau. The lower his voice, the more there is to worry about, say those who work for him.

"He has a funny way of pursing his lips, puffing them out and pulling them in that tells you he's ticked at something," one of his old friends and editors said.

Somewhat autocratic in manner, hard-working and involved, not afraid to dirty his own hands with grunt work, totally in touch with everything that goes on in all corners of the empire, direct, blunt at times, honest and forthright—all of these descriptions suit Murdoch well, according to many who have known and worked for him longest.

The telephone, his favored instrument of communication with his staff, took on even greater importance when Murdoch left for London in the fall of 1968; from here on in he would have to govern the Australian kingdom from halfway around the globe. Murdoch was determined to make good on his schoolboy promise to one day own the *Daily Mirror*, and he had been quietly acquiring stock in IPC, Cecil King's publishing conglomerate, which owned the paper. When he was ready to make his move, however, it was not the *Daily Mirror* but rather the *News of the World* that offered him the opportunity to gain a presence in the British publishing community.

"The *News of the World* gave Rupert his first chance to get started in the U.K.," an associate of Murdoch said.

The *News of the World,* whose six million circulation was the largest among the Sunday newspapers, was owned by the Carr family. It was considered to be the grandaddy of Sunday tabloid journalism, accenting the underside of British life. Sir William Carr was the tabloid's largest shareholder with 32 percent, followed by an investor named Derek Jackson who controlled 25 percent. When Jackson announced plans to sell his shares, Murdoch expressed an interest in them—only to find that there was a competing bidder in the market, a man who was to become an arch rival of Murdoch for the next two decades (as we shall see), a Czechoslovakian emigré named Jan Hoch, who had settled in England and changed his name to Ian Robert Maxwell.

In their first head-to-head competition, the stakes were

high for both Murdoch and Maxwell. The *News of the World* was highly profitable and would generate handsome revenues for both men's growing publishing empires. Among Maxwell's holdings was Pergamon Press, a publisher of scientific books and journals, and he was anxious to get into the newspaper business.

The ailing Sir William Carr was particularly concerned about keeping Jackson's shares from falling into unfriendly hands. Maxwell, a Socialist member of parliament, was politically unacceptable to the conservative Carr, who was afraid Maxwell would attempt to alter the newspaper's editorial slant. Murdoch, whose own political orientation was slowly evolving rightward, managed to position himself as an ally of Carr, with the understanding that both of them could find common ground in their joint ownership of the paper. The ploy worked after a good deal of maneuvering on both sides. At first Carr agreed to sell just enough shares to Murdoch to keep Maxwell from acquiring a majority. But Murdoch was in no mood to serve as anyone's buffer, and he eventually won control of Jackson's shares—plus others he bought in the market—at a shareholders' meeting, despite the fact that his bid was lower than Maxwell's. Maxwell succeeded in alienating just about everyone concerned, including members of the Carr family who originally supported him.

"Maxwell took the wrong approach," one of them told Thomas Kiernan afterward. "He flogged his obnoxious personality in front of everyone and then made it clear that he felt nothing but contempt for anyone who would even consider not throwing their vote to him."

"Maxwell accused us of stacking the meeting," Murdoch said to Kiernan. "I made sure that the hall was full of our people. We didn't turn anyone away, but we had our numbers there in case . . ."

The voting at the shareholders' meeting was not even close—299 to 20 in favor of Murdoch—and six months later he succeeded in forcing Carr out and replacing him as chairman.

"I had no choice," Murdoch said, according to Kiernan. "Once I got in there and saw how badly the organization was run, I had to clean house. Everything was dreadfully old-fashioned and stultified."

Murdoch's victory was especially stunning considering that he managed to achieve it with a surprisingly small amount of money. His acquisition of the shares he needed for control cost him only a few million pounds, a sum he was easily able to raise by borrowing from Australian banks against the assets of News Limited. Throughout his entire career, Murdoch has been an ardent believer in the use of leverage to finance his expansion.

"In effect, Murdoch does what all the big international operators do, and he does it better," Alun Jones, former chief financial officer of Olympia & York and J. Walter Thompson before that, explained. "The Saatchi brothers have built their entire advertising empire on the same principle. They're able to take advantage of different tax and accounting laws in the U.K., the U.S. and Australia to increase their borrowing power. It's all very clever. I can show you the balance sheets of the same company—one for Great Britain and the other for the U.S.—and you'd think you were looking at the finances of two different companies. That's why people like Murdoch are able to borrow more than their competitors."

Author and former publisher Gerald McKnight owned a newspaper in England called *The News Shopper* at the time.

When Murdoch expressed interest in buying the profitable trade publication, McKnight sent word that he would be interested in discussing it. As McKnight said in 1989, "The next we knew, a huge Rolls Royce rolled up to our rather crummy little offices. And a huge Australian guy, a man called Rich, who was his personal accountant and his then manager in London, and several others, all poured into the shop and said, 'Well, show us the books.' Without any appointment or anything.

"So we did, and they were duly satisfied with all that and we got to talking and eventually we had several sessions with Murdoch on the top floor of his building then in the *News of the World* . . . You know, when he negotiates, he sits sort of looking at his navel like a buddha, grunting slightly, and then the wheels of the mind are turning all on figures. And he'll go on and on and on with his figures, and eventually we got a very good price out of him. He was pretty good.

"And all his secretaries are about forty to fifty," McKnight continued. "They're Australian and they're motherly and they keep coming around giving him cups of tea . . . He did very well with [*The News Shopper*] and made a big success with the paper and sold it for millions."

Murdoch not only invaded England in the final days of 1968, but he did it more successfully than anyone thought possible only a few months before. With one brilliant coup he seized control of a hugely profitable Sunday newspaper whose gross cash flow could easily service the debt he took on to buy it. As long as the revenues from his various enterprises continue to outstrip the interest on his debt, he can continue to grow and expand the limits of his empire.

In winning the fight for control of the *News of the World,*

Murdoch also succeeded in launching a rivalry with the flamboyant Maxwell that persists to this day. So far Murdoch has managed to best Maxwell in most of their encounters, but the enmity lives on.

"He'd said some rather nasty things about me to the press," Kiernan quotes Murdoch as saying. "And some nasty things about Australians in general. I couldn't let him get away with that."

Chapter
Four

IN THE face of growing criticism that his newspapers were catering to sensationalism, Rupert Murdoch maintained that he was only giving the public what it wanted. The fact that the circulation of his papers was increasing while that of many of his competitors was stagnant or declining was proof that his formula was working.

"He's not in newspapers to make the world a better place," Sir William Rees-Mogg, former editor of the London *Times*, told William H. Meyers of the New York *Times*, as reported in his June 12, 1988, article.

Others defend his style of journalism, saying that he would go out of business in a hurry if he didn't publish a product that people wanted to read.

"He has a right to do anything he wants with his own publications," says Steve Dunleavy, a former editor of the New York *Post* who currently works at Murdoch's Fox-5 Television in New York City. "Rupe doesn't dictate public tastes, you know. He has lots of bosses out there. Millions of them. The public tells him what they want to read and Rupe gives it to them."

Murdoch got involved in one of the most controversial episodes of his life shortly after his acquisition of *News of the World.* In 1964 the paper had published the memoirs of Christine Keeler, the call girl whose simultaneous relationships with a Russian spy and British defense minister John Profumo nearly toppled the Conservative government of Harold Macmillan. Five years later, Keeler, apparently in need of money, was shopping around an updated, tell-all version of the affair. Murdoch bought the new memoirs and published them in a series of weekly installments beginning in the late summer of 1969. His gamble paid off in terms of circulation—an increase of 300,000 copies above the usual six million—but the move backfired in another way.

Murdoch succeeded in unleashing a storm of controversy over his role in reviving the incident. Profumo had evidently devoted himself to social work during the previous five years in an attempt to rehabilitate his reputation, but the publication of Keeler's memoirs stirred up all the unpleasantness once again. The British establishment—society, the press, members of the clergy—castigated Murdoch, and in his own defense he decided to accept an invitation from the peripatetic David Frost to appear on his London television program. (Frost, after having made a reputation as a satirist of sorts, was commuting back and forth from London to New York to host his own interview shows.)

"Murdoch admitted at the time that he walked straight into a trap," a friend of his said. Naively perhaps, he thought he would be given a fair chance to explain himself by answering straightforward questions. But David Frost had more than a taste for the sensational himself. In 1988 the media created the term "tabloid television" to describe such provocative programs as "The Morton Downey, Jr. Show," Geraldo Rivera's "Geraldo," Murdoch's "Current Affair" with Maury Povich, and David Frost's "Inside Edition," which aired on the NBC network. Like a hunter looking for a kill, Frost went straight for the jugular. According to Kiernan and Michael Leapman, another biographer, the nervous, ill-at-ease Murdoch was no match for the silky smooth Frost, who cut him up badly. Murdoch knew he had been beaten, and quickly regretted accepting the performer's invitation. At the end of the program he stalked off the set, accompanied by his wife Anna, who had viewed the proceedings in the "green room." Whether or not he actually vowed then to get even with Frost someday by buying London Weekly Television, the company that sponsored the show, and sacking him, that's essentially what happened a short time later.

When this author caught up with David Frost at the "Inside Edition" set this year, the British broadcaster denied that he had intended to embarrass Murdoch.

"That wasn't the intent at all," he said. "You have to understand what was happening at the time. Everyone in England was incensed. Profumo had already paid dearly for his indiscretions. The man will stop at nothing to sell his bloody newspapers."

If Frost saw any similarities between what Murdoch did in 1969 and the kind of tabloid television journalism that he himself was doing in 1989, he didn't say.

"After he launched the *News of the World,*" a Murdoch associate said, "Rupert's printing plant, with its large unionized labor force, was idle six days a week. His paper was only published on Sunday, don't forget. That's the sort of thing that drives him mad."

The best way for the Australian to get full value out of the unions was to publish a daily and keep them busy full time. Since the long-coveted *Daily Mirror* was not up for sale, Murdoch decided to compete with it and attempt to beat the tabloid at its own game.

A struggling newspaper called the *Sun,* whose circulation had declined from one and a half million to 850,000, struck Murdoch as the vehicle to do just that. During the previous eight years the *Sun* and its predecessor the *Herald* had racked up losses for International Publishing Company (IPC) totalling nearly thirteen million pounds. When the board of IPC announced plans either to sell or shut down the failing newspaper, Murdoch's nemesis, Robert Maxwell, came forward with an offer. He intended, he said, to revamp the *Sun* into a pro-labor journal with reduced circulation—a suggestion that, ironically enough, did not sit well with the unions, who were more concerned about a loss of jobs than they were about leftist ideology.

Once again, Murdoch sensed an opportunity and he wasted no time in capitalizing on it. IPC had offered the *Sun* to Maxwell for next to nothing in order to cut its losses. With the unions completely opposed to Maxwell's downsizing plans for the daily, they suggested Murdoch as a possible buyer for the *Sun.* At least he would attempt to turn the newspaper into a profitable enterprise. Murdoch was still smarting over Maxwell's slurs on Australians, and he couldn't resist the urge to enter the fray and bloody his rival's nose once again. He stepped in with the unions' blessing and bought the *Sun* for less than a million pounds (about $1.5

million at the time), with a downpayment of $120,000 and the balance payable over the next six years only if the paper showed a profit.

In beating Maxwell to the punch for the second time in less than a year, the Australian pulled off the coup of his career, although he didn't know it yet. One of his executives described it later as "the steal of the century." Under Murdoch's tutelage, the *Sun* outdid the *Daily Mirror* in its emphasis on sex, sports and crime. The new, regenerated *Sun* ran excerpts from flashy bestsellers such as *The Sensuous Woman* by the anonymous "S" and Jacqueline Suzanne's *The Love Machine*, and Murdoch titillated his readers with the first-ever pictures of topless women to appear in London newspapers in his popular Page Three features. Inside of a year, the *Sun*'s circulation rocketed from 800,000 to 2,000,000, mostly at the expense of the *Daily Mirror*. Today it is one of the most profitable dailies in the world. The *Sun* is essentially the cash cow for Murdoch's entire empire, with a circulation of 4.1 million, about a million more than that of the *Daily Mirror*.

"The great success story on the print side is what he's done in the U.K.," Gordon Crawford, media analyst with Capital Research in Los Angeles, said. "If you go back and look at the history of what he bought the *Sun* and *News of the World* for . . . and you look at what their cash flow is now, I mean it's just an enormous coup that literally made billions of dollars and created billions of dollars in stockholder value."

Some have argued that Murdoch, in outmaneuvering Maxwell for control of the *Sun*, deprived his arch rival of the victory of a lifetime. What is overlooked in this analysis, however, is that Maxwell's plans for the *Sun* were totally different from Murdoch's, and most likely would not have been nearly as successful.

"Maxwell can be very tough," Murdoch said to William H.

Meyers of the New York *Times,* according to his previously mentioned article. "He's brilliant, but knows nothing about publishing newspapers."

There was no question in anyone's mind that Rupert Murdoch knew a thing or two about publishing newspapers.

"You see opportunities," Murdoch said to me, "you're young and you get silly and buy the *News of the World* in London which was nearly bankrupt. And seizing opportunities, we started the London *Sun* virtually for nothing. With the arrogance of the early success of that, we said, 'Well, we'd better come to America.' And we found it very difficult here."

Before he left for America, however, Murdoch had an old score to settle.

"Rupert is not one to quickly forget old grievances," a long-time friend of his told me. "You definitely don't want to get on the wrong side of him."

Tucked away in the back of his mind, but apparently not forgotten, was the embarrassing television encounter of a year earlier with David Frost. The Sicilians have a proverb that says, "Revenge is a dish that is best served cold." In the Australian's case he may well have thought that luke-warm was cool enough, for he decided to extract his revenge while the incident was still fresh in his mind.

London Weekend Television (LWT) was a money-losing subsidiary of England's General Electric Corporation. It was founded in 1966 by David Frost and several other people, and was on the verge of financial collapse when Murdoch bought a controlling interest in it toward the end of 1970. Government regulations prohibited any one person from gaining total ownership of a commercial broadcasting company, but Murdoch's shares entitled him to a seat on the board of directors. Frost, with 5 percent of the shares himself, also had a seat on the board.

Murdoch wasted no time in assuming executive control over the policies of the company. He alone of all the board members had the financial clout and expertise to keep the broadcasting company solvent and independent. The major problem, as he saw it, was that LWT was licensed to broadcast from Friday to Sunday night, a period best suited for light entertainment rather than the intellectual, sophisticated programming the company offered. During the next twelve months Murdoch cut staff, hired new managers and downscaled the programming without "tabloidizing" it to the extreme many critics feared, and before long the company was showing a profit.

Murdoch's motivation for taking on the challenge of LWT is open to some speculation. Did he want to punish Frost, whom he effectively deprived of influence and forced out a short time later, or merely prove to his critics that he was capable of surmounting all obstacles? Certainly, the money involved was insignificant compared to the revenues generated by the *Sun* and the *News of the World*.

There was a bizarre and tragic footnote to this episode with David Frost. Shortly after seeing Murdoch on television and reading interviews with Anna in the London press, two immigrant brothers named Hosein devised a plan to kidnap Anna and hold her for ransom.

The brothers set their plan in motion in January 1970. After following Anna through the streets of London for several days as she made her daily rounds in her chauffeur-driven Rolls Royce, they forced their way into the car at gunpoint and seized the woman riding alone in the back seat.

Unknown to the kidnappers, however, was the fact that

Anna and Rupert had left for Australia the previous day. Rupert had lent the car and its driver to Muriel McKay, the wife of his close associate Alex McKay, and it was she whom the brothers actually abducted. In frustration or panic—possibly, a combination of both—the Hoseins murdered Muriel McKay and abandoned her body. They were eventually tried and convicted for murder. It was a horrifying conclusion to a uniquely morbid episode in the Murdochs' lives.

Murdoch's whirlwind overhall of LWT was nothing short of dazzling, but no sooner did he turn the company around than he lost interest in it and set his sights on a more distant horizon. More and more, the idea of establishing a newspaper presence in the United States appealed to him. His friendship with Leonard Goldenson had strengthened over the years, and, according to a friend of theirs, Anna was unhappy living in London in the midst of the controversy surrounding her husband's media acquisitions. Their first child Elisabeth was little more than a year old and Anna was pregnant with their second—a boy they would name Lachlan.

Politically, Murdoch was becoming more conservative after his battles with the British unions, and he regarded the United States as a more hospitable climate for conducting business. Conventional wisdom held that a national daily would not go over in the United States because of its cultural and demographic diversity (the Wall Street *Journal* was not yet distributed nationally, the National Enquirer was hardly a newspaper in the conventional sense and was published weekly and *USA Today* would not be published until a number of years later).

Murdoch had never been one to accept consensus thinking

blindly. The experts were often wrong, afraid to gamble on the unknown. On the other hand, as Murdoch told me, gambling was something he enjoyed, possibly a genetic trait. He had gotten where he was by following his instincts—and taking on the risks.

Chapter
Five

WHILE MURDOCH was formulating his American battle plan, an opportunity presented itself in his native Australia that commanded his immediate attention. Sir Frank Packer was getting on in years, losing some control of the family organization to his son Kerry, who wanted to sell the *Telegraph* and concentrate on their television and magazine interests. The likely buyer for the newspaper was the Fairfax organization, which could then eliminate its major competition by merging it with the *Herald.*

Murdoch flew back to Australia early in 1972 and, in a lightning-quick stroke, went to a boxing match with Kerry Packer in the course of which he offered to take the *Telegraph* off his hands for its goodwill value, which he put at the equivalent of $17.5 million in U.S. currency. Murdoch positioned himself as the lesser of two evils alongside the Fairfax people, and the deal was set. In acquiring the *Telegraph,* Murdoch now owned one of Sydney's leading morning dailies as well as its leading afternoon paper, the *Mirror.*

The deal with the Packers typified one of the major distinctions between American and Australian accounting rules. "According to Australian accounting rules," Maxwell Newton explained, "Rupert can put a money value on goodwill . . . Very important. Whatever else he earns is really not worth a pinch of shit compared with the value of the goodwill."

In somewhat less colorful language, media analyst Gordon Crawford put it to me this way, "When you make an acquisition in [the United States] you have a goodwill charge, assuming that the price you paid is more than the stated book value of the company. You have got to write that off over forty years and so what happens is, in the media business you have very, very large goodwill, because in most media businesses the actual physical assets aren't that important. What you're paying for is the franchise, or the list or whatever. A big goodwill charge dilutes your earnings per share. Now, some of us don't really care what the reported earnings are, and really follow the cash that's generated by the company. Which, I think, is a proper way to look at the company, but you know other people look at earnings per share.

"You're really at a disadvantage when you have to write off that goodwill," Crawford continued. "Foreign companies don't have to do that."

Crawford's comments require some elaboration. Goodwill is an amorphous, intangible value that is difficult to measure accurately. It represents the value of a company's reputation within its industry, its "franchise" to operate as Crawford put it, the weight and clout of its name in the marketplace. Because it is intangible and subject to change (a company's reputation can be damaged overnight), in the United States goodwill is deducted from earnings, weakening the balance sheet. In Australia and England, however, it is considered an asset that the banks will lend money against, whereas American banks prefer to lend against tangible assets such as plant and equipment.

The goodwill value of a company can be fixed by a potential buyer who takes it to a bank and tries to borrow against it. The bank will either accept it as is, or say in effect, "No, we think you're overstating it 25 percent. Here's what we're prepared to lend you." Or a seller looking for a good price on his holding might estimate its goodwill value at a certain amount during negotiations with a buyer. It is up to them—and ultimately the bank that is financing the deal—to arrive at a figure acceptable to all parties.

Because of different accounting rules in various countries, the Murdochs and Saatchis of the world, the Reichmanns, Bronfmans and Campeaus of Canada, all the international financiers, have been able to outmaneuver their American counterparts whose assets are located solely in the United States. They have more borrowing power because of these accounting differences. Murdoch, in buying the *Telegraph* for example, could then walk into a Melbourne or Sydney bank and use the *Telegraph*'s goodwill (which he most likely bought on credit since none of the professionals use their own money for these deals) and borrow against that to finance another acquisition. In a way, it can be viewed as a kind of pyramiding of leverage that works as long as the cash flow from the acquired properties covers the debt service.

Within the Murdoch empire at this time, the only unprofitable operation was the *Australian,* his national daily, which he continued to subsidize with the profits of his cash cows. The *Australian* was his most upscale publication, and it served as an influential political forum for Murdoch. The *Australian* had been an effective vehicle in the election of the leftist government of Gough Whitlam, and it would prove to be even more instrumental in engineering his downfall a few years later.

During one of his scouting trips to the United States to search for newspaper possibilities, Murdoch met President Richard Nixon and several of his aides. While he had not yet moved completely to the right politically—he supported the Labor government of Gough Whitlam in his own country through the 1974 election—there was no question that he was moving in that direction. Murdoch was impressed with Nixon and his policies, and lent editorial support to them in his British and Australian newspapers.

The seeds of his disenchantment with the Whitlam government were planted as early as 1973, when the Australian maritime unions, in a protest against U.S. bombing in Vietnam, refused to service American ships, and Whitlam at first refused to intervene at Nixon's request. Whitlam eventually caved in to pressure from both Washington, D.C., and Murdoch's editorial barbs. He ended the strike within days, thereby earning Murdoch's support in his campaign for reelection a year later. Shortly afterward, however, Murdoch turned against him in earnest.

Murdoch claimed that he had grown disillusioned with Whitlam because of the failure of his policies; the Australian dollar had been sharply devalued, the economy was sagging and key members of the government were tainted with financial scandal. Whitlam's version of the incident was markedly different; he stated publicly that his refusal to grant Murdoch a bauxite development license in Western Australia was the true reason for the publisher's change of heart. Other observers thought Murdoch was acting at the behest of the U.S. State Department, which promised him support in his negotiations with American banks.

Quite likely, as in most high-level affairs, there was no one simple explanation. Murdoch's political perspective was taking on a genuinely more conservative cast. He was developing a valuable political relationship with the Nixon administration, whose influence could possibly help him advance his own business interests. And it is reasonable to assume that he was incensed over Whitlam's refusal to grant him a lucrative mining license. It would seem that all these currents came together in a roiling fury that culminated in Whitlam's downfall in 1975.

Sensing defeat, Whitlam attempted to shore up his strength by tapping into the anti-Americanism that surfaced during the war in Vietnam. The United States maintained a radio facility at Alice Springs in the Australian outback, ostensibly to transmit information between Washington, D.C., and the Far East, and to monitor NASA space operations. Whitlam publicly labeled the Alice Springs operation a CIA installation whose true purpose was to collect intelligence data on the Soviet Union and China.

In the midst of the controversy, Whitlam was forced to call for a new election, and during the campaign that followed the *Australian* and the other Murdoch papers launched a series of attacks on the prime minister, accusing him of everything from sexual improprieties to nefarious financial dealings with Iraq and Pakistan. In the end, Whitlam suffered a resounding defeat at the hands of the Conservative, Malcolm Fraser. The vitriol of the campaign spilled over into the following year. Whitlam denounced Murdoch as the instrument of his defeat, while Murdoch lashed back in an editorial, "Mr. Whitlam is going out not with a stance of dignity but with a whimper."

The *Australian*, a money loser since its inception, had finally paid Murdoch back in the form of political capital. If he had any doubts about its influence prior to the campaign of 1975, they were permanently laid to rest from that moment on.

Preoccupied as he was with the political climate in his homeland during this period, Murdoch had not lost sight of his plans for the United States. His empire in 1973 encompassed some eighty newspapers, eleven magazines, television and radio stations, printing, paper and shipping companies scattered throughout Great Britain, Australia and New Zealand. These interests were controlled by his two major companies: News Limited in Australia and News International in England. For the time being, Murdoch had expanded about as far as he could into the media of those countries. Now the United States, a country the size of his native Australia but with nearly ten times the population, lay sprawled across the horizon with all its promise and opportunity. He could not resist the call.

Anna had already given birth to Lachlan and was pregnant again. It was around that time, after James was born, that Rupert moved them all to the States.

The growing family moved into a duplex apartment on Fifth Avenue in the Sixties, next door to Temple Emanuel. (Ten years later they moved twenty blocks north on Fifth into the triplex directly across from the Guggenheim museum, where they still live today.)

"The old *Sunday Times* published a front-page cartoon of Rupert," Newton said, "with a plasticene model of him hold-

ing open a raincoat, and they called him the 'Dirty Digger.' "
A digger is an English slur for Australian.

The Dirty Digger and Murdoch of the Mammaries were just
two of the nicknames the British media bestowed on Rupert,
according to several sources.

"Great Britain will accept you," Anna Murdoch told William H. Meyers, according to his New York *Times* article, "if
you're willing to join and play by the rules. Rupert wasn't
willing. He went to Great Britain to challenge Fleet Street,
not because he loved Great Britain."

So, the move to New York—a business venture for Murdoch—was a welcome change of residence to a more hospitable climate for Anna. She was beginning to develop an interest in a literary career of her own, and attended New York
University, where she earned bachelor's and master's degrees
in literature and mythology. Her attempts at fiction were not
successful at first.

"I was told by an editor that my stories didn't fit into the
formula that women's magazines were running," she said to
Cynthia Cotts of The Illustrated London News. "Perhaps that
means I'm not a short-story writer unless I'm going into the
small press. Perhaps I'm not a short-story writer at all."

Perhaps. But she was later to prove that she was a gifted
novelist. *In Her Own Image* was published to generally good
reviews in 1985, and her second novel, *Family Business,* followed three years later.

In addition to the publishing opportunities Murdoch saw in
the United States, he also saw a political vacuum developing
as a result of Richard Nixon's Watergate problems. If Nixon
was forced to resign, Murdoch believed the American public
would welcome a conservative voice to counter the attacks

on him and his administration from the liberal press. His primary interest remained the creation of a national daily newspaper, similar to the *Australian* in format but with the virtue of profitability. One money-losing newspaper was more than enough of a drain on his resources.

Chapter Six

MURDOCH'S INITIAL foray into the United States was on a smaller scale than he originally envisioned, and it cost him more than most financial analysts thought prudent at the time.

In the early 1970s, the newspaper industry in the United States was going through a major shake-out phase. A series of strikes, coupled with rising production costs, forced many dailies out of business. In New York City alone, such long-standing institutions as the *Herald Tribune,* the *Daily Mirror,* the *Journal American* and the *World Telegram* had fallen by the wayside by that time, leaving America's largest city with only two morning dailies (not counting the Wall Street *Journal,* a specialty paper) and one afternoon publication. Throughout the nation, newspapers were being shut down or merged into others, drastically reducing the overall supply.

Quite simply, there were not that many up for sale when Murdoch came upon the scene.

"It was John Newcombe who put Rupert on to Texas," an associate of Murdoch said. "Rupert and John were friends, he taught him something about the game, and Newcombe was developing a tennis center in Texas at the time."

Through the Australian tennis star, Murdoch heard about a promising situation in San Antonio. The major newspaper in town at the time was the *Light,* an afternoon daily owned by the Hearst organization with a circulation of 120,000—not bad for a city with a population of under a million. The competing afternoon paper was the San Antonio *News,* owned by the smaller Harte-Hanks chain, as was a morning daily called the *Express* and their combined Sunday edition. The Harte-Hanks newspapers, with a total circulation of 140,-000, were only marginally profitable.

Murdoch, anxious to break into the American market, paid slightly less than $20 million for the three Harte-Hanks publications, a considerably higher sum than he would normally have paid for comparable newspapers in Australia and England. Newspaper acquisitions in the United States are usually based on a multiple of earnings—not goodwill value. Since net profits in this instance were negligible, Murdoch was paying an extraordinary multiple by American accounting standards.

The morning newspaper, the *Express,* was the most profitable of the three; the San Antonio *News,* with its relatively puny 61,000 circulation against the *Light*'s 120,000, was the biggest drain on reserves, and it was there that Murdoch decided to concentrate his energies. In the beginning, the Australian attempted to beat the *Light* on the downscale end of the market, out-tabloidizing it, so to speak, with an even heavier emphasis on sex, crime, comics, puzzles and contests.

The strategy proved modestly successful as circulation jumped to 75,000, but at this point Murdoch had a rude awakening.

In England and Australia, increased circulation normally results in greater profitability. In the United States, only twenty-five percent of gross revenues are derived from circulation. The lion's share comes from advertising revenues. Murdoch, in going after the low end of the market, failed to realize a corresponding increase in advertising dollars as circulation went up. (This was a mistake he was to make again later with the New York *Post;* despite his success in dramatically increasing the *Post*'s circulation, he never attracted the advertising he needed to turn a profit.

"He apparently did boost the circulation," said an associate of Murdoch who requested anonymity, "but he didn't make it up in advertising . . . They deserted for reasons that had nothing to do with the paper's circulation. They deserted because the other media told them they shouldn't be in his paper.")

Not one to let his losses run interminably—no good gambler does—Murdoch quickly changed directions and upscaled the *News,* figuring if he beat the *Light* on the higher end of the market, it would be more attractive to advertisers. This strategy was more effective than the first, and slowly the revenues increased. Rupert Murdoch was getting a crash course in American newspaper publishing. The real battle, he learned in short order, was not for readership so much as it was for those coveted advertising dollars that paid the bills.

This exercise in San Antonio served as a valuable tune-up fight to prepare him for the main event. His primary goal remained the creation of a national daily. But the risk was also great since it had not been done before and American publishing analysts considered the concept unfeasible. His

Texas start-up operation was not yet an unqualified success, and his national daily in Australia had never turned a profit, so prudence dictated that he follow a more familiar path.

He was still committed to the idea of establishing a national presence in the United States. His greatest successes to date had occurred in the tabloid field, and it was therefore only natural that he took a close look at America's leading national tabloid, the National Enquirer. There was nothing comparable on the market at the time, no imitators had yet been spawned, nothing remotely similar available for purchase. Until now he had preferred to acquire an existing publication instead of starting one up from scratch. Invariably, the costs were lower, the chances for success greater with a known product. But now Murdoch was faced with an unusual situation for him: The asking prices for American newspapers were far higher than he was used to paying in Great Britain and Australia, and, in any event, the area he wanted to get into was monopolized by a single publication—which was not for sale.

"It was the first time in his life that Rupert was faced with the prospect of creating a product out of whole cloth," said one of his associates. A weekly along the lines of the National Enquirer made more economic sense than launching a daily of that type, and the production costs would be lower. If he could tap into the National Enquirer's five million circulation with a snappier format, perhaps adding a dash of color, he could gradually eat away at his competitor's market and eventually dominate the field.

The effort was an expensive one, and it appeared at first as though it would not succeed. Adding up advertising, distribution and production costs, Murdoch spent some $12 million just to launch his American weekly, the National Star, and after a year his financial advisors were telling him to cut his losses and shut it down. His circulation failed to climb above a million copies a week, and the future looked less than promising. The "National" was dropped from the title, shortening it to simply the Star (as it is known today), a mix of astrology and advice columns added to the format, but still the Star failed to tap a responsive chord among the American public.

Murdoch, however, was determined to keep rolling the dice on this one rather than crap out early and admit defeat.

"We have no intention of failing," he said at the time, according to Thomas Kiernan. "The only question is how great a success we'll have."

The turning point for the Star occurred when Murdoch brought one of his correspondents, Ian Rae, up from Australia to take over as publisher.

"I was primarily responsible for transforming the Star from black-and-white into a color magazine," Rae, currently executive vice president of news at Murdoch's Fox Television, said recently. "It seemed to work wonders in distinguishing us from the competition."

Within a couple of years of Rae's arrival upon the scene, circulation was climbing steadily and those all-important advertising dollars were flowing in to Murdoch's coffers. Readership has continued to increase over the years to the point where it is virtually even with its arch rival, the National Enquirer, and far ahead of the slew of clones that have been hatched since the Star's inception. It stands today as Rupert Murdoch's most profitable American publication.

If the Star was not up to the journalistic standards Murdoch envisioned for his now-aborted concept of a national daily newspaper in America, it at least established him as a presence to be reckoned with. Through Leonard Goldenson and his friends in the Nixon administration, the Australian was introduced to rich and powerful people who were destined to play important roles in his life in the years ahead: bankers, lawyers, real estate developers, business executives, other newspaper publishers and media lords, politicians, members of society.

Among them were Howard Squadron, the well-connected New York attorney, today a partner in the firm of Squadron, Ellenoff, Plesent & Lehrer, who remains Murdoch's friend and primary attorney; Howard J. Rubenstein, who handles public relations for many of the rich and famous, including Murdoch and Donald Trump; Katharine Graham, owner of the Washington *Post;* Dorothy Schiff, another powerful newspaper woman who owned the New York *Post;* Clay Felker, creator of New York, a magazine originated as a section of the Sunday Herald Tribune and later spun off when the newspaper folded; and Stanley S. Shuman, a managing director of Allen & Co., which became Murdoch's investment banker in the United States.

With the Star safely launched and his Texas publications beginning to show modest profits, Rupert Murdoch started to look for a major daily newspaper to acquire—perhaps in New York or Boston—much as he had looked toward Sydney after establishing a presence in Adelaide and Perth. He and Anna struck up a friendship with Clay Felker and Gail Sheehy, a New York writer who was later to become Felker's wife; the couples visited the Hamptons together on weekends, and planned joint skiing vacations. The Murdochs even bought a house in East Hampton, their first real estate investment after the Fifth Avenue duplex, not far from Felker's summer home. It was Felker who suggested to Rupert that the New York *Post,* a money loser subsidized by Dorothy

Schiff to the tune of nearly a million dollars a year, might be available.

Schiff invited Murdoch to lunch in her sixth-floor suite in the old *Post* building looking out over the East River. She understood what she had to do to make the *Post* profitable— its antiquated plant and machinery needed updating, labor and distribution costs were too high, and some suggested the newspaper would benefit from changes in format. But at seventy-three years of age, faced with tax law changes that affected her tax liabilities, she was open to an offer.

The September 1976 luncheon was a cordial affair; Schiff and Murdoch later expressed a genuine fondness for each other, but there were problems. Dorothy Schiff, an ardent Democrat, wanted the *Post* to retain its liberal editorial slant. Murdoch, who had been an increasingly outspoken supporter of Nixon and his conservative policies (prior to Nixon's resignation in 1974), would more than likely revamp the *Post* to suit his own interests. Dorothy Schiff had been publishing the New York *Post,* founded in 1801 by Alexander Hamilton, since 1939. It was and remains today the oldest continuously published daily newspaper in the United States. Schiff had shepherded the *Post* through the political wars in the 1950s, standing up courageously against the vicious Red-baiting onslaught of Senator Joe McCarthy. Her pending sale of the newspaper was more than a question of money; the *Post* represented a heritage and tradition of incalculable value to her.

Murdoch was more than interested in buying the paper, but when Schiff wavered at first he turned his attention briefly back to England. Murdoch made an offer for the *Observer,* a Sunday newspaper that competed with London's *Sunday Times* and *Sunday Telegraph.* According to both Thomas Kiernan and Michael Leapman, Murdoch's interest in the *Observer* started off as a negotiating ploy that turned into genuine interest once he arrived in England. Whatever the case, the tactic worked. When word of Murdoch's interest in the *Observer* traveled back to Schiff, she reopened her lines of communication with him once again and said she would give serious consideration to a firm offer. Murdoch responded quickly. He abandoned his quest for the *Observer* and offered her $32.5 million, a relatively high figure considering that the *Post* was losing money and could not be evaluated in terms of a multiple of earnings.

(If the ownership of a company is divided into a million shares, for example, and the company earns a million dollars a year, its earnings are a dollar a share. A potential buyer might offer $10 million for the company, or ten times earnings—one dollar in earnings per share times 10 equals $10 million. In this instance the *Post* had no earnings, was in fact losing money, so Murdoch in essence was paying for goodwill value, which is not a bankable asset in the United States. He was, however, able to present the *Post*'s estimated goodwill value to Australian banks to raise money for the purchase.)

The deal was consummated in November 1976, a little more than two months after his lunch date with Dorothy Schiff. Murdoch celebrated his prized acquisition with dinner at Elaine's, a trendy restaurant of the day, catering to writers and publishers on New York's upper East Side. Among the celebrants at his table that evening were Clay Felker, Felix Rohatyn, the investment banker who put together the plan to save New York City from bankruptcy at the time, Shirley MacLaine, the actress, and her then boyfriend, the writer Pete Hamill.

"I may have paid too much for it," Murdoch remarked to

Felker at one point in the evening, according to Gail Sheehy, "but it was the chance of my lifetime."

The Australian entrepreneur had shown himself once again willing to take a risk.

"If you're young and reckless, you take risks pretty easily," Murdoch said to me. "And then—it's in your nature, I guess— but if you have some degree of success, not always, but some degree of success, it emboldens you to do more. And I guess, if you have some gambling genes in you somewhere, you get some genetic enjoyment of risk. Some people enjoy risk and some people hate it."

Taking one of the biggest gambles of his life so far, Murdoch had broken into the big leagues of American newspaper publishing. Not only did he now have a major presence in America's premier city, but he was the proud owner of the nation's longest-running daily newspaper.

Chapter
Seven

IN THE beginning, there was no discernible change in the New York *Post*'s format except for the addition of Page Six, a somewhat titillating forum for gossip about celebrities and their doings. But by the middle of 1977 a series of less-than-subtle changes crept into the make-up of the paper. Headlines blared more loudly than before, the first three or four pages were taken up with the more provocative sex and crime stories of the day, the sports section was expanded, racetrack coverage increased. Many critics noted that Murdoch had revamped the *Post* into a slightly upscale daily version of the Star and the National Enquirer.

The *Post*'s circulation also began to increase, nearly doubling in time to an eventual peak of more than 900,000 copies a day. While Murdoch's detractors were castigating him for the style of journalism he brought to America, the public responded differently, and he had his defenders in the media as well.

"I think he has every right to do whatever he wants with his publications," said a long-time friend and colleague of Murdoch. "He took the New York *Post,* which was a very well-written, failing newspaper, and he shook up New York City. I was there when that was being done and I had a sneaking admiration for the guy. The old *Mirror* was screaming headlines as much as the New York *Post.* If you go back and look at them, they're actually bigger and more outrageous . . . People somehow laid this trip on him.

"Murdoch is still into old-fashioned news. I mean, look at Harold Evans now. He used to edit the *Times* of London and now he's editing a yuppie magazine. I think those things are just as much disinformation as the old New York *Post* headlines, and I think people forget that when they criticize Murdoch . . . I also wrote for [title deleted] that's coming from a liberal perspective, and it's as equally distorted as anything I went through when I was with Murdoch's people."

"If you get the idea that Rupert's a vulgarian," Maxwell Newton said, "you're wrong. He's a very well-read, extremely well-informed person with tremendous recall and with a desire to produce beautiful things as well as popular things."

Murdoch's new New York *Post* stirred up a storm of controversy that continued until the day he sold it, more than a decade later. The *Post* took on a decidedly conservative political tone in its editorials; it was firmly behind the Reagan administration throughout the 1980s, and actively supported Lewis Lehrman, a conservative Republican businessman, in his unsuccessful race for governor of New York against Mario Cuomo. It lobbied long and hard in favor of the death penalty against liberal opposition. Under Murdoch's aegis the *Post* was totally renovated into a right-wing tabloid that infuriated some of the old *Post*'s readers, but simultaneously attracted a broader readership than it had before.

Despite the increased circulation, however, the *Post* never turned a profit for Murdoch. It was the same old story: expanding readership with no corresponding rise in advertising revenues. By the time he was forced to sell it in 1988, the *Post* was losing about $13 million a year, a total loss of $150 million during the decade Murdoch owned it. This situation was, in part, due to a misperception on the part of advertisers.

"The paper was never read by shoplifters, as the joke goes," said one of Murdoch's writers who worked on the *Post* in the early days. She was referring to a joke making the rounds that department stores wouldn't advertise in the *Post* because the *Post*'s readers were their shoplifters. "The paper's always been read by commuters in the afternoon going home on the train."

This much was true. I remember commuting from New York City's northern suburbs to Wall Street throughout much of the 1970s, and observing that most of the brokers and investment bankers who read the New York *Times* and Wall Street *Journal* in the morning invariably bought a copy of the *Post* to catch up on the gossip during the ride home in the evening. But, whatever the reason, Murdoch failed to get this message across to the advertisers and the *Post*'s overall revenues suffered because of it.

Murdoch's association with Clay Felker was not strictly social. While Felker had been the one who originally encouraged Murdoch to go after the *Post*, he himself was having difficulties with the board of directors of his own company, which owned New York magazine and the *Village Voice.* Felker's problems stemmed from the fact that he did not enjoy exclusive ownership of the publications. When he took his company public to raise capital in 1969, he ended up diluting his equity and saddling himself with an independent—and sometimes recalcitrant—board of directors that monitored his every move.

The principal shareholder in the company, with 24 percent of the stock, was Carter Burden, a wealthy socialite and an elected member of the City Council of New York. Bartle Bull, a powerful New York lawyer, also owned a sizable block of shares. Felker's equity stake had been whittled down to 10 percent. New York magazine and the *Village Voice* were both profitable enterprises, but Felker created problems for himself when he persuaded Burden and Bull to let him launch a new magazine in 1976, a West Coast version of New York magazine called New West. Felker ran several million dollars over budget, seriously draining the parent company's resources, and straining his already faltering relationship with Burden in particular.

Unable to function as freely as he wanted to, Clay Felker sought to enlist Murdoch's aid in obtaining Burden's block of stock. Felker had long admired Murdoch's business acumen. The Australian's empire was worth over $100 million at this time—controlled primarily by Murdoch—while the market value of Felker's publications was in the neighborhood of $15 million and controlled by other people's money.

"The way to operate is with OPM—other people's money," Murdoch had repeatedly advised Felker, according to Gail Sheehy.

Felker's area of expertise was magazine publishing. He seemed to have a nose for the market, notwithstanding the failure of New West to get off the ground. Both New York magazine and the *Village Voice* were making money, and he had nurtured and cultivated some of the best writers of the era: Tom Wolfe, Jimmy Breslin, Gay Talese, Ken Auletta and others loosely associated with the New Journalism school of reporting. On the surface it appeared to be a marriage that could work; Murdoch and Felker got along socially and apparently respected each other; the former's financial skills and the latter's publishing expertise presumably were complementary strengths.

But in the end, the marriage was not to be. When the dust finally settled, Murdoch and Felker's relationship had degenerated from friendship to open hostility. The breach was total, the enmity all-consuming. Felker was outmaneuvered, outclassed, and Rupert Murdoch was the new owner of New York magazine, New West and the *Village Voice.* When I reached Clay Felker by telephone in his office at Manhattan, Inc.—where he presides today—in 1989, twelve years after his monumental struggle with his old friend, the battle wounds clearly had yet to heal.

"The guy is just . . . he's insatiable," Felker said in an outburst of emotion.

Exactly what transpired depends on whose version of the epic battle one subscribes to.

"The only accurate piece that I've seen written about it," Felker said, "was by Gail Sheehy in Rolling Stone . . . She knew Murdoch and she witnessed a lot of this first-hand."

This was hardly surprising, since their durable romance that spanned the better part of two decades had recently culminated in marriage. According to Sheehy in her Rolling Stone piece, ". . . Rupert Murdoch consummated the sneak takeover of *New York* . . . , *New West,* and the *Village Voice* . . ." within six weeks of being approached by Felker. Clay Felker himself said at the time that he had been "raped" by his old friend. Other observers, however, had a different view of the affair.

Sources at Allen & Co., Murdoch's investment banker, maintained that Murdoch carefully explored the feasibility of buying the New York Magazine Company before committing himself to making a move. Only when the report came back to him that the acquisition could probably be made for something under $10 million did the Australian decide to go ahead. The opportunity to establish a major publishing presence in New York City, with the New York *Post*, New York magazine, and the *Village Voice*, for a total of about $40 million was too good to pass up.

Other sources said that Murdoch had already grown somewhat disillusioned with Felker because of his extravagant lifestyle (Murdoch has frugal standards), and not least of all because of Felker's close friendship with the Australian's old nemesis David Frost. Those who knew both men say that Murdoch, rightly or wrongly, suspected that Felker had made less than complimentary remarks about him behind his back. Supposedly, Murdoch was willing to keep Felker on as editor because of his close association with his publications' major writers, but made it clear to Felker that there could be only one publisher making business decisions— Murdoch himself.

Profligate spending, Murdoch said to Felker, according to Kiernan, is "a lifetime habit with you. You're too old to change your spots."

"You and I could never work together," he told Felker another time, Sheehy reported in her Rolling Stone article.

According to Sheehy in the same article, Murdoch advised Felker to "borrow a lot of money in order to own something 51 percent. Then work your tail off for two years or three years, scrimp and save and pay off the thing, you'll own it 100 percent and then you don't have to take any crap from any-body."

This was sound advice from Murdoch's perspective. It en-compassed his whole philosophy of doing business; it was a formula he had put to work time and time again throughout his career to build his empire. But it simply did not suit Felker's style. Murdoch knew that and he also understood that because Felker was unable to follow his advice they could never work together as business partners.

The key to acquiring the majority portion of the New York Magazine Company was the block of stock owned by Carter Burden. Since the company was public and its shares were traded on the New York Stock Exchange, Murdoch began to build a stake by buying stock in the market. He also opened lines of communication with some of the other large share-holders and made an agreement to buy their shares. If he could only get Carter Burden to sell his 24 percent block to him, he could accumulate a 51 percent majority and effec-tively gain control of the company.

The struggle for Burden's shares continued at a frantic pace throughout the entire month of December 1976. Felker did not have the financial clout to fight Murdoch on his own, so he enlisted the support of Katharine Graham, publisher of the Washington *Post,* who expressed interest in buying con-trol of the company with him. Burden apparently enjoyed observing the titanic battle for his stock from his perch in the catbird seat. With both camps bidding for his stock, Burden took off for a skiing vacation in Sun Valley, Idaho, and kept the combined forces of Clay Felker, Katharine Graham and Felix Rohatyn, who was advising Graham, fuming in New York while he remained unreachable on the slopes.

"Get that yo-yo off the slopes!" Rohatyn screamed at Burden's lawyer over the phone, according to Sheehy.

Katharine Graham, who had been waiting in vain for two days for a telephone call from the elusive Burden, was not used to being treated like a wallflower at a dance. Neither, for that matter, was the high-powered Rohatyn. The Felker forces later maintained that they reached a verbal agreement with Burden's lawyer to buy Burden out at seven dollars and fifty cents a share, a price guaranteed by the Washington *Post*, not knowing that Burden had already drawn up an agreement with Murdoch to sell his stock for seven dollars a share. Bartle Bull, too, had arranged with Stan Shuman of Allen & Co. to sell his own shares to Murdoch.

The next few weeks were filled with charges of double-dealing on both sides, acrimonious accusations, threats of lawsuits—a generally unpleasant gnashing of teeth. But finally, by the early days of January 1977, Murdoch emerged the victor. In addition to the Star, the New York *Post* and his Texas newspapers, he now owned New York magazine, the *Village Voice* and New West. He had achieved in one fell swoop a major publishing presence in the United States. In doing so he lost the services of some of the leading writers for the *Village Voice* and New York magazine in particular, who felt obliged to depart for other publications following the demise of Felker. In short order he installed James Brady, former editor of *Women's Wear Daily* and the first American editor of the National Star, as editorial director of New York.

Despite its leftish political stance, Murdoch left the format of the *Village Voice* pretty much intact. It was showing a profit, and Murdoch, a shrewd businessman first and foremost, did not see any reason to tinker with success. The bottom line came first. If anything, his new editor at the *Village Voice*, Michael Kramer, wanted to return the downtown weekly to its former roll as an underground counterculture publication.

"As long as its making money I don't care," Murdoch said to Kramer, as reported by Michael Leapman.

The circulation of New York magazine rose to 415,000—90 percent of it subscription—during the next few years, and has remained at that level ever since. Murdoch hired a new editor, Ed Kosner, in 1980, and promoted him to publisher in 1986. Kosner attributed a good deal of New York magazine's success to the merger of New York and Cue.

"That helped a lot," Kosner told Jeff Marcus of Magazine Week, as reported in the May 15, 1989, issue, "because it gave the magazine a very strong listings coefficient. Starting with the acquisition of Cue, New York immediately began to publish more than thirty pages of listings every week. It helped everything. It meant that even if in any given week a reader was not terribly interested in the cover story or one of the feature articles, as a weekly buy and as a subscription buy, New York was still a very useful publication."

Useful enough to contribute an extra $44 million in advertising revenue to the magazine's already swollen coffers.

Chapter
Eight

IN AN interview given to Vartanig G. Vartan of the New York *Times* shortly after his conquest of New York, Rupert Murdoch described his success as "a pyramiding of power of control." The foundation of his burgeoning empire was News Limited, based in Australia. Murdoch owned 48 percent of the company with the remaining 52 percent scattered among thousands of shareholders, none of whom owned more than one percent. He was determined not to repeat the mistake of his father.

The Murdoch empire at this time was divided into three separate but interrelated fiefdoms. The headquarters remained in Australia under the banner of News Limited, and it encompassed some fifty Australian newspapers, two book publishers, commercial printing plants, mining interests and at least partial ownership of five television stations.

The British properties were under the umbrella of News

International Ltd. based in London, while the primary U.S. concern was News America Publishing, Inc. in New York City. Other American subdivisions included the City Post Publishing Corporation, publisher of the New York *Post*, and the New York Magazine Company.

To make matters even more complicated, all of Murdoch's companies owned shares in one another. News Limited owned 48 percent of News International Ltd., which in turn owned 50 percent of News America Publishing, Inc. News Limited and News International Ltd. each owned half of the City Post Publishing Corporation, and City Post Publishing and News America Publishing jointly owned the newly acquired New York Magazine Company.

There were a number of reasons for all this financial wizardry. Some of it had to do with accounting and tax considerations, but primarily it was a question of Murdoch keeping control of his sprawling empire. As Murdoch himself explained it, the overlapping partnership structure allowed him to reinvest profits back into his various operations instead of being required by the banks to pay out dividends to shareholders.

"In this way," Murdoch said, "a central bank in London or Australia can't order you to pay dividends, since you don't have control stock. It means you can plow back profits."

The value of being able to reinvest profits in production instead of paying out dividends to shareholders can't be overstated. Many stock market investors look for dividends in established companies like Ford and General Motors, for example, to help bolster their total return. But emerging growth companies—admittedly more speculative vehicles—can often provide a greater rate of appreciation by plowing back profits and using leverage to keep expanding. This is especially critical for companies like Murdoch's that have not yet reached their full market potential and have room to grow—unlike the Fords, GMs and GEs of the world, who have already carved out a substantial niche in the market and whose main concern is preserving market share.

"Rupert and Anna were comfortably settled in New York at that time," one of his associates said. "They were still living in their Fifth Avenue duplex with the three kids,"—Elisabeth, Lachlan and James—not counting Rupert's daughter Prudence from his first marriage. "They also bought a renovated colonial farmhouse near Chatham." Chatham is located in the Berkshire Mountains, south of Albany and close to the Massachusetts border.

By his own admission—as well as the opinion of those the author has spoken to who know him well—Murdoch was and is a conservative man in taste and lifestyle as well as political orientation. Unlike Anna, who had a more sociable side to her nature, according to family friends, Murdoch prefers to live quietly and frugally, spending time with old friends rather than mixing with strangers.

"I'm a bit dull and humorless," he told Time magazine in January 1977, "not the sort of person who makes social friends easily."

The little time he did take off for relaxation was spent skiing or on an occasional game of tennis, and he told me that these sports remain his primary form of exercise today. Chatham is within an hour's drive of half a dozen ski areas, including Hunter Mountain, Butternut, Catamount, Jiminy Peak and Brody. Some years later he sold his farm house in Chatham and replaced it with a spacious condominium on the slopes in Aspen.

To Murdoch, the pleasures of relaxing on a mountain were

always a distant second to those he found in the business world. His major preoccupation in New York City remained the reorganization and restructuring of the New York *Post*. To help him in these efforts, he appointed as executive editor Ed Bolwell, a fellow Australian who had worked for Murdoch's father years before and more recently served as an editor on the New York *Times* and Time magazine.

"Running a newspaper is a little like conducting a symphony orchestra," Bolwell told Time shortly after his appointment. "Some people have to be badgered and some coddled to get the best out of them. And you have to stretch. Not to stretch is not to live. I am very competitive."

Others Murdoch brought on board at the time were the two Steves—Steve Dunleavy, mentioned earlier, a rough-and-tumble Australian and Murdoch loyalist, and Steve Cuozzo, an American who is a managing editor of the *Post* today. Dunleavy still works for Murdoch at Fox-5 Television, and Cuozzo told me that Murdoch was very much involved in revamping the newspaper, and he regarded Murdoch as someone who was "good to work for."

Before Murdoch acquired it, the circulation of the *Post* had fallen below 500,000 while that of its only remaining rival, the *Daily News,* had risen to two million. The story that provided Murdoch with his first opportunity to narrow the gap with the *News* was the bizarre Son of Sam murders that preoccupied New Yorkers throughout the spring and summer of 1977. Otherwise known as the .44 Caliber Killer, a deranged murderer named David Berkowitz had terrorized the entire city by preying on young couples in automobiles parked in out-of-the-way lovers' lanes.

The story had all the elements—sex, violence, terror—that Murdoch knew how to cover as well as anyone in the business. While Son of Sam had New Yorkers cowering in fear, power blackouts, minority riots and a hotly contested political contest in the fall also provided Murdoch with further grist for his mill. Emotions were running extremely high, and that summer was a singularly unpleasant time for anyone living in or near New York City. I remember well the collective sigh of relief when Berkowitz, a postal worker living in Yonkers, was finally arrested in August.

The *Post* went head to head with the *Daily News* in its detailed—some said lurid—coverage of the story. The atmosphere was charged; it was Jack the Ripper New York style, with modern embellishments. *News* columnist Jimmy Breslin titillated the city by quoting from letters sent to him, signed "Son of Sam," and the *Post* retaliated by publishing several earlier letters Berkowitz had written to an old girlfriend. Many criticized both newspapers for their "high-pitched" style of journalism, but no one could argue with the results: the circulation of the *Post* started to climb.

Excessive heat, power blackouts followed by looting in the ghettos, a summer of uneasiness and fear were also covered in detail by both publications. To some the coverage was excessive, to others it was good old-fashioned mass-market journalism.

To his credit, Murdoch did attempt to defuse some of the tension in the air with a speech before the Rotary Club in which he stated, according to Kiernan, "The racial discord in the city is aggravated by demagogues playing cynical and political games . . ."

As summer lengthened and faded and some of the troubles receded with it, the hotly contested battle for the mayoralty of New York City replaced the other stories on the front pages. The main event in the Democratic primary featured a classic contest between a bland, generally inept incumbent named Abraham Beame and a fiery and colorful challenger, Congressman Edward Koch.

Murdoch had no use for Beame, whom he blamed for New York's fiscal problems, and he lent his support—as did the *News*—to Koch. Ed Koch went on to beat Beame in the primary, and was later elected New York's 105th mayor in the general election on November 8th. Koch said afterward that Murdoch's role was crucial in his election since the old *Post,* under Dorothy Schiff, would most likely have backed another candidate in the primary, someone to the left of both himself and Beame.

The *Post* also found itself in the midst of a controversy of sorts when it ran an article in late August protesting the release of Alice Crimmins from prison. The Crimmins case had been major news in 1971. A beautiful redhead with a taste for the seamier side of life, she had been convicted and sentenced to from five to twenty years for the murder of one of her children in 1965.

Murdoch was castigated in some quarters for pillorying Crimmins on the front page of the *Post.* After serving only six years of her sentence, had she fully paid her debt to society for the crime she was convicted of? Some thought not, Murdoch among them. And he was not alone in his assessment.

Chapter
Nine

B Y THE fall of 1978, less than two years after his first lunch date with Dorothy Schiff, Murdoch had managed to increase the circulation of the New York *Post* to about 900,000 copies a day. He had succeeded in narrowing the gap with the popular *Daily News*, but the paper continued to show significant losses despite some cost-cutting measures he took during the New York newspaper strike in August 1978. His other American operations were profitable, however, and more than made up for the *Post*'s losses.

With his sprawling empire firmly entrenched in the United States, Murdoch again turned his attention back to his native country. His big frustration in the land Down Under was his failure to establish himself as a major power in the television field. Until now, his dominance was in print media, while his electronic holdings were relatively minor and confined to smaller cities.

The big leagues in Australia meant Sydney first and Melbourne second. His first big opportunity to crack the Sydney market arose when Channel 10, the city's third-largest station, went on the auction block. The station was owned by United Telecasters Ltd., and early in 1979 two of the company's largest shareholders expressed interest in selling a substantial block of stock totaling 22 percent of the company. Sir Kenneth Humphreys, the head of United Telecasters, offered to sell part of the block to Murdoch and a smaller portion to another shareholder, effectively distributing the station's ownership in a manner that denied effective control to any one party.

Shared power was not a concept that appealed to Murdoch. Smelling blood upon the waters, Murdoch homed in for the kill. Establishing a monumental line of credit (again, using goodwill for collateral), the Australian started to accumulate stock in United Telecasters Ltd. on the Sydney All Ordinaries market, which is equivalent to the New York Stock Exchange. Within weeks, after buying stock publicly and arranging a private deal with one of the major shareholders, Murdoch found himself with the lion's share of the company, some 46 percent of the outstanding shares, which effectively gave him control.

Australian law prohibits any individual from owning more than 5 percent of two stations in the same market, so to comply with it Murdoch happily divested himself of his interest in the small station in Wollongong, a Sydney suburb. His successful raid on Sydney was now a *fait accompli*, but still had to pass approval by the Australian Broadcasting Tribunal, the television regulatory agency. His application was fought by representatives of the Labor Party, still fuming over his role in the 1975 election.

In his own defense, according to biographer Michael Leapman, Murdoch said in testimony before the tribunal, "Because I love this country, because my wife and children do, I bring them here as often as I can. Who else has risked everything to start a national newspaper which goes across the length and breadth of this country? Who employs more than fifteen thousand people with opportunities to work throughout the world? I started the *Australian* fifteen years ago as a dream. Nearly thirteen million dollars has gone into making that dream a reality."

Murdoch's performance was evidently convincing, and the members of the tribunal voted in his favor.

Three months after his takeover of Channel 10 in Sydney, Murdoch embarked on another TV campaign—this time for control of Channel 10 in Melbourne. Sydney and Melbourne, Australia's two largest cities, provided approximately 60 percent of the country's total advertising revenue. There were three major stations in Melbourne, one owned by the Packer organization, the second by the Herald and Weekly Times group that Murdoch's father had established and allowed to slip away because of its ownership structure and the third by Australia's second-largest airline company, Ansett Transportation Industries, which served the domestic market (Qantas, the largest, is an international carrier).

Since none of the three was up for sale, Murdoch decided that the best way to gain control of one of them was by acquiring Ansett, which was experiencing some financial difficulty. Its shares had fallen in price throughout the early part of 1979, making them an attractive target for an investor looking to buy them cheaply. Murdoch was not the only player in the market with an eye for stock at bargain basement prices. Robert Holmes à Court, relatively unknown at the time but a financier to be reckoned with today, owned about 5 percent of the stock, which he bought on the market. Thomas Nationwide Transport owned another sizable block of shares amounting to 15 percent of the company.

Murdoch had added about $50 million to his war chest following his takeover of Channel 10 by spinning off his bauxite mines in Western Australia, and he was now flush with cash. So armed, he entered the market and acquired Ansett shares, triggering a race among himself, Holmes à Court, and an oil company named Ampol, another interested party, for control of the airline—and ultimately, as far as Murdoch was concerned, the coveted Melbourne television station. Within weeks, Holmes à Court had upped his ante to 15 percent, equal to Thomas Nationwide Transport's holding. Ampol was up to 20 percent, and Murdoch, coming on strong, was a 9 percent owner.

The four-way stalemate resulted in a situation where no one had effective control of Channel 10's parent company. Frustration ran high in all camps, but the impasse would not last long. After a good deal of jockeying behind the scenes, Murdoch finally reached an agreement with Holmes à Court to buy his shares, guaranteeing the South African–born financier an $11 million profit. With Holmes à Court's shares in his treasury along with his own 9 percent, Murdoch teamed up with Sir Peter Abeles, managing director of Thomas Nationwide Transport, to jointly take over Ansett. He was now by far the company's largest shareholder. The rest was academic. He bought Ampol's 20 percent holding, giving him a total of 44 percent of Ansett. This, along with Abeles' 15 percent, gave both men—who have remained business allies to this day—effective control.

Another acrimonious session before the regulatory board followed, resulting at first in a decision against Murdoch.

But, after intervention from the government the ruling was reversed, and by the time the dust settled Murdoch not only owned two major television stations in Australia's two largest cities, but the country's second largest airline as well.

In 1979, Murdoch decided to alter somewhat the structure of his empire. He changed the name of his Sydney-based holding company from News Limited to the News Corporation Ltd. News International Ltd. continued to manage his operations in England, and News America Publishing, Inc. ran things in the United States.

(A detailed list of the various Murdoch properties throughout the world appears at the end of the book.)

The board of directors of News Corporation Ltd. also reflected the changing cast of players who were most influential in Murdoch's life. Members included himself as chief executive, Stanley S. Shuman of Allen & Co. and a relatively new face on the scene, Donald D. Kummerfeld, who was to be his chief operating officer at News America for seven years before assuming a new role as president of the Magazine Publishers Association.

The importance of the position occupied by Kummerfeld in Murdoch's empire cannot be exaggerated. His list of accomplishments and credentials, his contacts in New York and Washington, D.C., his influence in both the business and political spheres provided him with a résumé that is perhaps comparable in length to that of President George Bush. According to Elizabeth Harris, a New York socialite and friend of Kummerfeld, he had been the budget director for the city of New York. Prior to that he'd been at First Boston and was hired away by his old friend John Zuccati when he was first deputy mayor under Beame.

Kummerfeld loves public life, according to Harris, so he worked for Zuccati until he became the staff head of the Municipal Assistance Corporation. There he met Stan Shuman, who was Murdoch's investment banker, and Shuman realized how much Murdoch could use an assistant with Kummerfeld's credentials.

In brief, Kummerfeld was plugged in where it mattered, where he could do Murdoch the most good financially and politically. Hiring Kummerfeld was more than just a smart move on Murdoch's part. Having Kummerfeld on his team was an incalculable benefit that went way beyond his ability as a mere executive. I learned from another source that Kummerfeld had also served for a while at the U.S. Bureau of the Budget and the Government Research Corporation, and that he was the main architect of Murdoch's financial growth in the United States during the seven years he ran News America.

Chapter
Ten

MURDOCH'S ACQUISITION of Ansett led him inadvertently into his first major political contretemps in the United States. Both Ansett and Trans-Australia Airlines (TAA), another domestic carrier, had a long-standing agreement to buy wide-bodied Airbus A300B4s from a consortium of European manufacturers. At the end of 1979, with the fleets of both companies in need of restocking, TAA put through an order to buy four of the European aircraft and took an option on another eight.

Murdoch, ever on the lookout for a bargain, decided to shop around for a better deal.

On his way back to the U.S. he stopped off in Seattle, Boeing's headquarters, and reached an agreement to buy a combination of 767s, 727s, and 737s—some twenty-one in all—from the American company, provided he could get better financing than Airbus Industrie, the European conglomerate, was offering.

To put the matter into perspective, it is important to understand the economic climate that prevailed at the time. Jimmy Carter was running for reelection in a hard-fought series of Democratic primaries that included such formidable contenders as Senator Edward M. Kennedy of Massachusetts. Inflation was soaring into double digits, gold had run up to over $800 an ounce, silver to $50 with some assistance from the Hunt brothers of Texas, the interest on mortgages would eventually reach 17 percent, CDs were paying about the same and the prime rate would go as high as 21 percent.

I was an investment broker and financial analyst at the time, writing investment guides for the public and a market letter for my clients. I remember well the climate of fear and panic that gripped Wall Street at the end of 1979 and throughout much of 1980. When silver finally crashed—and stocks with it—in March 1980, several major brokerage firms were threatened with bankruptcy, including such venerable institutions as Bache, Merrill Lynch and Shearson Loeb Rhoades. The Hunt brothers of Texas had borrowed hundreds of millions of dollars from them to buy silver on margin (i.e., the investor puts down only a small percentage of the transaction and the brokerage firm lends the rest). When the price of silver plummeted, the firms asked the Hunts to pay back the loans and the brothers shocked Wall Street when they announced that they couldn't come up with the cash. This meant that the firms themselves would have had to meet the astronomical margin calls to satisfy federal regulations, an obligation that would have forced a number of them into bankruptcy.

With firms of that calibre strained to the breaking point, the end result could well have been a general panic that threatened the entire financial system. At that point, the Federal Reserve, under Paul Volcker, felt obligated to arrange a $1.1 billion loan for the Hunts from a consortium of banks so that they could pay the money they owed their brokers, and a modicum of stability returned to the markets.

In this highly charged financial atmosphere, with interest rates skyrocketing and inflation soaring, Rupert Murdoch came under attack for attempting to arrange a low-cost loan for himself to buy the Boeing aircraft. But everybody was scrambling for whatever edge they could get.

The incident that invited the wrath of the Senate Banking Committee involved a series of events centered around the Democratic primary in New York City. It began with the New York *Post*'s endorsement of Carter over his chief rival, Senator Kennedy, in the New York primary. It culminated six days later when Murdoch's Ansett received approval of a $209 million loan from the Export-Import Bank at 8.1 percent—the same day he had lunch with President Jimmy Carter in the White House.

"In reality, the deal was much more complicated than that," said one of Murdoch's financial advisors. "The loan was made in the form of a basket of currencies—French francs, German marks and American dollars—at varying rates of interest that blended together at a shade over 8 percent."

Questions were raised regarding the propriety of the loan, as well as its timing, coinciding as it did with the White House luncheon.

Senator William Proxmire, who was then chairman of the Senate Committee on Banking, Housing and Urban Affairs, the watchdog agency that regulated the activities of the Export-Import Bank, called for a full investigation of the incident. The hearings were conducted over two days, May 12th and 13th, 1980, on the fifth floor of the Senate office building next to the Capitol. Murdoch agreed to testify, even though the committee lacked the authority to compel him to do so; he was accompanied by Donald Kummerfeld and Howard Squadron, his lawyer.

On May 13th Murdoch said in his defense that there was no quid pro quo. "My luncheon with the President was totally unconnected to the Ansett purchase of Boeing aircraft and accompanying Ex-Im loan," the New York *Times* of May 14, 1980, quoted him as saying.

"Neither at the luncheon," he continued, "or at any other time . . . did I or anybody else representing Ansett discuss the purchase of Boeing aircraft or the Ex-Im loan."

Robert Strauss, who was heading up Jimmy Carter's reelection committee, likewise denied any impropriety. Senator Proxmire had the last word when he stated that he saw an "incredible series of coincidences" that continued to trouble him. But in the end Murdoch was absolved of any wrongdoing. Proxmire's committee failed to establish any proof of collusion between the president and the Australian publisher, and the allegations were dropped.

There was some irony in that Murdoch's first choice in the race for president that year was the Republican Ronald Reagan, whom he supported in the general election in November. Aside from any financial considerations, Murdoch endorsed Carter over Kennedy in the New York Democratic primary because he regarded Carter as the most conservative in a field that also included Jerry Brown of California.

With the brouhaha over the loan finally put to rest, Murdoch and Abeles, his friendly partner at Ansett, went on to transform the airline into a highly profitable aircraft leasing company as well as a domestic carrier. By 1989, it was carrying six and half million passengers to sixty ports within the country. It owned a luxury resort on Hayman Island, near the Barrier Reef in Queensland, and was expanding further into the resort field. A subsidiary, Ansett New Zealand, was competing strongly with Air New Zealand on domestic flights within that country. Ansett also owned a 25 percent interest in Ladeco, a private Chilean airline, 20 percent of America West, based in Phoenix, Arizona, and managed Polynesian Airways for the Western Samoan government.

Not incidently, Ansett's fleet of aircraft still included Boeing jets, as well as European Fokker F50s and Skystar A320s.

"It was shortly after the Ansett flap," said one of Murdoch's associates, speaking off the record, "that Rupert launched what I like to call 'his Second Invasion of Great Britain.' I mean, there were others in the interim, to be sure, but in 1981 he returned with a vengeance.

"I think he was getting bored at the time," she continued. "He was well established in the U.S., he had that big success in Australia with the television and . . . well, what was there to do? Go down to the stone and write more headlines, fire some editors, drive everybody crazy with questions about the cost of newsprint? He's a terrible fidget. When he doesn't have a deal to do, he travels around and checks up on his people, gives them fits until he leaves.

"The *Times* of London was always a thorn in his side. They didn't like him from the start, even made some racialist jokes about his Aussie background. The *Times* represented everything Rupert disliked about England—class consciousness, snobbery, that sort of thing. The paper was never that profitable but it did have cachet. It was upper class, it had the kind of acceptance Rupert envied.

"I don't believe he really entertained, wasn't really all that serious about owning it until this time. It was something for him to do. I mean, for sure it wasn't the money. The *Post* was draining him, so was the *Australian*, and while overall he was sound, he definitely did not need another strain on his resources. It was more a vanity thing, I'm sure of it. He needed to show them he was more than just the Dirty Digger they portrayed. That Murdoch of the Mammaries stuff bothered him very much."

Apparently it did. Murdoch himself was quoted by William H. Meyers of the New York *Times* as saying, "Part of the Australian character is wanting to take on the world. It's a hard, huge continent inhabited by a few European descendents with a sense of distance from their roots. They have a great need to prove themselves."

"Part of it was Harold Evans," said my source, elaborating on her earlier comments. "Rupert never liked him much, I don't think. But people who read the *Times* revered him. Look what he owes Murdoch now versus what Murdoch owes him. He used to edit the *Times* and now look where he is."

In 1989 Harold Evans was heading up Conde Nast Traveler in New York City. His wife, Tina Brown, had a similar post at Vanity Fair, another Conde Nast publication. Harold Evans was destined to play a major role in Murdoch's life in 1981 and the years following.

"Harold Evans used to work for Rupert at the *Times*," said Maxwell Newton "and Rupert gave him the sack. He wrote a book about Rupert also, sticking the boots into him."

Newton was referring to Evans's book, *Good Times, Bad Times*, which he wrote after he was fired from the *Times*, telling his side of the story. In 1989, the former editor of the *Times* of London did not see any reason to change his mind about his old boss.

"People began to think that the only thing in my life was Rupert Murdoch and I was obsessed by him," Evans said to me, "and I'm not obsessed by him. I still happen to be highly critical."

The *Times* and the *Sunday Times* were two separate newspapers owned by Times Newspapers Ltd. which was controlled by Kenneth Thomson, a wealthy Canadian. The two publications were struggling financially following a series of debilitating disputes with their labor unions. In January 1981, the small and wiry Harold Evans, then fifty-two years old, was the editor of the *Sunday Times,* while his counterpart on the daily *Times* was the tall, aristocratic Sir William Rees-Mogg. Murdoch, two months shy of his fiftieth birthday, reached a conditional agreement to buy the two publications from Times Newspapers Ltd. The conditions were, according to the New York *Times* of January 23, 1981, that he reach a settlement with the unions within three weeks, and that the British government approve the transaction.

The Thomson organization also stated that its agreement with Murdoch was contingent upon a guarantee from the Australian that he would do nothing to lower the tone or character of the one-hundred-and-ninety-five-year-old newspaper. Besides the daily *Times* and the *Sunday Times,* also included in the sale were the Times Literary Supplement, the Times Education Supplement, and the Times Higher Education Supplement, all weeklies.

At a news conference in London, Murdoch stated according to the January 23, 1981, New York *Times,* "I am not seeking to acquire these papers in order to change them into something entirely different. Whatever proposals for progress may be developed, there will be no fundamental change in the characteristics."

Denis Hamilton, editor-in-chief of both the *Times* and *Sunday Times,* commented, "I believe that Rupert Murdoch is one of the greatest newspaper executives in the world today. These newspapers, in the tough situation they are in, will be best in the hands of a fellow professional."

The labor force of the newspapers, some four thousand strong at the time, was governed by seven unions. Joe Wade, the leader of one of the printers unions, was quoted in the same New York *Times* article, "I know from personal experience that Mr. Murdoch can be a tough and ruthless negotiator. But at the end of the day I know we can get a fair agreement with him."

The losses sustained by the Thomson organization at the time totaled more than $30 million a year. The circulation of the prestigious daily *Times* was only three hundred thousand a day, far less than a tenth of that of Murdoch's highly profitable *Sun*.

"There was a huge flap at the time," said a close associate of Murdoch, "over how much power Rupert would command if the sale went through. Much of this was outright snobbery, I think. Those who read the *Times* considered themselves the elite. They took pride in small numbers, that they were better than the rabble, and Rupert was going to change all that."

Murdoch was not without his supporters in the press, however. Prior to an emergency debate in Parliament over the pending sale, about a hundred of the *Times*'s two hundred and ninety journalists issued a statement saying that Murdoch's bid was the best hope of saving the newspaper. The parliamentary debate resulted in a favorable decision for Murdoch, clearing the way for the negotiations to continue. The February 9, 1981, New York *Times* quoted Murdoch's seventy-year-old mother as saying she received a phone call from her son regarding the imminent purchase.

"He has always tried very hard to warn me as each crisis has arisen. He was very enthusiastic about it and very anxious that we should all be pleased and happy. We as a family always support him up to the hilt."

Murdoch completed an agreement with the unions, according to the February 13, 1981, New York *Times*, calling for the elimination of about seven hundred jobs and the introduction of new printing technology, including the use of so-called "cold type" to replace the slower and more costly lead-type or "hot type" system. The unions had resisted cold type for years, but Murdoch said they had finally come around to accepting economic reality. "The fear of losing jobs concentrates one's mind," he said.

With the union agreement now behind him, there was nothing left standing in the way of the sale. It was consumated at a final price of $28 million, turning Murdoch into one of the most powerful Fleet Street publishers of the twentieth century. Murdoch also had to pay out an additional $15 million for employees who were to be dismissed during the following weeks. Even so, the price was regarded as a bargain by many publishing professionals. The *Times* building alone was worth an estimated $40 million, and even though the newspapers had been losing money for years, Murdoch had a clearly established track record of turning losers into winners.

After the sale was completed, Murdoch moved the aforementioned Harold Evans from the *Sunday Times* over to the daily *Times* as its new editor. Evans succeeded William Rees-Mogg, the daily *Times* editor for the past fourteen years, on March 1, 1981. Evans, who began his journalism career on provincial newspapers in the north of England, had subsequently earned a reputation as a hard-hitting and somewhat controversial investigative journalist.

Murdoch's relationship with Evans was destined to go down in history as one of the stormiest publisher-editor conflicts in recent history. Evans told me that the Australian interfered with the editorial side of things from the start, but the fiery editor was not immune from criticism himself. Other publications, including Harpers and Queen magazine and Private Eye magazine, denounced the changes the new editor imposed.

Harpers and Queen called the new *Times* "a fallen lady whose heart has been plucked out by whiz kids and replaced by a more up-to-date model," and Private Eye had a field day parodying some of Evans's innovations.

In his defense, according to the New York *Times* of November 30, 1981 Evans replied, "These people must be joking, or else they're the kind of people who confuse pomposity with seriousness—a common type in Britain."

Chapter
Eleven

THE FEUD between Murdoch and Harold Evans evolved into a *cause célèbre* that intensified considerably during the early months of the following year. Evans's resentment of Murdoch continues unabated until today. The former editor of the *Times* articulates the "downside" of Murdoch—the barrage of criticism that has been hurled at him over the years—perhaps more eloquently than anyone else I've spoken to, and it is worth evaluating the comments he made to me in March 1989 to get a full picture of Murdoch the man and Murdoch the publishing magnate.

"It's got more important, the Murdoch story in America," Evans said, "particularly with Channel 5 and Fox and all that . . . If you look at what's happened to the *Times* in London since I left, or the *Sunday Times* for that matter, the points that were important to me about independence as a paper, and nonpolitical bias and noncommercial bias—all those points have now been lost in London. The editor of the *Sunday Times*, for instance, has accepted a position as chairman of Murdoch's Sky Television—which is an amazing thing—while staying editor of the *Sunday Times*, so that the *Sunday Times* is promoting actively in its pages Sky Television, which is owned by Murdoch and whose chairman is the editor of the paper.

"I mean, an appalling mix of commercial interests there. The *Times* itself, it's now pretty well documented . . . went extreme ideologically right wing and stayed that way, lost its independence in that sense. It's all come true, you know. That's why the independent newspaper's done so very well in London, because it's taken over the *Times'* independence.

"Somebody said to me the other day . . . Mr. Murdoch couldn't possibly dominate editors all over the world. Well, in fact, he can because they know what he wants and they live in fear. And so you'll find, in all his papers, by and large they reflect his tendencies . . . If I were a Murdoch editor now, I would know exactly what position to take on any civil rights controversy, anything to do with the Contras, anything to do with the Soviet Union and so on . . . The general pornography of Murdoch's papers in London is appalling. I couldn't believe it when I got back to see what they were doing."

"You mean the *Sun* primarily?" I asked.

"Well that's *him,*" Evans said. "He's responsible for every piece of fabricated news which they do regularly, every piece of sadism and distortion that gets in the paper—it's not something from which Murdoch can dissociate himself. In fact, he doesn't dissociate himself from it. It's *him.*"

When I discussed these issues with a number of editors and writers who currently work for Murdoch, the portrait they painted was decidedly different.

"The idea that Rupert is some sort of a vulgarian is a canard that's been put out by those people who are trying to denigrate his achievements," Maxwell Newton said. "He began [the *Australian*] at the age of thirty-five, and it bloody near put his whole company into a loss. Since that time he's made tremendous gains in tabloid publication, but really not on a particularly large scale in relation to his whole business.

"He's got a very considerable, realistic skill in understanding what the masses of people are interested in. And this gives fits to a lot of people."

Another of Murdoch's writers, speaking off the record, said, "Frankly, I think he has every right to do whatever he wants with his publications. [Murdoch] is in the Hearst tradition, which is an American tradition . . . I'm not so sure that we have any option but having the Murdochs in this business. And therefore, I feel very differently about the sorts like Evans who get in snits. I happen to dislike yuppie journalism as much as I dislike a lot of his journalism, and I think there's perhaps more to be said in defense of [Murdoch's] journalism . . . I think his politics has a lot to do with the criticism, too. I mean, the whole Ted Kennedy affair was directed largely toward [Murdoch]. If I owned a paper, I know myself that I would do what he's doing. It *is* a capitalist society. I think he ought to have the right, if he owns something, to do what he wants, at least on the editorial page."

So, we have two contrasting views of Rupert Murdoch—a man who incites a high degree of passion from different quarters. Perhaps we should not be surprised that someone who has been able to accomplish so much also has the capacity to spark such controversy wherever his presence is felt. Like many men and women of great achievement Murdoch seems to be a complex individual, with many facets to his nature.

Whatever view of Murdoch one forms, it is usually a highly

charged one. There is little in the way of middle ground where the Australian media lord is concerned.

He and Harold Evans, a man of strongly felt and strongly voiced opinions himself, were apparently destined to clash right from the start. Murdoch kept him on as editor of the *Times* for a year, but by March of 1982 he was gone.

While Rupert Murdoch was enmeshed in his battle to buy the *Times,* his fiftieth birthday was looming just beyond the horizon.

"Anna was determined to make it a gala event," a friend of the Murdochs said. "She organized a lovely bash at the Cavan Ranch, the Murdoch estate near Canberra. It was mostly for family, but some friends were there as well.

"Quite a turnout it was, too. Lasted a couple of days as I recall, over the weekend. There was a sumptuous dinner the first night with live music and fireworks. Anna put together a film showing highlights of Rupert's life. The partying continued the next day, plenty of food and drink—and then a big surprise: a plane flew overhead pulling a streamer that said 'Happy Birthday, Rupert.' Two jumpers popped out and landed in the middle of the festivities. Very nicely done.

"One of the nicest touches was a portrait of Rupert Anna commissioned from one of his favorite artists. He was quite moved by it. I don't think I'd ever seen him so moved."

By this time Murdoch had already rehired Maxwell Newton, his former editor of the *Australian,* and brought him up to the States. Newton started writing his financial column for the New York *Post* (later it was syndicated throughout the Murdoch system), and the publisher made other changes in his continuing circulation war with the *Daily News.*

In addition to pushing the *Post* in a more conservative

political direction, he added other features, including a game called Wingo, which required readers to buy the paper every day in order to qualify for certain prizes. He also began to publish the *Post* around the clock, adding several new editions in the morning and at different times in the afternoon, changing the headlines each time in an effort to keep abreast of late-breaking news.

This was an expensive innovation, but it paid off in terms of circulation. The circulation of the rival *Daily News* dropped off in the beginning from two million copies a day and three million on Sundays to a million four hundred thousand daily and two million on Sundays. Meanwhile, the *Post*'s circulation had risen from a low of below five hundred thousand when Murdoch bought it to its peak of nine hundred thousand a day. The problem was that the costs of publishing all those new editions skyrocketed with the circulation and Murdoch continued to run into a stone wall with advertisers. Try as he did to attract additional advertising revenue, it failed to materialize.

This was the view expressed to me by many who worked there. But Murdoch himself has a somewhat different perspective on the problem. As he explained it, the *Post* could very well have turned a profit had he been able to boost its circulation beyond that of the rival *Daily News.* Had he done that, he said, there would have been no problem with advertisers.

"Murdoch's critics," one of his writers said, "always point to the headlines in the *Post* or the contents of the *Sun* to show what kind of man he is. They never mention the finer things he's done. For instance, how many people have bothered to point out that he was one of the producers of *Gallipoli?*"

He was referring to Murdoch's first venture into feature films when he teamed up with fellow Australian, Robert

Stigwood, to produce the movie *Gallipoli*. Actually, the movie had been released a couple of years earlier in Australia to general critical acclaim, and was distributed in the United States and elsewhere in 1981 and 1982.

Gallipoli is a poignant and searing portrayal of the massacre of Australian troops by Turkish forces in the Middle East in 1915. It received mostly rave reviews during its release in the United States, and was commercially successful as well. Murdoch said later that he had been attracted to the story because of the role his father played as a journalist during the Gallipoli campaign, exposing the atrocities of the war. Keith Murdoch's dispatches from the front established his reputation at home, earned him fame as an Australian patriot and intrepid reporter. There was more than mere coincidence in Rupert Murdoch's interest in the production of the film. To a great extent, he was paying homage to his father's shining moment as a journalist.

The artistic and commercial success of *Gallipoli* sharpened Murdoch's appetite for more of the same. His investment banker, Allen & Co., had established a major presence in Hollywood when it gained control of Columbia Pictures in 1973, and later found itself ensnared in the David Begelman embezzlement scandal of the late 1970s. Herbert (Herbie) Allen, who was now president of the company that had been controlled by his uncle Charles Allen for years, was married at the time to the actress Ann Reinking, and he was anxious for Rupert Murdoch to expand his empire further into the film industry. Several years later the Australian would do just that when, largely under the guidance of Herbie Allen and Stan Shuman, he acquired control of 20th Century Fox.

So, while it was true that Murdoch did depend to a great extent on tabloid journalism to pay his bills, there was another side to the man as well—a side reflected in his continuing support of the *Australian,* as well as in a number of additional publications such as the Times Literary Supplement and Educational Supplement, Mirabella, In Fashion, New York, New Woman and other magazines.

Murdoch continued to support Israel and Jewish causes around the world. In recognition of this fact, the American Jewish Congress—then headed by Howard Squadron— hosted a dinner in his honor at the New York Hilton in April, 1982, naming him Communications Man of the Year. Seven years later, on April 6, 1989, Murdoch had a chance to reverse roles with his lawyer when Yeshiva University's Benjamin N. Cardoza School of Law honored Squadron at its annual dinner in New York City, during which it established the Howard M. Squadron Program in Communications Law. Rupert Murdoch was the chairman for the event.

Chapter
Twelve

ON APRIL 12, 1982, Rupert Murdoch announced that he would be willing to buy the *Post*'s primary rival in New York City, the *Daily News,* in an effort to keep both papers afloat.

The competition between the *News* and the *Post,* Murdoch said, according to the New York *Times* of April 13, 1989, was "a dance of death which must end with the disappearance of one or both newspapers."

"It was quite amusing," one of Murdoch's associates said, "to hear the squalling that went on in some quarters when people got wind of that. I mean, they were in a snit already because he owned the *Post.* Now they were faced with the prospect of his buying up the competition. It was too funny, really."

The Tribune Company of Chicago, which owned the *Daily News* and had been negotiating its sale with Texas financier

Joseph Allbritton, did not find Murdoch's interest quite so amusing. It regarded his bid as "a transparent attempt to destroy and shut down" the *News,* according to the February 13, 1989, New York *Times.* This, of course, would leave Murdoch without competition and virtually guarantee the *Post*'s profitability.

The unions were caught in the middle, since the quid pro quo for any sale would be a loss of jobs at the printing plant. The *Post* was not the only newspaper losing money in New York; despite its higher circulation, the *News* had lost $12 million the previous year and was expected to lose substantially more in 1982.

And the Tribune Company of Chicago was not alone in its failure to find humor in Murdoch's bid for the *News.* In an article published in the July 13, 1982, New York *Times,* Sydney H. Schanberg—a reporter whose coverage of the war in Vietnam was made into the movie *The Killing Fields*—was nearly apoplectic on the subject. The article entitled, "The Tasmanian Devil," accused Murdoch of making "politicians afraid of him and his power to sway minds . . . Put simply, Rupert Murdoch seems willing to go on losing many millions annually on his generally trashy tabloid so long as it provides him the platform to wield power in the city and be a political kingmaker."

In the same Op Ed piece, Schanberg managed to stretch the bounds of logic by saying, "The *Post* has expanded its political coverage of late, improving it quantitatively and sometimes qualitatively, thereby further staking out its role as a political force." In one sentence, Murdoch's *Post* is "generally trashy," while a few sentences later the quality of its political reportage has improved "qualitatively"—to serve sinister ends.

"He doesn't win either way," one of Murdoch's editors said.

"I mean, fair is fair. What it comes down to is which side of the fence one is on politically, doesn't it?"

A real note of humor was injected into the situation when Donald Trump announced that he might be interested in acquiring the *News* if the Tribune Company failed to find an acceptable buyer. A Trump takeover of the *News* would have virtually guaranteed the closing of the newspaper, since he was primarily interested in the real-estate value of its new building on Forty-second Street and Second Avenue. But in the end Murdoch's—and Trump's—critics were able to breathe more easily when the Tribune Company concluded its negotiations with Allbritton, and the Texan became the new owner of the *Daily News*. The rivalry between the two newspapers continued as before, with the *Post* gaining on the *News*'s circulation—but never able to turn a profit.

Always a man of extremes, Murdoch next turned his attention to the opposite end of New York State, to the *Courier-Express* of Buffalo.

"There are many theories about why Rupert was interested in a failing newspaper in Buffalo of all places," one of Murdoch's associates said. "Some saw sinister designs in his need to control public opinion everywhere. Well, what's wrong with using one's power to sway people's thinking? Newspapers have always backed one candidate or another, but only when Murdoch did it did it strike some people as malevolent."

Buffalo, the second-largest city in New York State, is always a pivotal city in state-wide elections. Its role in capturing the upstate vote is as critical as New York City's is in the metropolitan region. While Rupert Murdoch never stated publicly that he was looking to buy the *Courier-Express* in order to establish an upstate presence in the gubernatorial election, it had to be at least one of the factors.

The 1982 New York gubernatorial campaign was a particularly critical one ideologically. The key contenders that year were Mario Cuomo, a witty, articulate and outspoken liberal Democrat, and Lewis Lehrman, a wealthy businessman who had the support of conservative Republicans such as William F. Buckley, Jr., and those with a more libertarian bent like the author and columnist William Safire. Murdoch, never a fan of Cuomo to begin with (he supported Koch against Cuomo in the Democratic primary, during which Koch self-destructed when he referred to upstaters, in a Playboy interview, as "rubes" and described living in Albany as "a fate worse than death"), was solidly behind the Lehrman candidacy.

When the *Courier-Express* was put up for sale by Cowles Media, the Minneapolis chain that owned it, it presented Murdoch with an ideal situation. The newspaper had been operating at a loss of approximately $8.5 million a year. The unions were unwilling to go along with job cuts that were deemed necessary for the paper to turn a profit, and Cowles announced it would shut the paper altogether if it could not find a buyer. Here was another opportunity for Murdoch to acquire a failing newspaper cheaply—this one in a politically strategic location—and then attempt to turn it around as he had done so many times before.

"At first glance, he wasn't interested," a Murdoch associate said. "Rupert had Don Kummerfeld take a look at it, and the numbers just didn't add up right. But when the staff got wind that Cowles was serious about shutting it down, we figured they would be more reasonable."

For the unions, which had not been willing to yield before, it became a question of facing economic reality or losing jobs. Murdoch thought they would opt for the former, and he flew to Buffalo in September 1982 with Kummerfeld to negotiate a deal. At a news conference conducted on September 13, Kummerfeld announced that the Murdoch organization had agreed to buy the *Courier-Express* from Cowles if the unions would go along with cuts in labor and operating costs. Present with Kummerfeld during the announcement was Otto A. Silha, chairman of the Cowles Media Company. Aggregate losses at the newspaper had totaled $25 million since Cowles took over in 1979. Silha reiterated his intention to shut down the *Courier-Express* by the following Sunday, according to the New York *Times* of September 14, 1982, if the unions failed to accept Murdoch's proposals.

The newspaper employed 850 full-time and 250 part-time workers. Murdoch was seeking to cut 400 of the 1100 jobs, which would result in a reduction of $8 million in the $22 million annual labor cost.

"I made an offer," Murdoch told biographer Thomas Kiernan. "The fools'll probably reject it."

His premonition, if that's what it was, proved correct. Murdoch's proposal was turned down by the rank-and-file, and Cowles made good on its promise to shut down the newspaper if no agreement was reached.

"We voted to die with dignity," a *Courier-Express* reporter stated in an interview with Editor and Publisher, according to Michael Leapman.

Whether with dignity or otherwise, another American newspaper faded into oblivion that week, less than two months before the general election in November. Cuomo edged out Lehrman by a slim margin and became the new governor of New York; he was reelected by a larger majority four years later.

In politics, it is always interesting to speculate on "what-ifs." What if Murdoch had been able to buy the *Courier-Express* and establish his political voice in Buffalo with six or seven weeks left in the campaign? Would it have been enough to tip the balance into Lehrman's camp and put his candidate in the governor's chair? If so, would it have made any difference in the end?

"Rupert has never been one for second-guessing himself," one of his associates said. "He's never worried himself with what might have been. He's always looking ahead, two or three deals ahead of what he's doing now."

His next deal—another newspaper in another city—was already on his mind.

Chapter
Thirteen

T HE OTHER city was Boston, and the other newspaper the
foundering Boston *Herald-American.* In the 1950s, the
Herald-Traveler had been that city's leading newspaper, with
a larger circulation than that of the *Globe.* But it entered a
period of decline during the 1960s, and was acquired by the
Hearst Corporation in 1972. Hearst merged the *Herald-Traveler* with its own existing tabloid the *Record American,* and
changed the name of the new broadsheet to the *Herald-American.* The formula failed to work, and for the next decade the
Herald-American continued to lose ground to its rival the
Globe.

In the fall of 1982 Don Forst, the editor of the *Herald-American,* received a phone call from News America executive Bob Page during which he was told, "Rupert's coming to
town. He wants to talk to you," according to Michael Leapman.

Murdoch invited Forst to visit with him at his country

home near Chatham, New York. Murdoch was dressed casually, according to Forst, and he offered Forst a cup of tea, a beverage Murdoch can't seem to get enough of. As the editor of the *Herald-American* lifted the cup to his lips, "all of a sudden the cup was on the floor and the handle was in my hand," Forst recalled in 1989.

"It was not a swell feeling as a cup of tea rolled onto the Oriental rug. [Murdoch] mopped it up, he was very nice, and he said, 'Oh, it must be Ann's, she's always gluing handles onto cups.' And then she came back in and he told her what happened, and she said, 'It's the Scottish in me. I can't bear to throw anything away.' He was very gracious at that moment."

During their day together, Murdoch told Forst that he intended to make a bid for the *Herald-American,* and offered him a choice of assignments within his organization, including editorial slots at the *Village Voice* or the New York *Post.*

"It was like he was a waiter bringing the dessert menu," Forst was quoted as saying by Michael Leapman. "I didn't know whether I wanted the éclair, the chocolate mousse or the strawberry tart. I wanted it all."

In the end, however, Forst decided against any dessert at all when Murdoch suggested that he might be happy as the third managing editor at the New York *Post*—a paper that was probably already overstaffed with two managing editors. As Forst described the situation to me, "It would be like going into a shark tank without a repellent or a knife."

What did he think of Murdoch?

"I think he's terrific, I really do," he said. "He's a hell of a businessman. He has guts, he obviously runs his business out of his head. He has a few managers and that's it. He does what he wants. He's one smart son of a bitch, definitely his own man. He can be a very charming guy."

It didn't take Forst long to understand that he did not fit

into Murdoch's plans at the moment—at least not as far as Boston was concerned—and he departed on his own for other pastures. Today, he is the editor of the New York City edition of *Newsday*.

Under Forst's editorship, the circulation of the *Herald-American* had leveled off at approximately 225,000 copies a day, less than half of the *Globe*'s. Murdoch offered the Hearst Corporation $1 million for the newspaper, plus an additional $7 million to be paid out of future profits, if any. A memorandum of understanding was announced by Hearst in New York, according to the New York *Times* of November 18, 1982. This deal, like the aborted one in Buffalo, was also contingent on Murdoch reaching an agreement with the *Herald-American*'s eleven unions. A spokesman for Hearst stated that it would close down the newspaper on December 3, 1982, if no union agreement was achieved by that time. Murdoch was looking to cut about eight hundred jobs from the work force of the *Herald-American*, which was losing about $12 million a year.

"We've come to this city to try to preserve this newspaper," said Robert Page, vice president of News America, according to the same New York *Times* article. "Our interest here is to try to preserve as many jobs on the *Herald-American* as is humanly possible."

This time the strategy worked. The deal was sealed on December 2, just hours before the December 3rd deadline. The unions granted Murdoch the concessions he asked for— much to the consternation of the *Globe*, which asked for, but did not receive, the same type of manning agreement—and the *Herald-American* became the latest addition to Murdoch's empire.

Within weeks, the revamping process began. Murdoch shortened the name back to the Boston *Herald*, sent Bob Page up to Boston to take over as publisher, and Leslie Hinton from the *Star* and Joe Robinowitz from the *Post* to run the editorial department. The layout of the new *Herald* went from four to seven columns, the sports coverage was increased, as was coverage of the stock market and Boston was treated for the first time to its own version of Wingo.

Murdoch Magic succeeded in attracting new readers right from the start. Circulation went up by 100,000 during the first year, and another 50,000 to 380,000 within two years. The Sunday edition also saw a jump in readership, from 227,000 to 319,000 over the same period.

"I think the Boston *Globe* is vulnerable," Murdoch told a reporter, according to Michael Leapman. "It has an allegiance to the upper class, to the liberal attitude. Now there's nothing wrong with that. That's fine. But I think it causes resentment. We, on the other hand, can't and won't pander to a particular group. We will appeal to everyone—white collar, blue collar, and those in the middle . . ."

Regarding the type of reporting that he considered responsible for the failure of many American newspapers to attract readers, Murdoch said in the same interview, "There's an elitist attitude out there. One problem is that journalism students today are taught that papers like the New York *Times* and the Washington *Post* are the models, that what those papers do is responsible and what someone else does is irresponsible . . . Their goal seems to be to have Robert Redford play them in a movie."

To eliminate this "elitist" attitude in his own publications, Murdoch brought many writers and editors up from Australia and over from England—Steve Dunleavy, Frank Devine, Ian Rae, Sharon Churcher and others—and surrounded himself with what has come to be called his Australian Mafia. They were schooled in Murdoch's brand of journalism, and many shared his political views as well. Most of those to whom I've spoken say that Murdoch is steadfastly loyal to the people who have stayed with him longest.

Murdoch has been accused of distorting or inventing stories to sell newspapers—something he has denied to me as well as to other interviewers over the years. When I spoke to one of his writers about this, she said off the record, "I've written for many publications. I've seen stories that are invented in the *News* and I've seen them in the *Times.*"

"Actually made up?"

"Not actually made up, but . . . I mean, I'm having a piece edited right now and I'm convinced in the back of my mind, though they say not, that the editing is coming from a liberal perspective and that it's as distorted as anything I went through when I was with Murdoch's people."

She agreed with my assessment that this type of situation is quite prevalent in politics, where the networks don't so much as invent stories, but slant them to represent a point of view and thus create an alternate perception of the news.

"That's exactly what it's all about," she said. "Rupert Murdoch was much more up front about it, plus he was a foreigner."

She attributed much of the criticism leveled at Murdoch to his conservative political views, as well as his foreign heritage.

"I went through that when I first came here twenty years ago," she said. "This country was much more chauvinistic and xenophobic in those periods. It's almost gone too much the other way, where people can get off the boat one day and edit a major magazine here now the next day.

"What Murdoch went through up here was partly unfair," the reporter continued. "By then I had lived in this country a long time, but I remember getting calls and people would say, 'What right have you to be working for a newspaper in this country?' "

Today Murdoch's publications in the United States—as well as his television and film companies—are still heavily staffed by Australians and Brits, but he has hired many more American writers and executives over the years. It is worth noting that Murdoch became an American citizen three years later, in 1985, prior to acquiring Metromedia and Fox Broadcasting, in order to comply with a law prohibiting foreigners from owning U.S. television stations.

Regarding his change of citizenship, Anna Murdoch said to William H. Meyers, as he reported in a 1988 New York *Times* article, "I was shocked. I never thought he'd do it. I realized then how strong his ambitious drive was."

Murdoch's first attempted venture into the electronic media in the United States occurred in 1983, two years before he filed for U.S. citizenship, and it was not as successful as he hoped. The citizenship requirement for ownership of a television station did not apply to cable and satellite transmission. On the advice of his bankers at Allen & Co., Murdoch signed an agreement with Satellite Business Systems (SBS) to use a communications satellite in order to broadcast television programs to subscribers.

According to the May 6, 1983, New York *Times,* a spokesman for SBS announced that it had leased five transponders to Inter-American Satellite Television, Inc., a newly formed Murdoch company, primarily to service rural customers in the United States who were not wired for cable. The Murdoch system would provide five channels, including one for movies, another for sports and the remaining with programming similar to that of cable television. Subscribers would pay a monthly fee for the programs, which would be beamed to rooftop or backyard dish antennas from a satellite that had been launched the previous November from the spaceship Columbia. Murdoch paid SBS—a company jointly owned by Aetna Insurance Co., IBM, and Comsat—$75 million for the lease.

The Australian appointed Harvey L. Schein, the former chief executive of the Sony Corporation of America, as president of the satellite company, which he named Skyband, Inc.

Speaking of Murdoch, his new boss, Schein was quoted in the New York *Times* of September 1, 1983, "He truly has the courage of his convictions. He's prepared to back his dreams and instincts with resources."

The dream included a start-up date by the end of 1983, with a goal of one hundred thousand satellite subscribers within a year. Alas, this was one Murdoch dream that would not get off the ground.

"Given new developments in satellite technology," Schein announced two months later, according to the *Times* of November 8, 1983, "Skyband has decided to delay inauguration of its service."

The delay evolved into permanent postponement shortly afterward, when it became apparent that the technological shortcomings would be too expensive to overcome. The logistics of supplying all those rural households with dishes for their roofs and backyards were difficult enough. Then, there was the question of limited programming and how many households would actually sign up for it. In the end Murdoch cancelled his lease with SBS, taking a $20 million loss on the project. His first venture into electronic media was something less than a success, but the defeat did not deter him from pursuing his dream. Even while he was struggling to launch Skyband, he was actively engaged in simultaneous battles on other fronts—in the Chicago newspaper arena and in the entertainment field, in California and New York.

At the time, I wrote a financial newsletter for my investment clients, and followed closely the price movements of various media stocks as they fluctuated wildly, buffeted in the market by one takeover rumor after another—many of them centered on Murdoch.

"The weaknesses to me," media analyst Gordon Crawford said, "are that Rupert for years and years has been dying to get into the electronic media. And I would say most of his moves in the electronic media either have been easily overpaid, or the jury's still out . . . I think you can argue that he's overpaid and done some very high-risk things there that may come back to haunt him."

If there is any weakness in Murdoch's financial structure today, there is no question but that it rests in the electronic side of his empire. Basically, his empire is sound, but 1983 was the year he took on greater and greater risks than ever before to expand beyond print in the United States and break into movies and television.

"There's an electronic revolution which we're still living through," Murdoch said to me. "We haven't seen the end of it at all yet. The electronic revolution is happening in communications, in instant communications. But you need to have the ability in entertainment as well as in pure news. I'm still trying to sort that puzzle out, trying to see how the pieces fit."

The year 1983 marks the end of Murdoch as mere newspaper magnate in the Hearst and Beaverbrook tradition, and the emergence of Rupert Murdoch as one of the most powerful and influential media lords in the world today.

Part Two

STAR WARS

Chapter
Fourteen

THE YEAR 1983 did not start out well for Rupert Murdoch.
Even before his ill-fated venture with Skyband in the
United States, the Australian media lord had troubles of a
different variety across the Atlantic Ocean in England.

On Monday, February 21, the *Sun* commenced a series of
articles based on interviews with one Kieran Kenny, a former member of the Buckingham Palace staff. Kenny, who
was evidently privy to a lot of hanky panky involving members of the royal family, titillated the *Sun*'s readers with his
account of a torrid romance between Kathleen (Koo) Stark
and the libidinous Prince Andrew. The first installment, entitled "Queen Koo Romps at the Palace," sent shock waves
throughout the country. Koo Stark, it was noted, was an
American actress who specialized in sexually explicit films.

Prince Andrew's mother, Queen Elizabeth II was somewhat less than amused by the article. She was so unamused,

in fact, that she took legal action against the *Sun*, the first time she had ever done so against a newspaper. The Queen, following discussions with her press secretary, Michael Shea, left Mexico aboard the Royal Yacht Britannia and filed a legal action on the grounds that "the servant has breached an understanding of confidence" that all employees sign, according to the New York *Times* of February 24, 1983, in which they agree not to make any disclosures about their work at Buckingham Palace.

The Queen was reported to be similarly incensed a year earlier when the *Sun* published photographs of a pregnant Princess Di wearing a bikini on a Carribean beach. Now, threatened with a pending lawsuit over the Koo Stark flap, Murdoch agreed—somewhat reluctantly, one imagines—to suspend publication of the series, thereby depriving the *Sun*'s readers of a promised installment dealing with Princess Di's finesse in buttering Prince Charles's toast. As one of Murdoch's editors in New York said to the author, "Rupe doesn't invent the news, you know, he merely gives people what they want to read."

Even while Murdoch was fending off the Queen of England and dreaming of beaming television programs down to rooftop dishes from satellites in the sky, he already had his eye trained on another newspaper in a major Midwestern city in the United States. In April 1983, Field Enterprises announced that the Chicago *Sun-Times*, the eighth largest daily in the country, was up for sale. Marshall Field V and his half-brother Frederick each owned fifty percent of Field Enterprise's voting stock.

The decision to sell the *Sun-Times* apparently grew out of

a fight between the brothers over their joint business interests, according to the New York *Times* of April 16, 1983. The newspaper's circulation of 649,000 was concentrated primarily in the city, and a media analyst with Lynch, Jones & Ryan estimated the market value of the *Sun-Times* at about $250 million. Rupert Murdoch was not mentioned as one of the potential buyers.

"Most people thought it was too big a price for him," said Frank Devine, whom Murdoch later sent out to Chicago to work on the *Sun-Times*. "The heavy speculation was that Knight-Ridder or somebody like that would take it on. But Rupert proved everyone wrong in the end."

At that time Devine was working for Reader's Digest in New York, where I first met him. He also served as an editor on the New York *Post* for a while, and is currently the editor of the *Australian* in Sydney, where he returned after suffering a massive heart attack. Devine, Maxwell Newton, Steve Dunleavy and Ian Rae are all part of Murdoch's original Aussie Mafia.

Besides Knight-Ridder, the Times-Mirror Group was a leading buy-out candidate, as I recall from following the industry at that time.

"With deep regret I confirm that the anticipated sale of the *Sun-Times* is part of the Field Enterprises' restructuring," said Marshall Field V, grandson of the company's founder, according to the New York *Times* of April 16, 1983. "Had this decision been mine alone to make, I probably would not have taken this action. However, the paper will now be available to someone who will have a commitment to continue publishing a vigorous, outstanding and highly respected newspaper."

His half-brother Frederick was described by the *Times* as

a bearded amateur race-car driver living in California, who invests in real estate and movies, and Marshall as a more conservative and civic-minded Chicago businessman.

Mike Royko, perhaps the best-known columnist for the *Sun-Times,* had a somewhat cavalier response to the proposed sale when he first learned of it.

"Different owners. What's the difference?" he was quoted in the same *Times* article. "The building will still be here."

Six months later, when he discovered that his likely new boss would be none other than Rupert Murdoch, the man from Down Under, his flippant attitude gave way to one of unrestrained outrage.

In October the Field brothers announced for the first time that Rupert Murdoch was indeed close to reaching an agreement with them to buy the *Sun-Times.* Few other publishers had come up with serious offers of their own since the previous April; while the *Sun-Times* was profitable, it faced considerable competition from its major rival, the Chicago *Tribune,* which may have been a contributing factor. The Toronto *Sun* had been one of the interested parties, then dropped out of the bidding when it acquired the Houston *Post* instead.

A few days later, Field Enterprises accepted an offer of $90 million from Rupert Murdoch after turning down one of $63 million, according to the New York *Times* of November 2, 1983. The low bidder was a consortium of investors put together by the paper's publisher, Jim Hoge.

Murdoch had won the bidding war "fair and square," a tired-looking Hoge said at a press conference held in the fourth-floor newsroom overlooking the Chicago River, according to the same *Times* article. "I have no complaints."

Murdoch declared at the same gathering that he had "no set strategy" as yet for the *Sun-Times.* The newspaper had origi-

Murdoch's father, Sir Keith Murdoch, who was sixty six when he died in October, 1952. (PHOTO-GRAPH: COURTESY OF NEWS CORPORATION LTD.)

Murdoch's mother, Dame Elisabeth Murdoch, busy
in her garden at Langwarrin near Melbourne in
1963. (PHOTOGRAPH: COURTESY OF NEWS CORPORA-
TION LTD.)

Rupert and Anna Murdoch with their 15-month-old daughter Elisabeth in October, 1969. (PHOTO-GRAPH: COURTESY OF NEWS CORPORATION LTD.)

Rupert at age twenty nine holding the first edition of his recently purchased Sydney Daily *Mirror* in June, 1960. (PHOTOGRAPH: COURTESY OF NEWS CORPORATION LTD.)

Murdoch shaking hands with Sir William Carr in
1969 after the Australian acquired the News of the
World in London. (PHOTOGRAPH: ASSOCIATED PRESS.)

Clay Felker in 1976 and Murdoch as
he looked in 1969. Murdoch won
the battle for control of the New
York Magazine Co. in January,
1977. (PHOTOGRAPHS: AP WIREPHOTO.)

Murdoch and New York *Post* publisher Dorothy
Schiff as they signed an agreement in November,
1976 for the Australian to purchase the oldest
continuously published daily newspaper in the
U.S. (PHOTOGRAPH: AP WIREPHOTO.)

Murdoch being presented with the B'Nai B'Rith
Anti-Defamation League's Torch of Liberty award
by League director Benjamin R. Epstein in March,
1977. Another recipient, Louis Rubin of Troy
News Co., Inc., is on the left. (PHOTOGRAPH: ASSO-
CIATED PRESS.)

Murdoch and New York mayor Ed Koch shaking hands in 1978 at a party marking New York magazine's 10th anniversary. Governor Hugh Carey is between them and the magazine's publisher Joe Armstrong is on the right. (PHOTOGRAPH: ASSOCIATED PRESS.)

Murdoch testifies before the Senate Banking Committee in Washington in May, 1980 in connection with a low-interest loan granted to Ansett Airlines after the Australian lunched with President Jimmy Carter. (PHOTOGRAPH: AP LASERPHOTO.)

Anna and Rupert leaving the office of the Boston *Herald American* in 1982 after Murdoch agreed to buy the newspaper. (PHOTOGRAPH: AP/ WIDE WORLD PHOTOS.)

Murdoch announcing to newsmen in Chicago in 1983 that he had just purchased the Chicago *Sun-Times* from Field Enterprises, Inc. for $90 million. (PHOTOGRAPH: AP LASERPHOTO.)

Murdoch enjoying a laugh before addressing the Public Relations Society of America in New York in 1984. At the time he was engaged in litigation with Warner Communications over his attempt to buy the company. (PHOTOGRAPH: AP LASERPHOTO.)

Anna and Rupert Murdoch enjoying a light moment with Prince Charles and Princess Diana in London. (PHOTOGRAPH: COURTESY OF NEWS CORPORATION LTD.)

Murdoch pictured with Maury Povich and his wife, newscaster Connie Chung, at the premier party for "A Current Affair" in July, 1986. Povich hosted the show. (PHOTOGRAPH: AP/WIDE WORLD PHOTOS.)

Murdoch keeping up with the news by reading
one of his favorite weekly newspapers in August,
1987. (PHOTOGRAPH: COURTESY OF NEWS CORPORA-
TION LTD.)

Murdoch sitting in the editorial room at his brand-new Wapping plant on the London docks in 1988. (PHOTOGRAPH: COURTESY OF NEWS CORPORATION LTD.)

Queen Elizabeth with Murdoch, attending a news
conference during the London *Times* bi-cententary
in 1988. (PHOTOGRAPH: COURTESY OF NEWS CORPO-
RATION LTD.)

nally been founded as a liberal alternative to the more conservative *Tribune* in 1941 by the Field brothers' grandfather, Marshall Field III.

Marshall Field V stated during the news conference, "I have nothing to go on, but he is going to give the *Tribune* hell," in response to a question about Murdoch's intentions.

If Jim Hoge and Marshall Field the younger had no qualms about Murdoch's pending acquisition of the *Sun-Times,* such was not the case with columnist Royko. He took a leave of absence from the paper in December.

"I've been reading about his journalistic endeavors," he was quoted in the December 21, 1983, New York *Times,* "and he doesn't sound like my kind of guy."

A few days later his vitriol reached even greater heights—or depths, depending on how you want to look at it—when he stated Murdoch could "go kick a kangaroo someplace," according to the New York *Times* of December 25, 1983. Regarding the Field brothers, Royko added, "Now the name Field ranks with the name Capone in Chicago history."

With those utterances, plus others he made later on when he moved his column over to the *Tribune,* Royko joined Harold Evans among the ranks of those whose hostility toward Murdoch was virtually boundless. As usual, Murdoch would have the last word. When the *Tribune* also hired Jim Hoge away from the Murdoch camp and sent him to New York to orchestrate the *Daily News*'s ongoing circulation war with the *Post,* Murdoch retaliated by offering more money to several of his columnists and bringing them over to the *Post.*

"While Jim Squires [the *Tribune*'s editor] is taking his siesta," Bob Page, Murdoch's new publisher at the *Sun-Times,* told the Wall Street *Journal,* according to Michael Leapman, "we plan to eat his lunch."

Other columnists came and went. Ellen Goodman's liberal

commentaries were replaced by the conservative views of Patrick Buchanan. Garry Wills, a former conservative turned liberal, was dropped after writing an anti-Murdoch piece for Vanity Fair, edited by Harold Evans's wife Tina Brown.

"The skirmishing was ceaseless," Frank Devine said, "but Rupe did what he wanted and it's worked out well. It usually does for him."

According to Maxwell Newton, Murdoch took on the Chicago *Sun-Times* and resolved its problems, then his interests changed. Even while he was negotiating with the Field brothers, he was already going "over toward magazine production and the movies."

The stock of Warner Communications, the entertainment and broadcasting company, had taken an interesting ride during the fall of 1983. I was tracking it closely at the time, and remember well the rumors circulating about a possible takeover of the company. After hitting a high of 63¼ in 1982, Warner stock had fallen as low as 19⅞ in early 1983, then started moving up again into the low 20s on unusually high volume. Clearly, someone was accumulating the stock in a big way.

At the end of December 1983, as Murdoch was concluding his acquisition of the *Sun-Times*, Chris-Craft Industries announced that it planned to buy more than 25 percent of Warner, while Warner would simultaneously acquire a 42.5-percent stake in a Chris-Craft television subsidiary, BHC, the fourth-largest non-network television broadcast company in the nation. Media analysts speculated that the unusual move may have been an effort by Warner to avoid a takeover attempt of the company by Murdoch since he had announced earlier in the month that his holding company, News Corporation Ltd., had already accumulated 6.7 percent of Warner's stock, making it the company's single largest shareholder.

"There's no question that it's an anti-Murdoch move," industry analyst Harold Vogel of Merrill Lynch was quoted as saying in the New York *Times* of December 30, 1983. "There's no other clear reason for exchanging assets with Chris-Craft."

Barbara Russell, one of the leading female investment bankers in the country, who was at Prudential Bache at the time, agreed with that assessment. The marriage between Warner and Chris-Craft, a plastics and chemical company, seemed unlikely at best. Warner was in a financial tailspin in 1983, a victim of an enormous bloodletting sustained by its Atari division, which lost $424.7 million during the first nine months of the year alone.

Analysts first noticed the unusual volatility in Warner stock as early as September, when Murdoch announced that he had purchased a million shares. This announcement was somewhat unusual since disclosure rules require that investors notify the Securities and Exchange Commission as soon as they accumulate 5 percent or more of a company, and Murdoch's stake amounted to only 1.6 percent. When the Dow Jones News Service asked Murdoch if he intended to take over Warner, he replied, "No, it's too big for me," according to the September 30, 1983, New York *Times.* He added that the stock looked like a good buy to him at $20 a share, and he might buy more if third-quarter earnings were strong.

Third-quarter earnings were dismal that year thanks to Atari which, as mentioned, had been hemorrhaging money. Warner lost $122.4 million for the quarter compared to earnings of $17.7 million for the same quarter a year earlier. Gross revenues were off 27.5 percent during the period. Atari's operating loss alone was $180.3 million for the quarter contrasted with earnings of $109.6 million for the third quarter in 1982. In all, Warner had lost a total of $424.7 million in the first nine months of 1983.

So, if Rupert Murdoch was waiting for third-quarter results as his gauge of future buying activity, it is difficult to see what he found encouraging in these numbers. Yet, according to the New York *Times* of December 3, 1983, Murdoch revealed that his holding company had upped his stake in Warner to 6.7 percent, following a $98.1 million buying spree. It was nothing more than "an investment," he said, according to the same *Times* article, and he was not seeking to take over Warner.

Most of this buying had been financed through extensive bank borrowing, Murdoch's traditional modus operandi. As of June 30, 1983, News Corporation's total long-term debt was estimated at $234 million. (To give you some perspective on how much Murdoch's empire grew during the next six years between 1983 and 1989, his debt had soared to $7 billion while his total assets were valued at $12 billion.).

Lee S. Isgur, a media analyst at Paine Webber Mitchell Hutchins—as it was then known—speculated at the time that a Murdoch takeover of Warner might be better for the company than a hostile bid from someone else. Speaking of Murdoch, Isgur said, as reported in the *Times* of December 3, 1983, "I think he would like to own Warner, but he can't afford premium prices. He can afford to pay $1.2 billion for Warner, but not $2 billion."

Isgur was referring to the price advance in Warner's stock throughout the fall despite its miserable earnings for the third quarter, and the fact that Murdoch would be forced to pay higher prices for additional stock than he had paid so far. Much of this was due to Murdoch's own heavy buying which, ironically enough, attracted speculators to the stock and made it even more expensive to accumulate. Isgur did remark at the time, according to the same *Times* article, that he didn't think the stock market would perform well the following year, and Warner's stock might drop to $15 or thereabouts. This may or may not have been an attempt to frighten speculators out of the stock and make a takeover more affordable; it's always interesting to speculate on other people's motivation.

Barbara Russell, my contact at Prudential Bache mentioned earlier, described Warner as "attractive on the longer term," according to the New York *Times* of December 3, 1989. The stock had closed the day before at 23⅝. She also speculated that the stock could rise from the low 20s as a result of a takeover attempt by someone other than Murdoch.

As it developed, Barbara Russell's projection was right on target. The stock did jump to a high of 29⅝ early the next year following additional buying by Murdoch that raised his equity stake in Warner to 7 percent. And, in the convoluted way that the market has of humbling us all sooner or later, Isgur's projection of 15 was nearly realized when Warner stock subsequently plunged to 17. As one wag once put it, over the long run most analysts are bound to be right at one time or another.

Notwithstanding Isgur's comment that a takeover of Warner by Murdoch might be beneficial for the company, Warner's stock-swapping arrangement with Chris-Craft at the end of 1983 effectively barred Murdoch from taking over the company. By acquiring a 42.5 percent stake in BHC, the Chris-Craft television subsidiary, Warner put itself beyond the Australian's reach since he did not become a U.S. citizen until two years later, and was therefore prohibited from directly owning more than 20 percent of a television station.

Murdoch's immediate concern was that Warner's stock

would drop in price if its deal with Chris-Craft was permitted to stand, and he would be saddled with a substantial loss on the 4.4 million shares he had already acquired in the market. Responding to a suit filed against him by Warner, seeking to enjoin him from buying any more stock, Murdoch took legal action against Warner in an attempt to block the Warner/Chris-Craft cross-ownership arrangement. Among the allegations in his suit, which he filed in Delaware where Warner was incorporated, were those charging the company with engaging in a "pattern of racketeering," according to the *Times* of January 25, 1984. The racketeering charge was based on the claim that Warner executives, including Ross, had traded on inside information when they sold their own company's stock at a profit prior to Warner's announcement in December 1982, that problems were mounting in the Atari division.

"When someone's trying to run you down," Murdoch was quoted in the *Times* of February 6, 1984, "you try to protect yourself. So that, the next time, someone else doesn't try to run you down."

When the dust finally settled a month later, it was Murdoch who emerged the victor. On March 18, 1984, the *New York Times* reported a deal between Warner and Murdoch whereby Warner would pay the Australian $31 a share for all his stock, giving him a $40 million profit on the shares he had accumulated at an average price of $24 a share. The buying spree had cost him $130 million, and he was netting out a shade more than $170 million less than six months later. Warner also agreed to pay Murdoch's legal fees which amounted to some $8 million. It was a hefty settlement for Warner to make, but Steve Ross and company evidently thought it was worth paying in order to get their stock back out of Murdoch's hands.

The price of the stock fell back into the teens shortly afterward, and Warner shareholders were outraged, as many stock market observers would claim they had a right to be. I remember a similar incident involving Amax a couple of years earlier when its stock plunged from 48 into the high teens after that company paid off a potential suitor. This practice has been labeled "greenmail" and some say it should be outlawed.

My own analysis of the situation is markedly different. There can be no such thing as a "level playing field," despite the efforts of regulators to create one. The stock market always entails risk; no one complains when a stock is rising, largely because someone like Murdoch or possibly Carl Icahn or T. Boone Pickens is driving it up. Shareholders always have the option to sell at any time, locking in profits or cutting a loss. Greed takes over, however, and many investors won't sell at, say, 50 if they think a stock might go to 55. Only when it drops below their purchase price, giving them a loss, do investors look for someone—usually Washington—to make them whole.

When a big player like Murdoch cashes in his chips, as he did in the Warner deal, he is only exercising his own right to sell for a profit the same as everyone else. No one told other shareholders to hang on until the bitter end, trying to squeeze every last dollar they could out of the stock. Those who did took the gamble and lost, but they could have sold earlier. Indeed, if Murdoch—or someone like him—hadn't come along in the first place, the price of the stock, with its lousy third-quarter earnings report, most likely would have dropped. Murdoch drove it up, no one complained; and when the ride was over, the lawsuits started. Warner, as it turned out, was on the receiving end of five class-action shareholder lawsuits starting on March 19, 1984, the day after the Warner-Murdoch deal was announced.

When I spoke to Susan Carr, litigation attorney for Warner Communications, Inc. in 1989, she said, "Those cases are still pending, and they are, for want of a better word, dormant. There's been no activity in those cases for a substantial period of time."

Whatever the case, Warner stock did climb back up to more than $50 a share in 1989 when Warner announced its intention to merge with Time, Inc., a combination that would make the new company the largest media giant in the world. When Paramount Communications (formerly Gulf & Western) entered the bidding war for Time, the price jumped to more than sixty. The race for dominance of the media world was on in full force. Steve Ross may have lost his battle with Rupert Murdoch in 1984, but speculators were betting that he would play a major role in whatever media conglomerate he headed up in the future.

Chapter
Fifteen

MURDOCH'S PERSONAL wealth was estimated at $240 million in a March 12, 1984, New York *Times* profile of the media lord, making him the wealthiest Australian in the world. Shareholders in his company also fared well since the price of News Corporation Ltd. stock soared from $2 Australian in 1983 to just under $11 on the Sydney Stock Exchange (it was not yet traded on the New York Stock Exchange; by August, 1989, it was trading as high as $27 a share in New York, giving the company a total market capitalization of well over $5 billion.) The value of Murdoch's empire—measured in terms of assets owned—was placed at $1.52 billion in 1984, less than a sixth of its size five years later.

(Total compensation paid to directors of News Corporation and its subsidiaries, including salaries and benefits, amounted to almost $34.6 million Australian in fiscal 1988. Barry Diller's package came to a little more than $4 million, two other directors received between $1 million and $2 million, two more between $600,000 and $700,000, while ten others ranged all the way from $20,000 up to half a million. These are relatively modest figures compared to many other major corporations.)*

For the six months ending December 31, 1983, News Corporation's profits were up 66 percent to $49.9 million, and industry analysts were projecting substantially higher profits during the following year.

"The analysts that follow us—and I guess we wouldn't disagree—," Don Galletly, Investor Relations Director of the News Corporation in New York City, said in 1989, "project Australian dollar earnings [for 1989] in the $490 to $520 million range . . . And the percentage increase would be similar in terms of per share, because there hasn't been any material change in the outstanding shares."

When asked if he expected pretty much the same percentage of revenue contribution from magazines, newspapers and other operations, Galletly said, "We will see a greater contribution from Australia and the Pacific . . . And we'll see an increase, I think, relatively speaking, in terms of newspapers and also film . . . We're sort of heading towards a record year."

On the political front in 1984, Murdoch's relations with the Labor Party government back home had improved considerably, despite his conservative leanings, and Prime Minister Robert Hawke rewarded him with his country's highest honor, the Order of Australia, in January of that year.

While Murdoch's worldwide empire was headquartered in Australia—and still is for legal and accounting reasons—he told New York bankers in 1984 that he saw his best oppor-

*See End tables for complete compensation figures and other financial details

tunities for future growth in the United States. As in the past, because of the accounting differences between Australia and the United States that I discussed earlier, much of the borrowing for that growth would be made in Australia. At the end of the fiscal year that ended June 19, 1983, $492.2 million of News Corporation's total revenue of $1.43 billion was generated in Australia; $618 million in Great Britain; and $323 million in the United States. But the U.S. portion was growing rapidly, so that by 1988 it commanded the lion's share, or 42 percent to Australia's 30 percent and Great Britain's 28 percent.

The geographical headquarters of Murdoch's empire remains in his native land, but in 1984 there was no question but that its financial center of gravity was shifting to America. His board of directors boasted three Americans: Don Kummerfeld, Richard Sarazen, the financial director of News Corporation based in New York and Stanley Shuman, Murdoch's investment banker at Allen & Co.

Murdoch "has put together a quite astonishing group of companies," said Ronald MacDonald, Rupert's brother-in-law, according to the New York *Times* of March 12, 1984, "but I don't see a thread. I think it's just him, and I wonder when he inevitably meets his maker, what will happen to that empire, because it requires someone of his talent, of his incredible energy, his use of the telephone to keep that group together."

Murdoch's foray into the stock market the previous fall, which resulted in a $40 million profit on his Warner Communications stock, evidently stimulated his appetite for more of the same. The New York *Times* of June 29, 1984, reported that companies owned by Murdoch had acquired 5.6 percent of the St. Regis Corporation—a forest products company: paper & building supplies—at a cost of approximately $65 million. When questioned, Murdoch denied that he was interested in any kind of greenmail.

"Under no circumstances would they accept any offer from the company to repurchase such stock unless the same offer were made to all shareholders of the company," he was quoted in the same *Times* article.

Murdoch had made his open-market purchases under the auspices of the News Corporation Ltd. and News International P.L.C. at an average price of $35.56 a share. According to Murdoch, this was "an investment" and there was no "present intention to acquire control of the company or to request representation on the company's board of directors."

In fairness to Murdoch, it should be noted that this is standard operating procedure for all the big players when they are looking to buy additional shares, with the view of eventually acquiring the target company. It would be foolish for any potential buyer to state unequivocally that he or she was going to make significant future purchases, since that would give a clear signal to speculators and arbitragers that the stock was in play and could only go up. As they entered the market, pushing the share price higher and higher, the would-be buyer—in this case, Murdoch—would be forced to pay more for the company in question. It's not a question of dishonesty, but of keeping your cards close to the vest in an effort not to show your hand, as any good poker player would do. A simple "No comment" is usually code language on Wall Street that a takeover really is intended.

Less than two weeks later, the New York *Times* of July 10, 1984 quoted a spokesman for St. Regis as saying that while Murdoch was stating publicly that he had no intention of acquiring the company, he was arranging a $750 million line of credit from the Midland Bank of London and other banks to do just that. St. Regis filed a thirty-one-page lawsuit against the Australian and his companies, seeking to block any future purchases of St. Regis stock and avert a takeover. Meanwhile, the stock was attracting the usual gaggle of arbitragers and continuing to move up, 2⅛ the previous day alone to 37⅞ in heavy trading. At this point Murdoch said that he had not firmed up his final plans for St. Regis, but he did want to position himself to buy enough stock to give him 50.1 percent.

"The line of credit has been established," one of my contacts at the Midland Bank said at the time, "but I can't say by whom."

Industry analysts estimated that the entire company was worth between $3.6 and $3.8 billion in 1984. Its timberlands alone wielded a market value of about $1.7 billion. Murdoch was not the only heavy investor in St. Regis, but he may have been one of the few who was *not* interested in greenmail. Sir James Goldsmith, the British industrialist, turned a $50 million profit when he sold his 8.6-percent holding back to the company. The Bass brothers of Texas also had 6 percent of St. Regis, and fallen arbitrage king Ivan Boesky had a substantial block of shares.

St. Regis lost its request for a court order blocking Murdoch from acquiring additional shares, according to the *Times* of July 11, 1984. As though in anticipation of Murdoch's legal victory, the stock rose another 1⅝ to 41½ on volume of 616,000 shares on July 10, the day the decision was handed down by federal judge Robert M. Hill. Two days later, St. Regis jumped another 2⅞ to 44⅜. Rumors were flying all over Wall Street that Murdoch had his financing in place and would shortly announce a bid to take over the entire company. Not one to miss jumping aboard anyone else's bandwagon, Ivan Boesky, through sources close to him, announced that he might have close to 5 percent of St. Regis himself, according to the New York *Times* of July 18, 1984.

Finally, the speculation was over. On July 18th Murdoch informed the directors of St. Regis that he was prepared to pay $52 a share, or $757 million in cash, for 50.1 percent of the company. At this point the Australian revealed that a consortium of banks headed by Midland Bank of London had provided him with a $750 million line of credit for this purpose.

"There was no greenmail intended at all," a friend of Murdoch said in 1989, "which is more than one can say for some of the others. St. Regis made perfect sense for him with its paper and newsprint operations. That's invaluable for any newspaperman."

As of July 18, 1984, Murdoch still owned 1.8 million shares or 5.6 percent of the company. One major player had already dropped out—Sir James Goldsmith, who, as mentioned, had sold back his 8.6-percent stake. Others included Lawrence A. Tisch, chairman of Loew's, whose company had acquired 8.5 percent of St. Regis for approximately $103 million, the Bass brothers, who disclosed on June 26th that they held 6 percent of the outstanding shares, and Ivan Boesky.

Among them, Murdoch was the only one actually offering to buy a major portion of St. Regis.

New York *Times* reporter Isadore Barmash revealed in a July 19, 1984, article that Murdoch's bid was the third attempted takeover of St. Regis in six months. The company was a plum, a ripe target for anyone with an acquisitive bent and the wherewithal to follow through on it. My own research at the time showed that St. Regis owned about 5.8 million acres of prime timberlands, boasted current assets of well over $700 million against current liabilities totaling less than half that amount, sat on a cash hoard of more than $150 million and had fallen in price from a high of $50 a share to the mid-30s, a more attractive level for potential suitors.

The major negative was that the company had taken on a lot of long-term debt, almost $900 million worth, which represented about 60 percent of capitalization (a healthier ratio would have been in the 30 percent range), a good deal of it to make St. Regis a less attractive takeover target.

William R. Hazelton, chairman of the company, said he was "not looking at white knights," according to the New York *Times* of July 19, 1984. The company was not for sale. A "white knight" is Wall Street terminology for a friendly suitor who steps in to save the target company from an unwanted bidder.

Just as Murdoch's original claim that he wasn't interested in taking over St. Regis is standard operating procedure on Wall Street, so, too, was Hazelton's assertion that he wasn't looking for a white knight while he was actively pursuing that very course. It didn't take him long. Barely two weeks later, on July 31, 1984, the *New York Times* reported that St. Regis and Champion International Corporation, another leading forest products company, had agreed to merge. The nearly $2 billion deal would create the largest company of that type in the nation. Hazelton had worked out the details with Champion's chairman, Andrew C. Sigler. In light of this development, Murdoch had no alternative than to back away from his own tender offer for 50.1 percent of St. Regis.

Once again, Murdoch had failed to gain control of a company he was legitimately interested in owning. But in the end he came out in better shape financially. The run-up in share prices gave him a profit of about $37 million for the stock he owned, not too shabby—particularly coming as it did so closely on the heels of his $40 million profit in Warner Communications.

"If it weren't for Rupert Murdoch, St. Regis would never be

part of Champion," Champion's chairman Andrew C. Sigler admitted, according to the New York *Times* of August 12, 1984.

And so another corporate marriage was ushered into existence, primarily through the efforts of a man who would rather be a bridegroom than a corporate marriage broker. It wouldn't take him long to realize that dream—less than a year, as it turned out. A couple of Wall Street analysts later said that Murdoch paid too much for his next big acquisition, but others disagree.

Whatever the case, the following year marked the beginning of Murdoch's expansion at a pace that dwarfed all he had accomplished in all the years of his life until this time.

Chapter
Sixteen

WHILE MURDOCH was setting the wheels in motion for perhaps the most significant acquisition of his life so far, competition in New York between the *Daily News* and the *Post* grew even more intense.

James Hoge struggled valiantly to reverse the *News*'s drop in circulation, largely at the hands of the *Post*. Expenses at the *News* were expected to rise about 1.7 percent in 1985. Circulation was running about 1.3 million from Monday through Saturday, down from 1.5 million since late 1982, and Sunday sales were 1.7 million as of September 30, 1984, according to the New York *Times* of December 10, 1984. The *Post*'s circulation had peaked at approximately the same level as that of the *Times*, around 930,000 a day.

After losing $14 million in 1982, the *News* turned a profit of the same size the following year, after cutting a third of the editorial staff and eliminating other personnel. The story was different at the *Post*, which continued to lose money—an anticipated $10 million in 1984—despite its expanded circulation.

"It was the old question of not enough advertising dollars," John Morton, newspaper analyst at Lynch, Jones & Ryan, said in 1989. "Murdoch had to spend money to get his circulation up, come out with all those extra editions. He cut expenses where he could, but when the advertisers didn't respond he kept on raising the price of the paper, a nickel or so at a time, but it just wasn't enough to make up the deficit."

When the Sydney Biddle Barrows "escort service" case broke toward the end of the year, the *Post* immortalized her with the sobriquet, "The Mayflower Madam," a reference to the fact that her ancestors had come over to America on the Mayflower. A reporter who worked for the *Post* at the time told me that Murdoch himself coined the term, and Murdoch would neither confirm nor deny it. According to those who worked for him, he was certainly intimately involved in every aspect of the newspaper. He was the nonpareil entrepreneur-newspaperman—owner, editor, journalist rolled in one—a man who surrounded himself with other editors and writers who learned the trade largely under his tutelage. In any event, the pithy epithet caught on immediately, and one could make a case that the title bestowed on Barrows by the *Post* will be remembered long after her real name has been forgotten.

The *Post* outmaneuvered the *News* in its coverage of this story, as it did in the coverage of the presidential campaign of 1984. Both the *News* and *Post* endorsed the incumbent, Ronald Reagan, over his hapless contender, Senator Walter Mondale, but it was the New York *Post* that unleashed a blizzard of articles favorable to the Republican president while the *News*, by and large, confined its support to the editorial page. At a 1981 dinner honoring Murdoch for his work on behalf of Reagan, then-congressman Jack Kemp stated, according to the December 10, 1984, New York *Times*, "Rupert used the editorial page and every other page necessary to elect Ronald Reagan president."

Other Republicans I spoke to said that Murdoch played a critical role during the 1980 campaign, not only in New York City but everywhere else he wielded influence.

"The biggest asset Rupert's got," Maxwell Newton said, "is his own intellectual and emotional energy. Well, he was spending a lot of it on the *Post* and it was not providing him with results."

As hard as Murdoch tried to put the newspaper into the black, to his continuing frustration he remained unable to do so.

With losses at the *Post* still very much on his mind, Murdoch's stock market profits during the previous twelve months provided him with at least a substantial consolation prize. But profits alone were not what he was after. Warner had eluded him a year before, but he was still as determined as ever to expand his empire into the entertainment field.

The roots of Murdoch's interest in electronic media can be traced back to his friendship with John Kluge, the German-born chairman of Metromedia, Inc., which owned television and radio stations in Boston, New York, Chicago, Washington, D.C., Los Angeles, Houston, Dallas and other areas of the country. It also owned Coles Publishing Company, which published the cross-reference directories that are popular with sales organizations and law-enforcement agencies.

It was Kluge who had been urging Murdoch to become a U.S. citizen and get into television, as he himself had done in

the late 1950s. For several years Murdoch had jokingly replied that he might think seriously about it if the older Kluge
ever wanted to sell him Metromedia.

With Kluge not quite ready to unload the company he had
taken private a year earlier in a $1.6 billion leveraged buyout,
Murdoch turned his attention west to Hollywood. Twentieth
Century Fox was struggling financially after releasing a
string of box-office clunkers such as *Rhinestone*, starring
Sylvester Stallone and Dolly Parton; *Blame it on Rio*, with
Michael Caine and Peter Falk; and *Unfaithfully Yours*, featuring Dudley Moore. The entertainment company's last hit
had been *Romancing the Stone*, an adventure flick with Michael Douglas and Kathleen Turner that owed a lot of its
appeal to the huge success of *Raiders of the Lost Ark*, which
it mimmicked.

The rotund Denver oil and gas magnate, Marvin Davis, and
a commodities dealer named Marc Rich had acquired control of the 20th Century Fox Film Corporation in 1981 for
$722 million. Davis bought out Rich in the summer of 1984
for a reported $116 million after Rich was indicted for tax
evasion and other charges in connection with his commodities operations. In March 1984, Murdoch reached an agreement to buy 50 percent of 20th Century Fox from Davis for
$162 million, plus an advance of $88 million to Fox's parent
company TCF Holding Company Inc., to pay down corporate
debt and help finance operations—a total cash outlay of $250
million.

"They need the capital to get back on track with production." said Harold Vogel, the Merrill Lynch media analyst,
according to the New York *Times* of March 21, 1985. "It's
been a rough period for them for the past one and a half or
two years."

Lee S. Isgur, the Paine Webber analyst quoted earlier in

connection with Warner Communications, was quoted in the same *Times* article, "He likes the idea of having a film library and a production arm. If he can have 20th Century's film library and distribution rights, that's not bad. He's also got an ego, and he wants to get into the business."

Murdoch was not immediately available for comment, but he said in a prepared statement: "Twentieth Century Fox is one of the world's few great film and television companies, and with its new management, under the outstanding leadership of Barry Diller, it is positioning itself for a significant growth period."

Putting the film company back on the winning road was not going to be easy. Twentieth Century Fox lost $85 million in the fiscal year ending August 25, 1984, plus another $12.4 million for the next quarter, which ended November 24th. As of that same first quarter, the film company's bank debt totaled $414 million, up from $363 million at the end of the previous quarter.

Marvin Davis had learned a lesson in Hollywood, according to Robert Lindsey writing in the New York *Times* on March 21, 1985, when he discovered that the movie business, like the oil industry, is capable of turning up dry holes. The Denver oil man had established a flamboyant presence on the west coast, buying a mansion in Beverly Hills once owned by singer Kenny Rogers and staging elaborate parties with his wife that invited comparisons with a character straight out of "Dynasty."

No sooner did Murdoch reach his agreement with Marvin Davis to buy half of the oil man's interest in 20th Century Fox, when he and Davis met with his old friend John Kluge and arranged to buy jointly seven television stations owned by Metromedia for a total of $2 billion. A year earlier Kluge took his company private in a $1.6 billion leveraged buyout, as previously mentioned, and was drowning under a sea of interest payments. Murdoch and Davis had both been members of Boston Ventures Ltd., a group that invested in the buyout.

At this point, things really got interesting. To begin with, Murdoch and Davis were the original odd couple; Murdoch was frugal and conservative while Marvin Davis was almost the prototypical oil man—flashy, flamboyant, freewheeling with his money. Second, the size of the deal alone was enormous for Murdoch, and many Wall Street analysts wondered out loud if he had finally taken on more than he could reasonably handle.

"I sure wouldn't want to step into his shoes for what he got," media analyst Gordon Crawford said in 1989. "I particularly cite the Metromedia television stations, which I think he grossly overpaid for."

Many other analysts agreed with Crawford's assessment. But Murdoch would not be dissuaded. He had wanted to expand his empire into American television for several years, and now that Kluge was disposed to sell he had the opportunity to do so in a big way.

The first indication that he was seriously interested in buying Metromedia's television stations occurred in early May. On May 2, 1985, the New York *Times* reported that Murdoch and Marvin Davis were engaged in serious negotiations with Kluge. The main sticking point was the law barring a foreigner from directly owning more than 20 percent of a television station, and more than 25 percent through indirect ownership. The second was an FCC regulation prohibiting any single owner from having both a television station and a newspaper in the same city.

Murdoch told me that he knew all along he would have to sell the *Post* once he acquired a television station in New

York City. But the FCC rule, as it stood then, contained provisions for appeal in certain situations where there was a lot of media competition. As we saw briefly in Chapter One, and will discuss in more detail a bit later, the legislation enacted in 1988 by Senator Ernest F. Hollings—with the approval of Senator Edward F. Kennedy—effectively curtailed the government's flexibility to review situations such as Murdoch's. It changed an FCC ruling without debate into law.

The precise wording of the law is quite murky, as most legal documents are, but in effect it restrained the Senate Commerce Committee—the regulatory body that is empowered to enforce FCC regulations—from reexamining the rules as they applied to Murdoch. Murdoch had been hoping to get an exemption, and the Kennedy-Hollings bill eliminated that possibility.

Two days later, Murdoch's friend and public relations man, Howard J. Rubenstein, announced that the Australian empire builder would apply for U.S. citizenship, which would effectively wipe away the first sticking point and allow him free entry into television. Until now, Murdoch had been a resident alien since his arrival in the United States more than a decade earlier, the proud possessor of a green immigration card like all other aliens in his position. Under the terms of Murdoch's and Marvin Davis's deal with Kluge, the two men would buy the seven Metromedia television stations in a $2 billion package, then sell the Boston station, WCVB-TV, to the Hearst Corporation for $450 million for a net cost of less than $1.6 billion. According to the New York *Times* of May 5, 1985, the sale to Hearst was believed to be the largest single-station broadcast transaction in history. Murdoch and Davis would keep the other six stations in New York City, Los Angeles, Chicago, Dallas, Houston and Washington, D.C.

"There's been no group sale of independent stations of this

size," said Howard E. Stark, an independent television broker, according to the May 6, 1985, New York *Times*.

"Rupert's a man who's always thrilled with a new challenge," the *Times* quoted Howard Rubenstein as saying. "He's always ready to climb Mount Everest. He has a broad attention span. Very broad."

The six stations Murdoch and Davis would keep were WNEW-TV in New York; KTTV in Los Angeles; WFLD-TV in Chicago; WTTG in Washington; KNBN-TV in the Dallas-Fort Worth area; and KRIV-TV in Houston. They were considered to be among the strongest independent broadcasters in the country. Some industry analysts thought they would provide Murdoch and Davis with a solid base to become major players in the field. But others, like Gordon Crawford of Capital Research, regarded the price tag as somewhat excessive.

In 1989, Crawford said that he doubted that Murdoch could "get his money back for" them now. "I think that ABC and NBC and CBS will tell you it's difficult having a three-network environment now, much less a four."

Richard J. MacDonald, media analyst with First Boston, said in 1989 that Murdoch's television empire was "in bad shape for a while," but he believed it was "coming back a bit," not losing "as much, a hundred million dollars, like it was."

But, at the time, analysts like Edward Atorino of Smith Barney were more sanguine about the Murdoch-Davis deal. "They are good stations in large markets," he said, according to the New York *Times* of May 8, 1985. "We're not talking about Podunk, Iowa, here." But even he had reservations about the price tag. "I have a theory that revenue growth and profit growth were falling short of what they expected," he added.

Still, there was much about the stations they were acquiring that looked attractive to Murdoch and Davis. WNEW (now WNYW) in New York had an average 12-percent share of the viewing audience in 1984, according to ratings compiled by A.C. Nielsen, putting it ahead of the other two independent VHF stations and trailing only the three networks. The Los Angeles station, KTTV, was tied for first place among the independents with a 9-percent share, and the other four were doing reasonably well in their own markets. Murdoch was not a man who liked to overpay for anything, but acquiring six television stations in one fell swoop, as it were, was a rare opportunity that he did not want to see pass him by.

With the Metromedia deal all but locked up, Murdoch announced in June 1985 that he was planning to marry 20th Century Fox's Hollywood production unit to a new television delivery system that would be linked to 18 percent of the homes throughout the United States. While the financial world struggled with the staggering monetary implications of Murdoch's moves, it overlooked—in the beginning, at least—his grand design. The 20th Century Fox and Metromedia deals were originally viewed as separate and distinct, but it soon become apparent that they were all of a piece as far as Murdoch was concerned. Movies, television ... it was all entertainment, a question of delivering news and movies and other programming to as wide an audience as possible via the electronic media.

As Murdoch himself stated in an interview published in the Winter 1989 issue of the Gannett Center Journal, "We're in the communications industry, and all that means. It's the exchange of ideas, it's news, it's just communicating with people, and there is no question that electronic communicating or television is getting bigger and bigger and bigger. With networks in and of themselves this is not so perhaps, but we are all spending more time in front of a screen, whether we're watching a videocassette or an entertainment program or news or even digitized information coming over. The electronic revolution is part of our lives, and if one wants to stay in communications, you can't turn your back on it."

Rupert Murdoch expanded further on the subject during a conversation with me in 1989.

"Entertainment you can take to be anything from a movie to a sporting event," Murdoch said. "The rest is a question of a distribution system. How do you distribute news, how do you distribute words? It's got to be a television screen, it's got to be a newspaper, it's got to be a magazine or a book. The same with entertainment. Is it cinema, a video cassette, is it the cable business or whatever?"

It all made good sense to Murdoch. But, just as he was about to cross the final Ts, dot the Is and turn his dream into reality, Marvin Davis clobbered him with a bombshell. In late June, the Denver oil man and Hollywood mogul announced that he was pulling out of his end of the bargain.

Chapter
Seventeen

"YOU CAN'T rely on anything he says," Murdoch said of Marvin Davis, according to William H. Meyers in the New York Times Magazine, June 12, 1988.

Marvin Davis would not comment on his reason for backing out of the Metromedia deal, but analysts speculated that the only reason he would have done so was because he considered the price excessive.

"We have decided not to exercise our option" to buy the stations, Davis said, according to the June 22, 1985, New York *Times*. "Instead, we will concentrate on the development of our other investments, including 20th Century Fox ... I look forward to continued association and partnership with Mr. Murdoch at Fox."

In light of what had just transpired, no one in his right mind truly expected that Murdoch and Davis would be continuing a partnership in anything, let alone in so complicated a venture as Murdoch's restructuring plans for 20th Century Fox.

Alan J. Gottesman, the media analyst at L.F. Rothschild, Unterberg, Towbin, speculated that Davis's problem "is probably that the economics of the deal elude him, just like they elude me."

Don Galletly, one of Murdoch's financial executives, did not have any problem with the economics of the Metromedia deal. In 1989, he said that Murdoch always had a long-range plan in mind, knowing that the television stations and film industry would pay off eventually.

"Last year film had a somewhat lackluster year," he said, but in 1989 and 1990 he expected to see "an increase."

Murdoch planned to move ahead on his deal with Kluge, with or without the help of Marvin Davis, which forced him to take on even more debt than he anticipated and raise additional cash. Raising cash meant selling off some assets, and in June he agreed to sell the *Village Voice* to Leonard Stern, the chairman of Hartz Mountain Industries, for approximately $55 million. As profitable as the sale of the *Voice* was, $55 million was a mere pittance against the staggering size of the deals he was on the verge of consummating: $1.55 billion net for six television stations, another quarter of a billion for half of 20th Century Fox (and as we will see shortly, Murdoch was already negotiating with Marvin Davis for the other 50 percent of Fox).

The banks would continue lending money to News Corporation, but only if he kept his debt-to-equity ratio within certain bounds. As Richard J. MacDonald, the First Boston analyst, explained in 1989, "His debt-to-equity ratio is defined under Australian accounting." Which meant it couldn't be more than "one-to-one." In 1989, Murdoch's debt was once again running high, 1.3 times equity, according to Mac-Donald.

Don Galletly also confirmed those figures to me. Murdoch was continually pyramiding his empire—taking on debt to expand it, selling off unprofitable pieces to pay down some of the debt, going in hock again to buy more, then selling off the less productive assets to keep the banks happy. It was Murdoch's way of keeping his empire financially lean as he expanded it, keeping all the cash cows and slicing off the fat.

In this instance, Murdoch was paying about fifteen times cash flow for Metromedia's six television stations, a price many analysts regarded as too high. Just the cost of servicing his enormous debt would put a tremendous strain on the stations' profitability. But he would not be thwarted in his dream of creating a fourth network of sorts, a marriage of film and television with the capability of reaching a huge cross section of the American public. In October Murdoch stunned the entertainment industry with an announcement that he would attempt to start a new network of affiliated stations. People within the industry were by turns skeptical, bemused and supportive.

Why not?

For years many others had dreamed of doing just that, but didn't know if it was possible. Now they would find out if it was, and Murdoch was taking all the risk. His plans called for a consolidation of 20th Century Fox and his six television stations into a single entity.

"You have tremendous obstacles in starting a network," said a television network executive who asked not to be identified, according to the October 11, 1985, New York *Times.* "You have program development, you have an infrastructure to collect, you have to gather the news, the equipment involved is expensive, you have thousands of employees. It's a big deal. The three networks pay more than a hundred million dollars each to their affiliates. That's pretty formidable."

The FCC gave its final approval in November to Murdoch's purchase of Metromedia's stations, as well as to an unrelated $3.5 billion takeover of ABC by Capital Cities Communications, Inc.—now known as Capital Cities/ABC. Both deals were said to be among the largest in the broadcast industry. The six television stations Murdoch bought reached about 22 percent of the American viewing audience. In giving its unanimous approval to Murdoch's acquisition, FCC chairman Mark S. Fowler read a statement attacking congressional critics of Murdoch for "misuse of government processes" because of their opposition to his "personal philosophy."

The man from Down Under was now U.S. Citizen Keith Rupert Murdoch. On September 4, 1985, he raised his right hand along with 185 other aliens and recited the oath of allegiance at Federal District Court in Manhattan. He was dressed characteristically in the usual dark suit, white shirt and dark tie that had become his trademark. His remarks to reporters who covered the ceremony were as sober as his attire. When asked why he had become an American, he answered, "Because I wanted to be, and I'm very happy and very gratified," according to the September 5, 1985, New York *Times.*

A week after changing his citizenship, Murdoch decided to take care of his unfinished business with Marvin Davis. Observers had been waiting for the other shoe to drop ever since the Denver oil man backed out of the Metromedia deal in June. It was apparent that these two men would never be able to work together; one of them would have to buy out the other's half interest in 20th Century Fox. The only remaining question was, who would be the buyer and who would be the seller?

Marvin Davis suggested that they flip a coin to see which man would buy out the other, William H. Meyers reported in the June 12, 1988, issue of New York Times Magazine. He backed down (once again) when Murdoch accepted the challenge. In mid-September, the public learned that Murdoch had been negotiating to buy Davis's remaining half interest in the company. Analysts speculated that the other 50 percent of 20th Century Fox was going to cost U.S. Citizen Murdoch in the neighborhood of $300 to $350 million—not a bad neighborhood to be in—or from $50 to $100 million more than he paid for the first half.

The analysts called it right this time. On September 24, 1985, the New York *Times* reported that the agreed-upon price was precisely in the middle of the "guesstimates," $325 million. Adding it all up, Rupert Murdoch's 1985 buying spree had cost him more than $2 billion so far, or about as much as the combined assets of his entire empire at the end of the previous year. According to an associate of Murdoch who requested anonymity the purchases were to be financed through existing bank credit lines, as well as from cash generated by current operations.

"This might not have been a good deal for film as little as six months ago," Merrill Lynch analyst Harold Vogel was quoted as saying in the *Times*. "But the integration of media and buyers has changed the nature of the broadcasting and movie connections."

What he was saying in a somewhat convoluted fashion was that a greater demand for film properties among interested buyers served to make them more valuable. The integration of film, television and assorted electronic media held enormous profit potential, and anyone who wanted to get into the industry had to pay a hefty entrance fee.

One of Murdoch's investment bankers, who asked not to be identified, admitted that the negotiations with Marvin Davis had picked up right after the oil magnate backed out of the Metromedia deal. "It's been a continuing discussion," he said, "but it intensified during the last two weeks."

(The relationship between any individual and his or her lenders and investment bankers is confidential. They are restricted by law from discussing the details of any deal while it is in progress, and many are hesitant to reveal information afterward for fear of jeopardizing an on-going business relationship.)

Murdoch has never been one to let any grass grow under his feet. No sooner had he swallowed whole six major television stations plus 100 percent of 20th Century Fox, than he revealed the details of the grand design that had been germinating in his mind right from the beginning. In November he announced a sweeping consolidation of 20th Century Fox with the six television stations under a new corporate umbrella called Fox, Inc. The fourth television network that he spoke of creating earlier was quite rapidly mushrooming into existence.

At the helm of the new enterprise would be the man whom Marvin Davis had appointed chairman and chief executive of 20th Century Fox a year earlier, Barry Diller. His plans called for dividing Fox Inc. into three separate but interrelated subdivisions: the 20th Century Fox Film Corporation, the Fox Station Group and the Fox Television Network.

Diller said that it would be "irrelevant" to call the Fox Television Network a fourth network, according to the New York *Times* of November 15, 1985, but he also added that Fox "definitely will be affiliating with individual stations."

"The opportunity," he continued, "is in the declining three-network share. The fragmented audience is not an audience that went down to play gin rummy. It went to watch independent stations, and it is an audience to be gathered."

The ink was barely dry on all the paperwork that established Murdoch as a towering figure in the electronic media world as well as in print, when Fox announced its earnings report for the quarter ended August 31, 1985. The company managed to squeeze out a profit of $1 million on revenues of $174.4 million. While a million dollars was mere walking-around money in a universe of $2 billion deals, it contrasted with a painful loss of $73.8 million for the same period a year earlier.

Puny as it was, it represented Fox's first profit in twenty-one months and came at a time when Murdoch had just taken over. For the fiscal year as a whole, the company was still in the red with a loss of $79.1 million, down from a loss a year earlier of $89.7 million. After suffering a series of box-office disasters, Fox seemed to be hitting its stride again with such films as *Cocoon,* with Don Ameche and Hume Cronyn, and *Prizzi's Honor,* starring Jack Nicholson, Kathleen Turner and Angelica Huston.

None of these, of course, had come into being as a result of changes Murdoch initiated himself, but perhaps—just perhaps—it was a sign that Fox's fortunes were taking a turn for the better.

The men from whom Murdoch acquired so much of his electronic empire in 1985—his old friend John Kluge and his erstwhile partner Marvin Davis—did not exactly fade out of sight once they sold their holdings to him. In 1989, at the sprightly age of 75, Kluge was still very much on the move with a newly created telecommunications empire. The first man ever to engineer a leveraged buyout of a broadcast company bought ITT's long-distance telephone unit in March 1989, thus positioning his company as the fifth-largest in that industry behind AT&T, Sprint, MCI and Telecom USA. Kluge also had interests in Orion Pictures Corporation, Ponderosa Restaurants, computer software and robotic painting firms.

Marvin Davis was also still larger than life in accomplishments as well as size, launching a $2.6 billion bid for NWA, Inc., the parent company of Northwest Airlines, in March 1989 and for United Airlines a few months later. The NWA bid came within days of Davis's announcement that he and the Prudential Insurance Company were jointly acquiring Spectradyne, a distributor of pay-per-view movies to hotels, for $635 million. Davis also owned resort properties in the mountains of Colorado and the Beverly Wilshire Hotel in Los Angeles.

Chapter
Eighteen

MOVIES AND television were not the only activities on Rupert Murdoch's mind in January 1986. While his wife Anna was busy writing books for publication, Rupert had been publishing books in Australia for some time, and now he extended his activities in this field into the United States.

Murdoch's Australian firm, Angus & Robertson, acquired Salem House and Merrimack Publishers Circle, two publishers and distributors of foreign books in the United States. Merrimack, founded in 1975, distributed about 250 books a year for British publishers, including Jonathan Cape, Virago Press, Chatto & Windus/the Hogarth Press, the Bodley Head, Quartet Books, the British Tourist Authority and Oxford University Press children's books, as well as books for Canadian publisher, Douglas & McIntyre. Salem House, the younger of the two publishers, was founded in 1986 and co-published some 250 books annually with various foreign publishers.

"Rupe was already keen on getting further into the book business," one of Murdoch's associates said. "Harper & Row or something of that size was already, I think, on his mind, and Collins in England, too."

Apparently so, for the following year Murdoch bought controlling interests in both of those publishers, eventually taking them over and merging them into a single entity.

Before he could do that, however, he had some serious problems of a different nature to deal with, both in England and the United States. The American problem concerned his financing arrangement for the acquisition of the six Metromedia television stations. In January 1986 the FCC extended the deadline for lining up his financing to March 16 and Murdoch came up with an ingenious arrangement that involved a substantial amount of risk as well.

His plan called for the exchange of the $1.6 billion worth of junk bonds that Kluge had floated when he took Metromedia private for $300 million in cash, and $1.15 billion in preferred stock issued by Fox Television Stations, Inc. The preferred stock carried a 13 percent dividend rate for the first year, 14 percent in the second, and 15 percent each year thereafter. The kicker was, if the company could not come up with the money to redeem the preferred stock at the end of three years, the shares could be converted into the common stock of News Corporation, effectively diluting Murdoch's control over the parent company of his entire empire.

For the uninitiated, preferred stock is a kind of hybrid security—somewhere between a stock and a bond. It is similar to a bond in that it pays a fixed rate of return, but it is also a stock since it represents equity (shares of ownership) in a corporation, but usually stripped of voting rights. The danger for Murdoch was the provision allowing Fox preferred to be exchanged for News Corporation common stock, giving shareholders voting rights in the parent company. Since Murdoch and his family owned nearly 50 percent of News Corporation—and he had vowed never to repeat his father's mistake and lose control of his own empire—he was taking an extraordinary risk. If new common shares were created, as would be the case if this exchange were to occur, Murdoch's control would be "diluted"—in other words, he would own a smaller percentage of a greater number of total shares.

"We don't want to be controlled by fund managers looking for quarterly results and bonuses," Murdoch told William H. Meyers of the New York *Times.*

As it turned out, he didn't have to submit to anyone else's outside control. Call it luck, call it genius, call it what you will. Murdoch had gambled all his life and won, and this time was no exception. Interest rates fell by the spring of 1987, and News Corporation borrowed $800 million by floating bond issues in Europe at the lower rates. It then used part of the money to pay down $200 million worth of the preferred stock. In the summer of 1987, some thirteen months ahead of the three-year deadline, Murdoch completed the redemption of all the outstanding preferred stock and eliminated the risk of dilution. His total debt still remained the same at $1.15 billion, but thanks to the lower interest rates the cost of carrying it was cut in half.

Murdoch received another benefit, too. Thanks to the differences in U.S. and Australian accounting rules that were discussed earlier, there were tax advantages to his moves. In the United States, the dividend payments on the Fox preferred shares were treated as debt and were, therefore, tax deductible, as though they were interest payments. In Australia preferred stock is treated as equity, not as debt, which looks better on the balance sheet. The Australian banks will lend you money based on the equity. Australia will also let you revalue your equity upward periodically to reflect appreciation, something you can not do in the United States.

As media analyst Gordon Crawford said, "Both U.K. and Australian companies can write up assets arbitrarily. Let's say you were MCA and you went to the December board meeting, and let's say MCA has a $20 book value. You could sit there and say, we think the real estate in California is worth $1 billion, not the $25 million we have it on the books for. So, let's mark it up to a billion dollars. And so, just with a stroke of the pen, mark it up to a billion dollars and the book value goes from $20 to $35. Then, all of a sudden, your debt-to-equity ratio looks much better."

This is how it's done in Australia and Great Britain, and since the News Corporation is an Australian-based company, that country's accounting prevails.

"Overextension isn't an issue with Murdoch," First Boston analyst Richard Macdonald said. "His company is very healthy. He likes using other people's money to increase the value of his own company."

The problem on the other side of the ocean that Murdoch faced early the same year was of an entirely different variety. This one had to do with the militant British trade unions that had virtually dictated terms to Fleet Street newspaper owners for as long as anyone could remember.

Murdoch was determined to have a showdown with them.

The big issue was Murdoch's introduction of new technology to replace the old labor-intensive method of printing newspapers by hand. The industry's two big printers unions—the National Graphical Association and the Society of Graphical and Allied Trades—went on strike against Murdoch's newspapers on Friday, January 24, 1986. They managed to shut down production of the Saturday editions of both the *Times* and the *Sun*, but a spokesman for News International said that he expected to print the *Sunday Times* and the *News of the World* at Murdoch's new plant in the Wapping section of London.

The plant at Wapping was at the very heart of the dispute; this was where Murdoch created a virtual *fait accompli* by establishing an entirely new production facility, complete with computers to replace the old typewriters and his new printing technology.

The unions were adamantly opposed to the introduction of the kind of labor-saving technology that Murdoch installed in his East London plant along the River Thames. Murdoch prevailed on Sunday, as his spokesman said he would, when both the *Times* and the *News of the World* were printed at Wapping and distributed throughout the streets of London. For the first time in Fleet Street history, reporters wrote their articles on the new computer terminals which were already widely used in the United States, and the newspapers were printed by computer instead of by hand. Murdoch had sunk $140 million into the Wapping facility, which was built in the old Dockland section of London, in his attempt to move British newspaper publishing kicking and screaming into the twentieth century. He intended to replace the 6,000 members of the printing unions with electricians who had been trained in the new technology.

The Wapping plant resembled a fortress in a war zone, with coiled barbed wire, steel fences and security guards surrounding the building. Built by French prisoners as a warehouse for spirits during the Napoleanic Wars, Murdoch's composing room had housed at one time thousands of barrels of wine and rum. The docks themselves were constructed in 1805 to handle the traffic from 10,000 coasters and

3,500 ocean-going vessels carrying exotic cargoes into London—coffee from Costa Rica, sunflower seeds from China, haricot beans from Ethiopia, apricot stones from Australia, agar from India.

Murdoch had the barbed wire and steel fences installed because British union members had a history of sabotaging machinery and other equipment to get their way, and Murdoch wasn't taking any unnecessary chances. This time, however, the unions were divided. The 6,000 printers had initiated the strike on their own, hoping that the journalists and distributors would join them. Anticipating such a coalition, Murdoch used a combination of threats and incentives to divide and conquer, according to the January 26, 1986, issue of the New York *Times*. Reporters and editors were given wage increases averaging $2,800 a year if they transferred to the new facility and learned to use the computers, and those who refused to do so were told they would lose their jobs.

The battle raged on, with both sides holding firm to their demands. The unions had two centuries of tradition to defend. For two hundred years, all the newspapers were printed and distributed from Fleet Street, and the unions had steadfastly resisted new printing techniques. Now Murdoch, the erstwhile Australian and recent American citizen, was changing all that. He had declared war on the unions and their power over the publishers.

His actions, according to Derek Terrington, a publishing analyst at the London firm of Grieveson Grant & Company, quoted in the January 28, 1986, New York *Times*, meant "the death of Fleet Street as a way of doing things, and as a way of life."

"We have a new era on Fleet Street," said Anthony Pennie, another analyst at James Capel & Company. "All the established papers will now have to respond in the face of new competition and get their costs down."

The move to Wapping was all the more provocative for the unions because of Wapping's proximity to Fleet Street, barely a mile and a half away. But Murdoch's divide-and-conquer strategy was working, with both the journalists and electricians refusing to join with their brethren in the strike.

"This has caused significant friction within the trade union movement," the New York *Times* quoted John Grant, director of the electricians' union as saying. "The only question now is whether it will get worse, and the outlook is not good."

Murdoch had apparently drawn up his battle plan well in advance, since he was able to transfer most of his production facilities to Wapping within twenty-four hours. Despite the actions by the printers unions, he was getting out about 70 percent of the normal press run, an amazing accomplishment in light of the wartime atmosphere that prevailed beyond the barbed wire defenses. Like a general directing the campaign, Murdoch issued orders from his office inside the plant.

"We are still learning the technology and perfecting our distribution system," Murdoch said, according to the New York *Times* of January 28, 1986. "It will be a few days, perhaps as much as two or three weeks, before we have everything running totally satisfactorily."

"It was a crazed situation, but Rupe was determined not to back down," one of Murdoch's associates said. "He felt he was right and he was going to win if it killed him."

Murdoch thought it was outrageous that printers with longevity on the job received an average of better than $40,000 a year, roughly three times the salary of the average British worker. The New York *Times* reported that featherbedding in the British newspaper industry had assumed legendary proportions. For example, on a typical night Murdoch was forced to pay for 500 printers while a head count indicated that only fifty—one in ten—were actually working. It took five men to operate a press with three reels in Chicago, four in San Antonio, six in New York City—and eighteen in London. This was a way of life that the unions were not about to give up without a fight.

"This time I'm not tapping on the window with a sponge," said Ron Todd, the leader of the Transport and General Workers Union, according to the January 30, 1986 New York *Times*. "I believe someone has got to say we are not standing for it."

The strike was ten days old on February 3, and still there appeared to be no way out of the impasse. Murdoch had his print run for the *Sun* pretty much up to capacity, and said, according to the February 4, 1986, New York *Times*, "We are pretty much unlimited in the number we can produce of the *Times* and the *Sun* every day."

Outside his office, the siege-like atmosphere still prevailed, with spotlights illuminating the gray London sky, steel gates barricading the entry points, security guards and policemen patrolling the streets, and a gaggle of cold and unhappy former printers picketing the building. Victory to Murdoch meant a saving of about $84 million a year in production costs, by his own estimate. An unidentified union member at the site stated, "If Murdoch gets away with this, it can go right through the country."

"A lot of these people, individually, are fine people," Murdoch replied, according to the New York *Times*, "But collectively, they seem to go mad. The London print workers have abused the system. They are not popular. And people are not prepared to risk their own jobs for the support of rackets."

"Rupert believed that public opinion was coming around to his side," a friend of his said. "He was never popular, as you know, but everybody was fed up to here with all the pampering and special treatment. It'd gone too far."

"We thought about it very hard," Murdoch told the New York *Times*, "and said we cannot have this huge operation just eating its head off and not producing. We decided we'd have to . . . set up a new newspaper with new practices."

Harry Arnold, a *Sun* reporter, said, "In this sort of a battle, you get the wartime spirit. There's a tremendous sense of camaraderie. There's a feeling we're witnessing a revolution, and it is terribly exciting." The printers, he continued, were "ostriches with their heads in the sand."

"It's all right to accuse me of being anti-union," Murdoch told William H. Meyers of the New York *Times*. "For sixteen years, we had the nightmare of mindless demonstrations. In the end, we said, 'You've lost the opportunity.' "

The publisher won the first legal skirmish when he took the issue to court and won a judgment whereby all the print unions' assets totaling $24 million were frozen under an order issued by Justice Michael Davies of the High Court in London. His directive was in response to the unions' attempts to halt distribution of Murdoch's newspapers by enlisting the support of the distributors union, a tactic that was not successful. He also levied a $35,000 fine against the printers.

"Our members come before money," said Brenda Dean, a union spokeswoman, according to the February 12, 1986, New York *Times*.

Justice Davies found the unions guilty of "flagrant contempt," and Ms. Dean called his decision a "swinging attack" on the unions and maintained that the future of all trade unions was at stake.

"It is not just money that runs a union," she said. "It is its members."

Perhaps, but she would soon learn that members can't run a union successfully without money—or a company either for that matter—and Murdoch understood that principle as well as anyone. He had already saved an estimated $56 million in severance pay, and he anticipated even greater savings the longer the strike continued. Also, thanks to his friend Margaret Thatcher, the new strike laws enacted under her administration favored the employer for the first time in decades. Unlike in the United States and most of Europe, there no longer was a "right to strike" in England. In the U.S. and Europe a strike is viewed legally as a suspension of a contract; in Great Britain it is a breach of contract—a significant distinction. In effect, the recently enacted law permitted an employer to dismiss a striking employee without notice or severance pay. Even some American conservatives regarded that reform as a touch extreme.

Under certain circumstances, striking unions could now be held liable for ruinous damages to the employer and subjected to fines as well, and their right to picket was severely limited.

"Fortress Wapping," as the British press called Murdoch's new facility, was humming along at almost full capacity five weeks after the strike began. As far as Murdoch was concerned, the striking union members were locked out "forever," according to the March 2, 1986, New York *Times*. He now controlled some 30 percent of newspaper circulation in Great Britain, far and away the largest segment of the market. Murdoch accused the unions of making serious tactical blunders since the beginning of the strike in January.

"The unions completely messed it up," he said to the New

York *Times.* "They read how we were buying television stations in America and they thought we needed the earnings here and that they could put me out of business for two weeks.

"What they should be doing now," he continued, "is saving their jobs at other newspapers rather than trying to get them back here because they won't get them back here."

"A lot of people were wondering," one of Murdoch's financial associates said, "if he had bitten off more than he could chew. He was $2.5 or $2.6 billion in debt at the time, leveraged all the way up, and a lot of people were waiting for him to fall on his ass. They thought he rolled the dice once too often."

The interest payments alone on his debt were expected to hit about $300 million in 1986. Murdoch's supporters maintained that he had been deeply in debt before and never defaulted, and this time would be no different.

"I'm a little nervous about it," said J. Kendrick Noble, Jr., an analyst with Paine Webber, as reported by the March 2, 1986, New York *Times.*

The big question on everyone's mind at the time was whether Murdoch, in his struggle to bend the unions to his will, would end up burying himself under the mountain of debt he had taken on to expand his empire even further. The fact that he is able to do so much simultaneously—take on debt to finance acquisitions, engage in drawn-out battles with unions, plan his next move—is a constant source of amazement to all observers.

Murdoch was doing all these things and more in the spring of 1986. When I spoke to some of his associates, people who have been with him longest and who know him best, they all maintained that he has been operating in that fashion all his life. As soon as you think you have a handle on where he is heading next, he does something to surprise everyone. His complexity makes him unpredictable, and that, apparently, is just the way he likes it.

Chapter
Nineteen

B Y JULY 1986 a few of Murdoch's publishing rivals were sufficiently encouraged by his successful stand against the unions to take action themselves.

"The move to Wapping was brilliant and courageous," Lord Rothermere, chairman of the Associated Newspapers, which published the *Daily Mail,* told William H. Meyers of the New York *Times.* "One can manage one's own newspaper for a change."

Apparently, Murdoch's fellow publishers discovered that the best way to manage their own publications was to follow him out to Wapping, and so the exodus from Fleet Street began in earnest. The prestigious *Financial Times,* England's leading business daily, announced plans for an $84 million plant complete with all the new technology in East London, near Wapping. In doing so, it lent its own support to the migration of major newspapers away from Fleet Street.

"Fleet Street as we knew it is gone forever," said Frank Barlow, the *Financial Times*'s chief executive officer, according to the New York *Times* of July 10, 1986. "That's inevitable."

All Murdoch's rivals were flocking to the Docklands. The *Daily Telegraph* was planning to make the move before the end of the year; the *Guardian* some time in 1987; and Associated Newspaper Holdings Ltd., publisher of the *Daily Mail* and the *Sunday Mail*, was building a plant of its own in the adjoining Surrey Docks.

"We have to eliminate Murdoch's cost advantage at Wapping," Barlow said. "Otherwise the *Financial Times* could be extremely vulnerable."

Unfortunately, few revolutions are accomplished without bloodshed, and this one proved to be no exception. With Murdoch's victory all but assured now that the other major newspapers had followed his lead, the unions still refused to give up the fight. Picketing continued throughout the year, and in January 1987, on the anniversary of the strike, a night of violence in Wapping resulted in injuries to 180 people, many of them policemen. An estimated 12,000 demonstrators had gathered outside the Wapping plant in an outburst of collective frustration. The police arrested sixty-seven of them, primarily for threatening behavior.

"We have witnessed the action of demonstrators whose sole intention was to attack the police," said Wyn Jones, Deputy Assistant Police Commissioner for Metropolitan London, according to the New York *Times* of January 26, 1987. "We took an appalling toll of very serious injuries."

Brenda Dean, the leader of the Society of Graphical and Allied Trades quoted earlier, disagreed. She blamed the police for charging the demonstrators on horseback, wielding truncheons, and said, according to the same article, "The police viciously attacked our people for no reason at all."

Whatever the case, the most vitriolic British labor dispute since the coal miners' strike of two years earlier finally ended in February.

"The dispute is over," Dean said. "To be honest, our options were very limited. It is a disgrace to our so-called democracy that working people can be sacked and treated the way our members were at News International."

"This has been a sad and unnecessary strike," Murdoch was quoted as saying in the February 6, 1987, New York *Times.* "It is in everybody's interest that it ends now."

Brenda Dean said the unions had agreed to call off the strike on advice from their attorneys, who said that they would most likely continue to lose in the courts. The unions had already paid out nearly $4 million in strike benefits and they were vulnerable to additional fines for disrupting work at the plant and violating a court order banning further picketing.

Murdoch won the war and, in doing so, he literally revolutionized the way in which newspapers are published and distributed in England. It was perhaps the greatest gamble of his life to date, and those watching on the sidelines, waiting for him to finally blow it all, must have grimaced in frustration as he emerged from yet another contest stronger than ever. In 1988, a year after he beat the unions, Murdoch's U.K. revenues had increased by another $280 million.

Even before final victory was his, Murdoch took measures to bring down the debt side of his balance sheet and raise cash in the aftermath of the Metromedia deal.

"He had to sell some assets, there was no way around it," analyst Richard MacDonald said. "There was speculation that it might be Ansett, but I didn't think so. The way he worked it was to unload the *Sun-Times* in Chicago."

Murdoch realized a pre-tax profit of $71.5 million when he sold the Chicago newspaper for $145 million in June 1986 to an investor group headed by the paper's president and publisher, Robert E. Page.

"The paper never became the New York *Post* despite all the fears," Page said, according to the July 1, 1986, New York *Times*.

The consortium of investors put together by Page included: Donald F. Piazza, the *Sun-Times*'s executive vice president; Adler & Shaykin, a New York investment firm; the Equitable Life Assurance Company of the United States; and Peers & Company, a merchant bank. Under Murdoch's ownership, the profitability of the *Sun-Times* increased from $3 million at the time he bought it to $9 million for the 1986 fiscal year. Some people speculated that the Page group might have been paying too much for the newspaper, but analysts the author spoke to thought otherwise.

"Newspapers normally go for forty times net income," Bruce Thorpe of Lynch, Jones & Ryan told me. "So, in this instance, the price could realistically have gone as high as $180 million using that yardstick. I think Page and his people got a fair deal."

News Corporation's enormous debt burden did not have a negative impact on its earnings for the year. Quite the contrary. For the fiscal year ended June 30, 1986, the company's earnings rose by 66.8 percent. Net income totaled $245.7 million in Australian currency, or about $171.5 million U.S. (At the exchange rates prevailing in April, 1989, that would translate into about $196.6 million U.S.) These latest earnings compared with net income of $147.3 million Australian the previous year. Operating revenue was $3.82 billion Australian, up from $2.44 billion.

Murdoch bought and sold properties at a dizzying speed. No sooner did he sell the Chicago *Sun-Times* to reduce his debt and raise cash than he was in the market for new acquisitions. In November his shopping spree took him to the Orient, where he bought a 35-percent interest in Hong Kong's largest English-language newspaper, the South China *Morning Post*, for $105 million. Murdoch took an option to buy an additional 15 percent of the newspaper, whose other owners included a Hong Kong bank, Dow Jones & Company and various smaller investors. Five weeks later, Murdoch's News Corporation further consolidated its hold on the South China *Morning Post* when it bought Dow Jones's 18.9 percent share, according to the December 18, 1986, New York *Times*. The reported price was $57.2 million.

A year earlier he extended his reach into the magazine publishing business when he bought a string of trade publications from the Ziff-Davis Publishing Company for $350 million. These titles included Travel Weekly, Hotel and Travel Index, Meetings and Conventions, the Official Hotel and Resorts Guide and other travel industry publications.

"It's astounding to me," one of Murdoch's associates said, "that he can keep it all straight in his head. He's juggling five balls in the air at one time when most people have trouble dealing with one or two. But he obviously knows what he's doing."

In December 1986 Rupert Murdoch embarked on the most emotionally charged venture of his life to date when he launched an all-out assault on the company his father lost control of thirty-four years earlier—even before he officially put to rest the dispute with the British unions. He stunned the Australian financial and business community with a $1.17 billion bid for the Herald and Weekly Times Ltd., the country's largest newspaper group. This was more than just another acquisition attempt. It was a psychic challenge as well, an attempt to redress the karmic balance in his own universe. When Sir Keith Murdoch lost the Herald organization in 1952, his son Rupert was enraged; now, three and half decades later, he was trying to get even.

"I don't think I'd ever seen Rupert so determined before," one of his associates said. "He'd gone after things and lost them, that was fine. But this time he was determined to win no matter what the cost."

If he did win, it would give Murdoch newspapers in every Australian state and capital city, as well as in regional areas, amounting to approximately 60 percent of the country's total circulation. Victory here would also reduce his major rival to one organization: the Sydney-based John Fairfax & Sons Ltd. Australia's anti-trust laws were relatively mild compared to those in the United States, but even so the bid had to pass muster by the Trade Practices Commission which administered them.

Sources close to Murdoch said the financing would be done through a package of new stock and notes issued by the News Corporation—a combination of equity and debt. Australia had cross-ownership laws involving control of newspapers and television stations in the same market, somewhat akin to their American counterparts, but Murdoch did indicate that he would be willing to sell his television stations in Adelaide and Melbourne, as well as some radio stations, to comply with them.

Murdoch admitted that there was an emotional nature to

this quest when he was quoted in the December 4, 1986, New York *Times.* "It's the challenge of the game," he said. "It gives me a great thrill, and it would be very wrong to deny that it is emotional."

This was a significant revelation coming from a man who usually spoke softly, sometimes in whispers when others would be shouting at subordinates—a man who was accustomed to concealing his emotions behind a steel facade.

As determined as Murdoch was to win this battle, it soon became apparent that he was not going to do so without a big fight. In one of life's little ironic flourishes, the subject of Murdoch's recent U.S. citizenship was raised immediately.

"The big concern," said Chris Warren, the acting federal secretary of the Australian Journalists Association, who was quoted in the New York *Times* of December 4, 1986, "is that it will make an American citizen more powerful in Australia than the editor of *Pravda* is in the Soviet Union."

Strictly from a legal perspective, Murdoch's U.S. citizenship did not prohibit him from acquiring any more newspapers, but it did constrain him from buying additional television stations. The man from Down Under, the quintessential Australian who was hell-bent on making his mark on the world at large, was now being taken to task after having done just that perhaps more successfully than any other Australian who came before him.

Chapter
Twenty

TWO DAYS after Murdoch announced his bid for the Herald and Weekly Times Ltd., the battle for control of the newspaper chain intensified. A formidable opponent entered the fray in the figure of Robert Holmes à Court, the transplanted South African, who indicated that he might be interested in topping Murdoch's bid with one of his own. Now that Murdoch was an American, Holmes à Court inherited the title of Australia's richest man and he had a reputation for aggressiveness that was a good match for Murdoch's.

With a bidding war looming on the horizon, Murdoch raised the stakes a few days later when he bought a 12 percent interest in the Herald organization from an institutional investor, Industrial Equity Ltd., a New Zealand firm. The block of stock totaled 18,370,000 shares and cost Murdoch $143.3 million.

Robert Holmes à Court officially tossed his hat into the ring just before Christmas with a $1.4 billion bid for the Herald and Weekly Times Ltd., topping Murdoch by better than $200 million. Before Murdoch had a chance to respond, Holmes à Court struck again, teaming up with Murdoch's arch rival in Sydney, John Fairfax & Sons Ltd., in a separate $610 million offer for the Herald organization's largest shareholder, the Queensland Press Ltd.

This flanking movement was significant from a couple of perspectives. If it succeeded, the speculation was that Holmes à Court would take control of Herald and its chain of newspapers while Fairfax, looking to expand its own operations, would acquire the Queensland Press, which published the Brisbane *Courier-Mail* and the *Telegraph*. Second, the offer for Queensland had strategic value since it had an interlocking ownership arrangement with the Herald organization— and also with the Advertiser Newspapers, another chain— with each company owning shares in one another.

"Australia's Battle of the Titans,"—as the January 8, 1987, New York *Times* headlined the event—was heating up in earnest.

"In the long run," the New York *Times* quoted Rosalie James, an analyst with McCaughan & Dyson & Company, an Australian securities firm as saying, "I think this country will have two newspaper barons and three television barons."

Among the so-called titans, Murdoch's News Corporation was by far the wealthiest and most far-reaching. In January 1987 it boasted a market capitalization of $2.9 billion U.S. currency and employed 25,000 people around the world. Robert Holmes à Court's Bell Group, J.N. Taylor Holdings Ltd., by comparison, had a capitalization of $1.3 billion, employed 4,316 workers and had interests in television stations in Perth and Adelaide, a weekly newspaper in Perth and in film, theater and music publishing. Holmes à Court also had a minority interest in Broken Hill Proprietary Company, a mining and natural resources firm, and a stake in USX Corporation, formerly U.S. Steel. The Fairfax organization was the pygmy of the group with a $723 million capitalization, newspapers in Sydney and Melbourne, as well as magazine, television and radio holdings.

"Rupert had nothing against Holmes à Court personally," a friend of Murdoch said, "but he felt he was out to get him because Rupert wouldn't sell him some properties he wanted. When he teamed up with Fairfax, Rupert was incensed. I think he would have gone ahead no matter how much he had to pay."

Murdoch countered the Holmes à Court/Fairfax bid a few days later with a new offer of $1.5 billion for the Herald group, plus a separate $700 million offer for the Queensland Press provided that the latter company accepted his offer without delay. The combined offer for the two companies was a clever as well as highly expensive maneuver to cut off the opposition on both flanks. To many it appeared as though the stakes couldn't possibly go any higher.

"There seems little doubt that this is the winning bid," said Lachlan Drummond, an analyst with MacNab Clarke, as quoted in the New York *Times* of January 10, 1987.

To be sure, it was a complicated coup Murdoch was attempting. Queensland owned 24 percent of the Herald and Weekly Times Ltd., while Herald owned 48 percent of Queensland. Murdoch's bid was akin to a military commander trying to conquer, simultaneously, two interconnected empires. Drummond can be forgiven for thinking that Murdoch's two rivals would drop out at that point, and it appeared for the moment that his judgment would be vindicated.

Murdoch called Robert Holmes à Court in Perth from his

base of operations in New York City and structured a deal whereby Holmes à Court would drop his bid for the Herald and Weekly Times Ltd. in return for the right to buy the company's two Perth newspapers, the *West Australian* and its afternoon counterpart, the *Daily News*. Holmes à Court would also acquire the Herald organization's television station in Melbourne.

"The television property was what he was after all along," an associate of Murdoch, referring to Holmes à Court, said. "That, and the two dailies. He was going to make life difficult for Rupert unless he got them."

It appeared as though Murdoch was on the verge of reclaiming the empire lost by his father. But, as it turned out, the war was not quite over. The Fairfax group was not about to be shunted aside so easily. A few days after the Murdoch–Holmes à Court agreement was announced, John Fairfax & Sons Ltd. upped the ante another notch with a $1.63 bid for the entire Herald operation. One day later, the Australian Broadcasting Tribunal muddied the already murky waters a bit more with a statement that it was examining whether or not Murdoch's bid breached Australian regulations prohibiting a foreigner from owning more than 15 percent of a radio or television station.

Murdoch was born in Australia, he spoke like an Australian, his empire, which employed thousands of Australians, continued to be headquartered there, but his U.S. citizenship now made him a foreigner in his native land.

The issue dragged on for another two weeks until Murdoch was finally able to claim victory in the one battle he was determined to win from the start. John Fairfax & Sons Ltd. dropped out of the bidding, Murdoch concluded his deal with Robert Holmes à Court and agreed to divest himself of the television properties that put him in violation of Australia's cross-ownership regulations, and in so doing subsumed the Herald and the contingent Queensland empires into the fold of the News Corporation. Murdoch now controlled about 60 percent of Australia's newspaper circulation. His was a sprawling conglomerate that included the *Herald,* the *Weekly Times,* the *Daily Mirror,* the *Telegraph,* the *Courier-Mail,* the *Advertiser,* the *Mercury,* his national paper the *Australian* and dozens of other publications scattered throughout Queensland, New South Wales, Victoria, Tasmania, the Northern Territory, South Australia and Western Australia.

"It was perhaps the greatest coup of his life," a friend of Murdoch said, "certainly the one that gave him the most pleasure. But, you'd never know it from talking to him. He showed nothing, acted like it was just another day's work. That's Rupert for you."

"I like Murdoch and respect what he's done," New York *Post* reporter, Bill Slattery, said. "But you never feel you really know him. You'd pass him in the hall, he'd smile, say a few words, but you never knew what was going on inside his head."

With the Australian campaign behind him and his company loaded up with debt once again, Murdoch went on the prowl immediately for new worlds to conquer. He trained his guns on his adopted home "Up Over," the United States of America.

Now that Murdoch was solidly entrenched in the newspaper and television industries, and his influence was growing in the magazine world as well, it was inevitable that sooner or later he would turn his attention to book publishing. In March 1987 he did just that in as dramatic a fashion as the world had come to expect of him. In a move that surprised just about everyone in the industry, he agreed to buy Harper & Row, the venerable 170-year-old publishing house, for $300 million. The price was regarded as a preemptive strike, since it exceeded by $15 a share a previous offer for the company by Harcourt Brace Jovanovich. Murdoch's ultimate goal, analysts speculated, was the creation of an international book-publishing network to complement his quickly growing communications and media empire.

"The ability to create a worldwide English-speaking book market has great potential," an unidentified industry analyst said, according to the March 31, 1987, New York *Times*. "Also, book publishing is the last medium Murdoch hadn't addressed in the U.S. in a major way."

"He already had Angus & Robertson in Australia," an associate of Murdoch said. "He had his sights set on America and the U.K. for a long time as well. It was just a question of timing it right."

The "conglomeratization" of book publishing worldwide was of great concern to everyone within the industry, and to many outside observers, too. The spectre of a handful of monster corporations controlling such a large segment of the book world conjured all sorts of troubling questions. The entire industry was being swept along in a frenzy of mergers, acquisitions and consolidations, and Harper & Row was a ripe takeover target since it lacked the financial resources of the giants.

"As the players in the publishing game get bigger and bigger," said Brooks Thomas, the chairman and chief executive of Harper & Row, as reported by the New York *Times*, "we couldn't go out and acquire another college textbook publisher, the way they could. But Rupert has deep pockets, and he's shown a willingness to back up his convictions with cash."

Herald Ritch, a managing director of Kidder, Peabody & Company, Harper & Row's financial advisor, was also quoted in the same article.

"Compared to any index of value," he said, "it's a great price."

"Murdoch's offer was about fifty or sixty times earnings," First Boston analyst Richard J. MacDonald said, "and three times book. A bit pricey, but it's worked out well for him. It made good sense, particularly since Murdoch already owned a good chunk of Collins."

He was talking about Murdoch's 41.7 percent interest in William Collins & Sons, a British publisher that was considered to be similar to Harper & Row in publishing style and temperament. There was already speculation that Collins might itself purchase an equity interest in Harper & Row, and participate in the management of the American publisher's day-to-day business. The numbers MacDonald quoted referred to Harper & Row's P/E ratio or price-to-earnings multiple, and the company's book value which represents assets minus liabilities.

At the time of Murdoch's bid for the company, Harper & Row was jointly owned by several large investors. The largest individual owner was lawyer and editor Theodore L. Cross, who controlled 5.3 percent of the 4.4 million outstanding shares; the counselling firm of Warburg, Pincus owned another 5.8 percent; 27 percent was held by about 1,500 employees in an employee stock ownership plan; some twenty-seven officers and directors of the firm owned an additional 17 percent; and Cass Canfield, Jr., the son of the man who was chief executive for thirty-six years, controlled 4 percent.

As is usually the case in buy-outs of this kind, top management walked away rich—or, at least, semirich—thanks to golden parachutes arranged by the company. Twenty of

Harper & Row's senior executives received cash payments equal to 2.99 times their annual income, according to a formula established by I.R.S. for takeover deals, and fourteen other executives got twice their base income. With such enticements difficult to turn down, it appeared as though the international merger and acquisition frenzy was not going to end anytime soon. Publishing was not the only business affected by it, of course, but there was little question but that the old days when editors took on books simply because they liked them—without too much concern about the bottom line—were rapidly fading away.

"It is either the apex or the nadir of a tremendous change in the industry and maybe the culture," said Juris Jurjevics, a former editor at Harper & Row who started his own independent publishing house, according to the April 5, 1987, New York *Times.*

Other publishing executives were more sanguine about the situation, maintaining that the infusion of huge sums of corporate cash into their enterprises would permit them to take even more chances on quality books than they could before. Richard E. Snyder, president of Gulf & Western's Simon & Schuster, said that publishing good books was good business.

"The idea is to sell books," he said, according to the same *Times* article. "Publish good books and the best of them will become blockbusters."

There was something prophetic in these comments, for two years later, in April 1989, Harper & Row won a bidding war for reprint rights to thirty-three books by Agatha Christie, the renowned mystery writer who had recently passed away. Harper's bid was $9.6 million for the titles—a figure that would have been beyond its ability to pay before Murdoch came along. Harper & Row also bought Len Deighton's next four novels for a reported sum of $10 million.

Ironically enough, Brooks Thomas, the chairman of Harper & Row, who approved the sale of the company to Murdoch, admitted that he had concerns of his own.

"If somebody has your string—even if they never pull it—maybe it has some effect on you," he said, according to the New York *Times* of April 5, 1987.

When I discussed the field of book publishing with Murdoch in 1989, he expressed some reservations about the industry.

"I think fewer books are being read and less time is being spent on books," he said. "I don't think any more books are being read. Take per head of the population or hours per week spent reading books per head of the population, or whatever. I'd make an uneducated guess saying it's going down not going up, certainly not going up."

For better or worse, the acquisition of old-line, formerly independent book publishers by corporate giants was continuing at a hectic pace. Even before Rupert Murdoch entered the arena, William Morrow & Company had been gobbled up by Hearst; Charles Scribner's Sons by Macmillan; Alfred A. Knopf and Pantheon had been incorporated under the Random House umbrella; Gulf & Western bought Simon & Schuster; the German company Bertelsmann A.G. acquired Doubleday & Company, no small enterprise itself, for $475 million, and merged it with Bantam and Dell, which it had also acquired.

"It's a white-hot environment" for book industry deals, said Herald Ritch, the Kidder, Peabody director quoted earlier.

"Anything that isn't pinned to the wall is being bought," said Roger Straus, president of Farrar, Straus & Giroux, according to the New York *Times*.

"If somebody offers you more money than you think you could ever make through earnings," said Brooks Thomas, according to the same article, "you have to take it."

There was no question but that Murdoch had British book publisher William Collins & Sons in mind when he went after Harper & Row. Others talked about the similarities between the two houses and, to be sure, the resemblance was not lost on so astute an observer as Murdoch. Five months after he won control of the American publisher, he sold a 50 percent interest in Harper & Row to William Collins & Sons for $156 million. This new arrangement meant that both Collins and Murdoch's News America Holding, Inc. would each own half of Harper, while Murdoch's British entity, News International, held a 41.7 percent stake in Collins.

"By more closely linking Harper & Row," Murdoch said, according to the New York *Times* of September 3, 1987, "one of the great publishing companies in the world, with William Collins, we have the opportunity to develop a truly international book-publishing network."

"We're very close in terms of philosophy of publishing," Collins's chairman, Ian Chapman, was also quoted as saying in the same article, "so I don't see huge changes taking place there, except that we may want to enter areas of the market they haven't been so much into."

"Joining with Collins," agreed Harper & Row vice president, Norman Pomerance, "gives us the possibility of worldwide publishing in the English language."

The following year, Murdoch further expanded his interests in the book-publishing industry when he acquired full control of Collins after a heated battle with Group de la Cité, France's second-largest book publisher. Murdoch outbid the French concern and bought the remaining 58.3 percent of Collins he didn't own for more than $700 million.

Once Group de la Cité withdrew and his victory was assured, Murdoch wasted little time in bringing Salem House and Zondervan, a publisher of religious books, into the Harper & Row fold. Critics of the move suggested that it was just a question of time before Murdoch imposed his own editorial style on his new book-publishing empire. But, in a 1989 interview, Zondervan president James Buick could not have been more upbeat.

"Everything is peaceful and quiet," he said. "We're getting all the possible support we can get, financial and otherwise. And virtually no interference at all, other than the kind you expect from a wholly-owned subsidiary in terms of financial controls and that sort of thing."

Was Zondervan profitable before?

"No. We went through four years, actually, of serious problems and restructuring, and we will be profitable this year and even more profitable next year in the trend that we're on.

As far as any kind of editorial interference was concerned, he said, "absolutely not . . . As I have seen it from the meetings I've been to in New York, the first amendment is sacrosanct . . . There really is no interference at all."

But P.J. Zondervan, the founder of the company, who retired several years back, did express some concerns of his own on the matter.

"I'm worried they might have different ideas for the company," he said to Associated Press correspondent Lisa Perlman. "I'm concerned about the future."

"Look, Rupert is a businessman first and foremost," a friend of Murdoch said. "If a publisher's making money, of course he'll leave it alone. And if it's not, he'd have to be crazy not to look in and see what's wrong. That's no more than anyone would do."

Murdoch's acquisition of William Collins & Sons led to a fair amount of turmoil within the Canadian trade-book publishing industry. Canada's Baie Comeau Policy, which dealt with the ownership of book publishers and received its name from Prime Minister Brian Mulroney's constituency in Parliament, required the ownership of book-publishing firms to remain in Canadian hands.

In February 1989 Murdoch was accused of altering the structure of William Collins Sons & Co. Canada Ltd. to reflect his ownership of Collins and Harper & Row. Murdoch proposed to change the name of the company to Harper & Collins Publishers and distribute the titles of both firms through the Canadian branch. Ostensible control of the firm would be given to a Canadian citizen, Stanley Colbert, a former Toronto literary agent who was born in the United States. But Murdoch's maneuver was viewed with some skepticism by other Canadian publishers.

"We have asked the government to investigate Harper & Collins to ensure that real control resides in the hands of Canadians," said Hamish Cameron, executive director of the Association of Canadian Publishers, according to the May 19, 1989, issue of Publishers Weekly. "By real control, we mean control of the board of directors, and control over assets, and control over appointment of managers.

"We have said that they haven't given up control over the distribution of books," Cameron continued, "and we believe that is critical."

Harper & Row's books were formerly distributed by Fitzhenry & Whiteside, a purely Canadian firm whose volume would be reduced by $13 million Canadian with Murdoch's new system.

Murdoch was not the only publisher involved in the Canadian controversy. Others included Grolier, which was owned by Hachette S.A. of France; Collier Macmillan, which was affected by Robert Maxwell's purchase of Macmillan in the U.S.; Time/Warner, whose pending merger would impact directly on a number of Canadian subsidiaries; and Gulf & Western, whose sale of Ginn & Co. allowed it to retain control of Prentice Hall Canada.

While the vast majority of Canadians were said to favor the spirit of Baie Comeau, there were a number of influential dissenters.

"I am against forced divestiture of foreign-owned subsidiaries," said David Galloway of Torstar, the parent company of Harlequin, according to the same issue of Publishers Weekly. He thought the policy could force U.S. companies to retaliate.

Stanley Colbert, Murdoch's man in Canada, was also cautiously opposed to the precise letter of the legislation.

"I've always supported the concept of a Canadian-owned publishing industry," he said, "but there is too much of a contribution made to Canadian publishing by foreign-owned companies to dismiss them or make them second class.

"To dismiss them suggests to me that it is not a cultural policy but a protectionist policy."

Cultural integrity or economic protectionism? The argument would no doubt rage for years to come—not only in Canada, but throughout Europe and the United States as well.

Chapter
Twenty-One

IN SEPTEMBER 1987 Murdoch turned his attention once again to areas other than book publishing. Even while he was putting the final touches on his Harper & Row/William Collins & Sons consolidation, he was simultaneously looking into a different segment of the British communications world. Those who were wondering where the transplanted Australian might strike next did not have to wait long for an answer. In another stunning move, he announced that he had already acquired a major stake in Pearson P.L.C., the English media and financial conglomerate.

Pearson was a diversified company whose holdings included the *Financial Times,* the Economist, two book publishers (Penguin and Longman), the merchant bank Lazard Brothers, Royal Doulton Porcelain, Madame Tussaud's Wax Museum, the Chateau Latour vineyards and other assorted operations. Buying under the aegis of his U.K. affiliate News

International Ltd., Murdoch acquired 17.5 million shares of Pearson stock, plus another 10.25 million shares bought through the News Corporation. These combined purchases gave him a 13.5 percent interest in Pearson, not enough for control, but more than enough to make a lot of people nervous. At the time this book went to press, Murdoch had increased his stake in Pearson to 20 percent.

"As the holder to more than 13 percent of our shares, Mr. Murdoch will certainly be listened to carefully if he wants to discuss any reasonable form of cooperation," an unidentified Pearson executive was quoted in the September 23, 1987, New York *Times*.

Murdoch already controlled about 35 percent of England's national newspaper circulation at this time, so it seemed unlikely that the Monopolies and Mergers Commission would permit him to obtain complete control of Pearson. His main rival in Great Britain, Robert Maxwell, also had a vested interest in limiting Murdoch's influence in the country.

Murdoch would not get "a free ride" if he tried to take over Pearson, Maxwell warned, according to the September 25, 1987, New York *Times*.

Notwithstanding Maxwell's vague threats, Pearson was regarded by analysts as a ripe takeover target because of the grab bag nature of its operations, which had been assembled haphazardly over 143 years without apparent design. The whole of Pearson was said to be worth less than the sum of all its diversified parts. Murdoch's investment in the company to date came to better than $400 million, and there was no question but that he wanted to increase his share.

"Anyone who assumes that Rupert Murdoch is a passive investor should have his sanity tested," said an unidentified financial advisor to Pearson, according to the New York *Times* of September 28, 1987.

The big question was what part or parts of Pearson was Murdoch primarily interested in? The *Financial Times*, Europe's leading financial daily, with a circulation of more than 300,000, made a great deal of sense for him since it would fit in neatly with the rest of his empire.

"They're fighting tooth and nail against him getting the *Financial Times*," Maxwell Newton said in 1989. "He doesn't want the *Financial Times*, all he wants is the right to publish in the United States.

"As I understand it, what he intends to do in the United States with the *Financial Times* is to make an American edition which—his idea was, it would sell 200,000 copies a day with no trouble at all. But I don't think they're going to let him do that."

By "they," Newton was referring to the British government.

"It's a problem he has all around the world with governments, I think, in relation to various markets," Newton said.

When I discussed the subject with Capital Research analyst Gordon Crawford, he said, "Pearson's told him in no uncertain terms that they don't want to do anything. That doesn't mean Rupert couldn't try something unfriendly, but it's very unlikely that the U.K. government would let Rupert . . . Not with owning the *Times* and the *Sunday Times* and *News of the World* and *Today* and, to pick up the *Financial Times*, too, would be too much concentration of power."

Crawford was referring to Murdoch's acquisition of *Today*, a financially troubled color tabloid, in July 1987 from Lonrho P.L.C. for $60.8 million. It was the only full-color daily newspaper in Great Britain, and had been losing money since its inception a year earlier.

Observers on the scene claim it is hard to imagine a more vivid contrast in styles than that between Murdoch and Pearson's chairman, Lord Blakenham, a 50-year-old scion of the Pearson family, a member of the House of Lords and past chairman of the Royal Society for the Protection of Birds. To his credit, Pearson earned more money under Blakenham's chairmanship during the past three years than it had in the previous forty, and he was not about to step aside for Murdoch without a fight—with or without any assistance from the British government.

By the end of 1987, Rupert Murdoch had already gone way beyond the legendary press barons who came before him—Hearst, Pulitzer and Beaverbrook most notably—and had established himself as the single most powerful media lord on earth. There were other media conglomerates that were larger than he was, but no other individual could boast of an empire that even began to approach his in the sheer value of the assets he controlled.

News Corporation's after-tax profits jumped another 31 percent in the quarter that ended September 30, 1987. Net earnings were $76 million Australian ($53 million U.S.), up from $58 million Australian a year earlier. Gross revenues climbed to $1.38 billion Australian ($960 million U.S.; at the rate of exchange prevailing in the spring of 1989, the U.S. equivalent would be $1.1 billion). Income from Australia and the Pacific Basin more than tripled, while profits rose 24 percent in England.

Murdoch had put his empire deeply in debt to generate such an incredible rate of expansion. Prior to engineering the largest deal of his life—the $3 billion takeover of Triangle Publications in 1988—the News Corporation Ltd. was already over $4 billion in debt. Murdoch was a legend on three continents, a man who continued to astound the financial world with the scope of his undertakings. Each time his critics thought he had finally overextended himself and was about to have a great fall, he emerged more powerful and successful than ever before.

Were there any limits on how far Murdoch could go, how much he could accomplish? Would his strategy for continued growth through increased borrowings work under any and all economic circumstances?

Those who thought not had so far been proven wrong. As he approached the eve of the most astounding financial coup of his life, Murdoch seemed undaunted by the warnings of critics who thought he had already gone too far.

Part Three

MEDIA LORD

Chapter
Twenty-Two

"THE CROSS-OWNERSHIP rule is a cornerstone of the First Amendment and free speech," Senator Edward M. Kennedy of Massachusetts stated on the floor of the U.S. Senate on January 28, 1988, according to a transcript of his remarks supplied to the author by the Senator's press deputy.

"The fundamental question is whether Rupert Murdoch is entitled to thumb his nose at that law and become the only newspaper publisher in America who can buy a television station and keep his newspaper in the same community.

"Mr. Murdoch was well aware of the law when he acquired his television stations in Boston and New York. He had a choice then, and he has a choice now. He can keep his newspaper—or he can keep his broadcasting station. But he can't keep them both. That's the law, and that's the way the law ought to be.

"I'm defending that First Amendment principle. The principle is right—and Rupert Murdoch is wrong to try to change it. Instead of attacking me, he should try to explain why he thinks he's entitled to an exemption from the law."

Senator Kennedy was responding to charges that legislation initiated by Senator Ernest F. Hollings, after consulting with Kennedy, was directed at Murdoch.

"I want to emphasize," Senator Kennedy said, "that the amendment was not directed specifically at Mr. Murdoch or his waivers, but at all persons who would be similarly situated . . .

"I went to Senator Hollings," Kennedy continued, "and urged him to save the cross-ownership rule. Senator Hollings agreed completely with my position on the issue, and he added a provision to the Continuing Resolution to accomplish this purpose.

"It is true that under the grandfather clause as it applies to New York City, the New York *Times* was able to continue to own an AM and an FM radio station (WQXR-AM and FM); and the Tribune Company continues to own the New York *Daily News,* a TV station (Channel 11) and a radio station (WPIX-FM). But those grandfather arrangements are hardly unfair to Rupert Murdoch. No new cross-ownerships have been permitted in New York City or any other city in America since 1975, and there is no justification to carve a special interest loophole in the law for Mr. Murdoch.

"I have no vendetta against the Boston *Herald* or the New York *Post,"* Kennedy continued. "I may not always agree with their editorial boards or their news coverage—but I do have genuine respect for the papers, their journalists, and their employees."

"Teddy Kennedy and Rupert Murdoch are a perfect match, just pure gladiators," William Rees-Mogg, former editor of the London *Times*, told William H. Meyers of the New York *Times*.

Senators Kennedy and Hollings won this battle, and forced Murdoch to comply with federal regulations. In March 1988 Murdoch sold the New York *Post* to New York real estate developer Peter S. Kalikow for $37 million, and in July he filed an application with the FCC to put his Boston television station, WFXT-TV, into an independent trust with former New York governor Hugh L. Carey and former U.S. Senator Edward W. Brooke as co-trustees. Under the trust agreement, Murdoch was permitted to retain beneficial ownership of the station, but not day-to-day control of it. This was a somewhat unorthodox settlement of the dispute, but not without precedent.

"The issues are whether or not the trust meets the stated requirements for insulation," said Robert H. Ratcliffe, assistant chief of the FCC division that had jurisdiction in cross-ownership cases, according to the June 23, 1988, New York *Times*. Among the requirements for insulation, Ratcliffe said, were "the crucial relationships between trustor and trustees. There may be no relatives or family members among the trustees. Additionally, all of an owner's interest, not just the controlling interest, must be placed in trust."

Final approval came on April 26, 1989, when the FCC granted Murdoch's request. Under the terms of the agreement—as reported in both the Wall Street *Journal* and the New York *Times* of April 27, 1989—Murdoch would receive the proceeds of any sale as well as dividends and additional payments that the trustees considered to be in excess of the television station's business needs. The FCC turned down a provision that any sale of the station had to be approved by

Murdoch, except that the price had to be for at least $35 million to a single buyer.

Murdoch lost the battle, but he was determined not to lose the war. Following the sale of the *Post,* he obtained a ruling from a federal appeals court that maintained Congress had unconstitutionally singled him out with its legislation.

"The Hollings amendment strikes at Mr. Murdoch with the precision of a laser beam," read the opinion, which was written by Judge Stephen F. Williams, according to the March 30, 1988, New York *Times.* "First Amendment values are implicated in the process and require even-handed treatment of all applicants."

The ruling came too late to save the *Post* for Murdoch, but it did open the door to further questions about whether the FCC cross-ownership ban would be allowed to stand.

Maxwell Newton maintained that Senators Kennedy and Hollings did Murdoch a good turn when they forced him to sell the money-losing *Post.*

"In the end," Newton said, "I think he did Rupert a favor, because it forced Rupert to get rid of the *Post,* which was absorbing quite a lot of his energy." Murdoch lost an estimated $150 million on the New York *Post* during the eleven years he owned it.

But Barbara Yuncker, the administrator for the New York Post Guild Insurance Fund, disagreed with Newton. "Don't go on the assumption that he wanted to do it," she said. "He was very upset having to do it . . . Murdoch didn't want to sell. He did benefit himself financially, but I think if you thought that he was trying to get rid of it, you're wrong. Because he still has a string on it if Kalikow can't make it go.

"Other organizations were either grandfathered or previously approved under the same provision under which he was appealing . . . In any event, the way the thing was drawn it applied only to him."

Murdoch himself had much to say on the subject during an unusually revealing interview conducted on the national radio program "American Focus," and published in the Winter 1989 issue of the Gannett Center Journal. In response to a question about whether or not cross-ownership of a TV station and a newspaper in the same market stifles diversity of opinion, Murdoch said,

"No, absolutely not. In New York there are eight or nine television stations, and I don't know how many newspapers, including major regional ones, and seventy radio stations. It's impossible to have a monopoly. I'm not against the spirit of the rule, not saying that it may not be necessary in small cities, but in the major markets in America we think that normal antitrust rules should be used."

Concerning the legislation brought into existence through the combined efforts of Senators Kennedy and Hollings, Murdoch stated, "The effect of that was to take an FCC rule which had provisions for discretion and for appeal in public hearings and to change it without debate into law. It went through a committee in one minute, and was then presented to the congress and the president as part of a two or three thousand-page budget. No one ever looked at it."

When asked for his opinion on the two senators' motivation for sponsoring the legislation, Murdoch replied,

"I think it was done with personal intent by Senator Kennedy. There was no doubt about that. It was done very willingly by Senator Hollings, who probably never heard of me, because he is having his own big fight with the FCC."

Hollings's dispute with the FCC, according to Murdoch, revolved around the agency's attempt to abolish the so-called

Fairness Doctrine, which Hollings believed in. The Fairness Doctrine required broadcasters to give equal air time to others with different editorial opinions.

"I think Senator Kennedy's motivation was quite different," Murdoch continued. "He saw us as an independent, conservative voice, if you like, in Boston and in New York, and one that had been critical of him. This was, you know, the good old Kennedy rule of don't get mad get even, so fair enough. But that's a pretty well-established fact now."

When informed that Senator Lowell Weicker of Connecticut (the liberal Republican who was ousted in November 1988 by the moderate Democrat, Joseph Lieberman) was also upset about being attacked in one of Murdoch's newspapers, the media lord said,

"Oh, I think some of the more liberal ones felt we were an opposite voice to theirs and would have acted against us. On the other hand, many liberals would say they believe in the freedom of the press, and would have been for us."

Murdoch was asked why he held on to the New York *Post* for as long as he did, considering how much money it was losing.

"When we did buy it," he said, "it was not losing money. It had been a break-even operation, if you like, but a very poor one. We'd intended to spend money on it. We doubled or tripled the news coverage, the sports coverage, everything in the paper, and tried to develop it. We took it as a great publishing challenge: to do the impossible, if you like, and make a success of it and find a viable place for it in the publishing spectrum in New York. So there was a certain amount of pride in keeping it going and fighting on."

Regarding the *Post*'s rivalry with the *Daily News*, Murdoch said, "There were also great difficulties at the *Daily News*, and we felt we could outlast them. I still feel that. The losses mounted, but they were containable until the last few months when the price of newsprint went up very greatly. With the Kennedy-Hollings amendment and the uncertainty that it led to, we just saw the advertising flying out the window. Our losses doubled overnight. We were holding on to the last minute, I'll admit."

When questioned about the criticism, in some quarters, that Murdoch was not beyond clouding the lines between fact and fiction to sell newspapers, Murdoch was adamant on the issue.

"Oh no, that's all fact," he said. "You cannot cloud fact and must not. I mean, some people love us for the New York *Post* headlines . . . The famous headline, which wasn't even on page one, I think, said, 'Headless body in topless bar.' Now, people have laughed about that or sneered at us or been shocked. The fact is it was perfectly true. There was a murder and the victim was decapitated and it was in some sleazy bar in New York City. It was a great headline, and it was true. If it was untrue you couldn't defend it at all."

What did Murdoch think those kinds of stories said about the American public?

"Oh, very little," he said. "It says a lot about our New York public. It says a lot about life in New York City, which is a hard life. It's a very exciting life. If you read the New York *Post* carefully, you will see it's tremendously into the arts and entertainment, into politics. This is a city of diverse views and tremendous political groups and pressures, and it's a city which is dirty and very depressing. It can be very hard if you're poor, but still attracts people like moths to the light, so to speak. And the New York *Post*, in its way, was part of that scenery, trying to report on it, comment on it, trying to be part of it, long before I came in."

And now that he was forced to divest himself of the newspaper by the power of the law, how did Murdoch feel about it?

"New York is our home and will remain our home, and this will be the first time in my life that I've lived in a city in which I haven't also been publishing a newspaper. I hope I'll overcome any withdrawal symptoms. It'll be good for me probably."

When I asked him in 1989 if he had put the *Post* completely behind him, Murdoch said, "Oh, yes. Absolutely. It was a nightmare chapter of my life. It was good and bad. I learned a lot. I should have put a lot more resources into it. Should have kept a steadier course with it. It was such a difficult, impossible position being the third paper out of three. We should have watched our losses more and held them down. It might have been better, who knows, if we had a handle on it from day one. But it's easy to say that now. We didn't have the money in those days. If we could have come up with another five million dollars a year we might've done better."

Was getting advertisers the big problem?

"It was getting readers," Murdoch said. "That was the problem. If we had more readers than the *Daily News,* we would have taken all their business away. No problem about that at all."

Circulation did go up quite a bit, didn't it?

"But not enough. I believe that unless—and they may find it with their new editor—if you can find an editor who'll make that so special, and so exciting that, that you can charge fifty cents a day, sixty cents a day, something of that order, then perhaps you can become sort of viable and build from there.

"But I think it's very, very unlikely," Murdoch continued. "We found that people had a tremendously settled attitude toward what the paper was. And the people we had to get to, which was the middle-class people of Queens, we had to broaden out beyond Manhattan. The paper was sort of a middle-class liberal paper which it had been, very liberal, in the early days. And it didn't matter that we became a bit conservative, and that we tried very hard with sports and that sort of audience, it didn't get across their doorstep. Equally, the Daily *News* which tried to be very liberal, coming the other way, didn't get across any doorsteps either. This is not a melting pot this place, it's not a landing ground. I mean, it's very ethnic. It's very settled in its attitudes. Just New York City, the city and all the myriad communities within it do not change."

What about Page Six, the celebrity gossip page that attracted a broad swath of readers?

"Page Six had one or two years when it was very good in the ten years we were there," Murdoch said. "Perhaps three or four years. But what people today misunderstand is that it was a highly edited page. We had a lot of tough times there. But in a sense you could say, with the hindsight of ten years, that it sort of put us on the map. And many things have happened there. Getting involved in the city, and the state, and the nation, the world."

You mean in establishing your presence here in the United States and getting your name out?

"Oh, yes."

On the subject of the Kennedy-inspired legislation that forced Murdoch to unload the *Post:*

"From the day we bought the television station we knew we had to sell the newspaper," he said. "There was never any question about that. And that was a deliberate choice. And I'll admit that I was enjoying it, I had become so attached to it that, instead of getting on with it and selling it then, we delayed and said maybe they would change the law. Something was going to happen and we could hang in there.

"We were in very active negotiations with Kalikow," Rupert Murdoch continued, "when Kennedy pulled that one, and we thought maybe he might change it. It's a damned silly law. But we'll see how the *Post* goes. This editor might be very successful."

Jerry Nachman had just been named the new editor of the New York *Post*, succeeding Jane Amsterdam.

"I don't even know him," Murdoch said. "I would say this is pretty much the last chance. There's a possibility that this summer the Daily *News* will go on strike. And that will give the *Post* new breathing room."

Would it affect the *Post*?

"They wouldn't take a strike, no," Murdoch said. "I don't believe they would, anyhow."

Was there a chance the *Post* could go under?

"Oh, yeah," Murdoch said. "I wouldn't say it's a chance, it's a likelihood. The Sunday paper's been a great mistake."

Rupert Murdoch was referring to the expensive and unsuccessful attempt to launch a Sunday edition a month earlier.

"I would say that to make the New York *Post* viable in the long run," Murdoch said, "it has to have a successful Sunday paper. And each time I came to that conclusion, I did my sums and said, 'I have to put in fifty to a hundred million dollars to have any chance to pull it off.' It's got to be the best launch ever seen, it's got to be the best paper you've ever seen and then people will discover the paper called the New York *Post*. And then if it fails, it doesn't matter that you've lost fifty million dollars. You've measured the credibility of the whole enterprise. And that's a risk that I think is very real. I might be proved wrong, but we'll see whether the failure of the

Sunday Post damages the daily *Post.* It may be that it won't. People could forget that pretty quickly."

If Murdoch did experience any serious withdrawal pains, he didn't keep them from slowing him down in his quest for further expansion. Even while his battle with Senator Kennedy was going at full tilt, he was already planning the greatest media coup of his life to date.

Chapter
Twenty-Three

THE ANNOUNCEMENT struck with the impact of a bomb-shell. Rupert Murdoch was buying Triangle Publications from Walter H. Annenberg for $3 billion—not only Murdoch's biggest deal yet, but the largest takeover in history involving the print-communications industry.

The announcement was all the more astounding since Murdoch's News Corporation was already over $4 billion in debt and most financial analysts thought he would not attempt another acquisition—let alone one of such mammoth proportions—until he had paid it down a bit. Instead, Murdoch was continuing his practice of revaluing his assets upward, as previously discussed, so he could use them as collateral for even greater leverage. Speaking of her boss, Carolyn Wall, the general manager of Murdoch's New York television station WNYW, said, according to the August 14, 1988, New York *Times,* "He's more an impresario than an emperor."

The Triangle publications Murdoch was acquiring included TV Guide, which had the largest circulation of any magazine in the United States, Seventeen, the Daily Racing Form and a magazine distribution business. The News Corporation was a giant prior to the Triangle deal; this latest acquisition elevated it to the ranks of a genuine colossus, with assets totaling more than $11 billion. Murdoch's empire was now roughly six times its size of only three short years before, and twelve times that of 1983. Only Bertelsmann A.G., the West German conglomerate, exceeded the News Corporation's $4.4 billion in revenues for its 1988 fiscal year.

Despite the immensity of his empire, Murdoch continued to run it as though it were a small family business. His management team consisted of a handful of close associates, many of whom had been with him from the early days. His key managers included Carolyn Wall, mentioned above; Richard A. Sarazen, the News Corporation's chief financial officer; John B. Evans, president of Murdoch Magazines; and Martin Singerman, the director of News America. Among them, the British-born Evans was a more recent arrival on the scene, having risen to his present post after starting as classified advertising salesman for the *Village Voice*.

"If you can claim affiliation with the Star," he was quoted in the New York *Times* of August 14, 1988, "it is like having come over on the Mayflower."

Murdoch's management style was to hire the right people for a job and then delegate a vast amount of authority to them.

"You can't build a strong corporation," Murdoch said, according to the same *Times* article, "with a lot of committees and a board that has to be consulted at every turn. You have to be able to make decisions on your own."

"He gives you great freedom," the article quoted Carolyn

Wall as saying, "but he lets you know from the beginning that you have no safety net under you."

"We talk all the time," Singerman said, as reported in the *Times* piece. "But then Rupert talks all the time to all of us."

Keeping close tabs on the empire's bottom line was the province of chief financial officer, Richard Sarazen. His was perhaps the most critical position of all, since the fortunes of Murdoch's entire empire rose and fell with the numbers Sarazen put on his boss's desk at precisely eleven o'clock every Friday morning. The figures were enclosed in a tan-colored book, and similar volumes from the British and Australian operations arrived in New York on Monday mornings. These books contained revenues and expenses for the week for every property in the empire, along with comparisons with the previous year's figures.

"If there's a problem anywhere," Sarazen said, "Rupert can spot it immediately. Usually, he'll want more information before he makes a decision."

With the acquisition of Triangle, Murdoch's American properties would provide the greatest share of worldwide revenues for the first time, according to Richard MacDonald and other analysts who crunched the numbers. Indeed, the figures I looked at in its 1988 annual report showed that News Corporation's U.S. operations accounted for 42 percent of total revenues in the fiscal year ended June 30, 1988. Australia and the Pacific Basin's contribution amounted to 30 percent, and Great Britain's 28 percent. Total assets carried on the books at the end of the same period amounted to $11.4 billion, while long-term debt was put at better than $4 billion, and rose even higher afterward when the company's assets were revalued to increasing its borrowing power.

In TV Guide Murdoch had a magazine with a circulation

of 17.1 million. Seventeen reached 1.8 million readers a month and the Daily Racing Form was considered the bible of racing publications, producing a wealth of information on horses and tracks. In expanding his empire to such dimensions, however, Murdoch had increased the company's debt to its present $7 billion from $237 million in 1983. The News Corporation was leveraged as it had never been before, and analysts began to speculate about what parts of the empire Murdoch would sell off to raise cash and reduce his debt. When I put that question to First Boston analyst Richard J. MacDonald in 1989, he replied,

"I've asked him that question frequently myself, and they always come back to me and tell me that it really doesn't make any sense to talk about businesses that might be sold, because it can be very disheartening for people who work there."

Since the News Corporation had a June 30, 1989, deadline to reduce its debt load to a level the banks found acceptable, the question could not go unanswered for too much longer. The answer, when it did come, was something of a surprise to many observers (as is reported below), but throughout the spring of 1989 the detective work continued apace.

The properties Murdoch would most likely want to hang on to, and those he would let go, would have to fit in with his long-range goal of creating a worldwide electronic and data base operation, providing subscribers with a welter of information about diverse topics, including financial markets, airline, hotel and travel data, and more. The great value of the Triangle Publications acquisition, in addition to its highly profitable print publications, was the amount of marketing data routinely gathered by both TV Guide and the Daily Racing Form. Murdoch envisioned a whole new generation of

customers—the travel industry, the airlines, hotels, etc.—
who had a need for this kind of demographic information
and would pay to receive it.

With financing for the Triangle deal pushing News Corporation's debt up to the $7 billion mark, a major concern was
just how much of the empire Murdoch would have to sell off
to satisfy the banks. I put that question to Don Galletly of the
News Corporation in New York, and he said they had to
unload well over $1 billion in assets by the end of June 1989.

"Eventual performance will depend on the speed with
which we sell assets to pay down debts," he said. "Our interest
expense is going to be fairly substantial this year because of
the new acquisitions, and although we have until the end of
June to sell off enough assets to meet our ratio test that the
banks watch, that's in progress. And if it doesn't take place
until June 29th, that's going to have a significant impact, you
know, versus February or March."

As to which assets in particular would go, Galletly said,
"Well, in general we have said underperforming assets and
we've sold some real estate, a building in Los Angeles, in
Century City, which netted us about $80 million in cash. We
sold our half interest in Elle magazine, which netted us $160
million, and we sold about $50 million in shares that the
company has owned in other companies.

"We've realized about $250 million dollars in net proceeds.
We need to sell another billion to a billion and a half dollars
worth of assets, actually realize cash proceeds of that amount
and pay down the debt by that amount."

News America publishing had launched Elle magazine
jointly with the French firm Hachette S.A. in September
1985. The publication, an American version of the French
fashion magazine, became a huge success with a circulation
of 825,000. Advertising revenues were also good, reaching

$23.8 million during the first half of 1988, a 59 percent increase over the same period a year earlier. Murdoch sold his 50 percent interest in the profitable venture for $160 million to Hachette, which also published *Woman's Day* through its Diamandis Communications division in the United States.

The building in Century City that Galletly spoke of was the 20th Century Fox Film building which went for $320 million and netted the News Corporation $80 million, according to him.

Murdoch denied speculation that he was also looking to sell the trade publications he bought from Ziff-Davis a few years earlier.

"We received an offer for Ziff-Davis for $800 million," he said, according to the January 23, 1989, issue of Adweek, "but we refused . . . We have no publications in the U.S. that are for sale. We have dozens of properties overseas that we can sell."

Some analysts also suggested that Murdoch would sell his interest in Reuters to reduce his debt load, even though the news and financial service company seemed to fit in perfectly with his long-range goals. Gordon Crawford of Capital Research was among them. He said, "I think he's selling his Reuters to fund the stuff he's doing now, like the Triangle properties. So, I would say he would be less and less of an influence on what they're up to."

But Meyers of the New York *Times* thought otherwise. He claimed that Murdoch wanted more of Reuters, not less, and might attempt to purchase the Australia Associated Press, which owned nearly 14 percent of Reuters and which would make Murdoch the single largest shareholder in Reuters.

And so, the guessing game continued during the ensuing months. The only thing certain was that the $3 billion acquisition of Triangle Publications was now the focal point of his empire. His battle plan for TV Guide, particularly, extended beyond U.S. shores into the international arena.

Early in 1989 Murdoch announced plans for a British edition of the publication. The English version of TV Guide would be different from its American cousin, largely because of a British copyright law prohibiting private publications from printing advance program listings. That function was reserved for the state-owned British Broadcasting Corporation, as well as ITV, a commercial television network.

BBC published Radio Times, which listed its own programming for the coming week, while ITV put out TV Times showing forthcoming programs on its own stations. Each magazine had a circulation of about 3 million, but, with an estimated audience of nearly 21 million homes with televisions in the U.K., the potential market that Murdoch hoped to tap was enormous.

"What we'll put together and launch in the next six months," said Elizabeth Rees-Jones, managing director of Murdoch Magazines in London, according to Advertising Age of January 9, 1989, "is a TV entertainment magazine based on programs and the people in them. We simply can't do TV listings, although we would like to."

Simultaneously, Murdoch launched an assault on the restrictive British law, and he was joined in his effort by his major U.K. rival, Robert Maxwell, and the West German firm Bauer Publishing, both of whom were planning television publications of their own.

In this fight to free up the television print media to more competition, Murdoch and other publishers were counting on support from an unexpected quarter: The European Commission, a division of the European Community that was setting the ground rules for Common Market trading that was to begin in 1992. The Commission had ruled recently against Irish broadcasters in their attempt to keep Magill TV Guide from publishing its own weekly program guide, and it appeared unlikely that the restrictive British copyright law would be permitted to stand as 1992 drew closer.

But commissions move slowly, and entrenched laws of all varieties take a long time dying. Murdoch had never depended on bureaucracies to pave the way for him. He had come this far by breaking new ground—as he had done at Wapping. Sweep out the old, bring in the new.

In this arena, too, he was planning to create a *fait accompli* and set a new standard for others to copy. The big loophole in the existing legislation was the emerging satellite television industry. Satellite programming was beyond the purview of the protective British copyright law. Murdoch had the right to publish satellite programming in his magazine, if he chose to do so, and satellite television channels were coming to Great Britain as they were to all of Europe.

Murdoch had no intention of taking a backseat to anyone in this industry, or any other. Rather, he would be one of its pioneers with a company named, appropriately, Sky Television. Another war was just beginning.

Chapter
Twenty-Four

O N THE night of December 21, 1988, a rocket lifted off its pad in French Guiana, illuminating the South American sky with a payload that would beam signals to homes on earth on six channels. The launch of the powerful Astra satellite marked Rupert Murdoch's entry into the European satellite television firmament. The programs would contain a mixture of movies, sports, news and entertainment that would put Murdoch in direct competition with his fellow pioneers.

Rupert Murdoch did not have the skies to himself.

In orbit already was a French satellite launched earlier in the year that was expected to carry five channels to earth, including programming offered by the W.H. Smith Group P.L.C. Also, British Satellite Broadcasting Ltd., a consortium of British, French and Australian companies, was planning a satellite launch of its own in August 1989. Murdoch's rival in Great Britain's print tabloid field, Robert Maxwell, started beaming his own programming from the same satellite Murdoch was using in February. And various groups from West Germany, Italy and France had announced similar projects.

The fledgling industry was already getting crowded, and would become even more so in the years ahead.

Even as the rockets were being readied on their launching pads, media analysts took their pencils and started toting up the numbers. If Sky Television was going to stay aloft, some predicted, Murdoch would have to spend a lot more money than the $184 million he had committed so far to the venture.

"In terms of a payback," one unidentified industry executive was quoted as saying in the December 21, 1988, Wall Street *Journal,* "I think [Sky Television] will be as long a road as the Fox network has been for him in the U.S."

Fox had continued to lose money since Murdoch started it, and rung up a pre-tax loss of $80 million in the 1988 fiscal year.

In addition to the overwhelming financial burden that satellite television imposed on its pioneers, there were the more mundane logistical snags of getting receiving dishes installed on time, as well as the problem of coming up with programming that would appeal to people from diverse cultures speaking a dozen different languages.

To circumvent the language barriers, Murdoch intended to limit his viewing audience, at first, to Great Britain and Ireland.

Still, initial confusion could make "the satellite market a much less attractive market from the consumers' and the distributors' point of view," said Geoff Powell, managing director of Granada P.L.C., one of the groups behind Murdoch's competitor British Satellite Broadcasting, according to the same Wall Street *Journal* article.

Murdoch had not entered the field blindly, however. His primary goals remained long-term, and he anticipated losses in the start-up years with the expectation of turning substantial profits down the road. Sky Channel, an existing cable television service that Murdoch offered in thirteen countries, was also losing money—almost $74 million since 1983—as was Fox Television in the United States. But these were hurdles that Murdoch fully expected to overcome.

"I don't believe people will be confused that much longer once there is product to sell," said Jim Styles, managing director of Sky Television, according to the Wall Street *Journal* of December 21, 1988. "It's like the first VCR or the first color TV. Until they see it and touch it and watch it and understand it, they will obviously be a little doubtful about it."

In an April 1989 interview, Don Galletly of the News Corporation said of Sky Television, "We're on air with four channels. At this point, in its very early days, there isn't much of a satellite population out there, not much of an audience watching. We expect by the end of the year to be up with at least five, and possibly six."

Toward that end, Murdoch began plugging Sky Television enthusiastically in his five U.K. newspapers in January 1989. The competition heated up in February among the major U.K. players—Maxwell, W.H. Smith Group P.L.C. and, of course, the media lord from Down Under—all serving up a new menu of programs for the viewing public. (British Satellite Broadcasting Ltd. was gearing up for a fall 1989 start.) Among the dishes offered by Murdoch was a concert featuring U.S. country and western singer Dolly Parton. The stakes were high: hundreds of millions of dollars worth of potential advertising revenues from U.S. and European concerns, with the largest portion going to the broadcaster with the largest segment of the audience.

In Great Britain alone "there is no doubt that five years from now, many millions of people . . . will be watching satellite TV," said Charles Jonscher, a London partner at the U.S. management consulting firm Booz, Allen & Hamilton, according to the February 2, 1989, Wall Street *Journal.*

How many broadcasters could the market support?

"I don't think there will be room for all," prognosticated Bob Marshall, associate director of London marketing consultant CIT Research Ltd., according to the same article. All the would-be broadcasters, he continued, "have inflated the market [size] they are going to reach."

Two long-standing competitors proved that they were not beyond teaming up in a joint effort when it suited both their interests. In May of 1989 Murdoch's Sky Television signed a five-year pact with Maxwell Cable TV (MCTV), allowing Murdoch's satellite channels to be distributed through the Maxwell cable system. Murdoch paid Maxwell, his old nemesis, "several millions" for the distribution rights, according to both the New York *Times* and Wall Street *Journal* of May 17, 1989. But the great significance of the deal was not the amount of money involved, but rather the edge both parties would have in promoting the new media technologies in Europe.

The benefit to Murdoch was a substantial increase in the number of households he would be reaching, from an estimated 500,000 to 750,000 by the end of 1989 to roughly 1.15 million. For Maxwell, the extra channels he distributed were expected to multiply his own market fivefold within two years.

"I know the rivalry between Murdoch and Maxwell is supposed to be intense," Maxwell was quoted in the same issue of the New York *Times.* "But we have chosen Murdoch because Sky is ready, willing and able to serve the customers who belong to our system."

Speaking of Murdoch, Robert Maxwell told financial journalist Adam Smith on his May 19, 1989, television program, "He is a genius. There's no question that he has achieved a tremendous amount all over the world. Like me he has built a global business."

On the same program, Maxwell biographer Tom Bowers said, "He's obsessed by Murdoch. Murdoch for him is everything he would have liked to have been. A man with a background, a man who has ruthlessness, a man with social connections, an insider and yet can pretend to be an outsider, or be a real outsider and pretend to be an insider, a man who has got a track record which has consistently been to beat Maxwell."

Their joint venture was given a boost of sorts when one of their major competitors, British Satellite Broadcasting Ltd., announced that it was delaying its own service until the spring of 1990—a full nine months behind schedule. The delay was blamed on technical difficulties in developing scrambling equipment to keep freeloaders from plugging in to British Satellite's programming without paying for it. The company's ability to raise some $400 million for the launch was also in jeopardy, according to the May 26, 1989, Wall Street *Journal.* The British-European version of Star Wars promised to get even more intense in the months ahead.

To be sure, there was a lot more than market share and advertising revenues at stake. What was taking place in Great Britain and Europe was nothing less than a modern-day revolution, one fought with computers and high technology rather than with guns and bombs.

It was all part and parcel of the general rush toward a unified Common Market in Europe by 1992. Considering the power inherent in the media to shape attitudes and tastes—some might argue, even political opinions to a degree—there was no question but that national styles and ethnic cultures would be undergoing significant changes in the coming years.

"This is a revolution in choice," said Murdoch, perhaps the most accomplished and feared revolutionary of the age, according to the New York *Times* of March 16, 1989.

The "choices" Murdoch mentioned involved an array of programming, the likes of which Europeans had never seen before. Until now, most European television was either state-owned or controlled, and the available fare was sharply limited—unlike American television, which offered something for almost everyone. Now, thanks to Murdoch and the other satellite television pioneers, all that was about to change. Virtually overnight, a booming new market opened up in Europe for program producers, film companies and advertisers looking to sell their products to Europe's 320 million consumers.

Politicians and social observers lamented the cultural impact that the new electronic revolution would have within their own borders. France, for example, was quick to impose restrictions on imported programming. Other countries promoted the view that deregulation was coming about too quickly, and they would soon be inundated by "wall-to-wall" American-style soap operas and game shows.

Some of the fear was justified, but a lot of it was blather—nothing more than ritualistic British and European reaction to anything carrying a U.S. label. In Great Britain, for example, while critics were voicing concern about "low-brow" American programs, the state-owned BBC was foisting upon the public endless hours of snooker (a form of pocket billiards) and lawn bowling coverage, which served as an effective soporific for even the most devoted fans. Programming choices were similarly limited in Germany, France and other European countries, with much of the content closely regulated by government. Murdoch and his fellow media barons may not have been offering to bring intellectualism and high culture to European viewers, but they were at least offering a measure of diversity.

"The idea that American television will vulgarize the high temple of European culture is nonsense and dreadful snobbery," said John Perris, worldwide media director for the advertising conglomerate Saatchi & Saatchi P.L.C., according to the New York *Times* of March 16, 1989.

Not all of Europe was in a snit over the burgeoning electronic revolution. Italy was fairly casual about regulating television—as it is about so many things—while West Germany, France and Denmark were more heavy handed. But any attempt to stem the floodtide of programming via satellite into the U.K. and Europe seemed as destined to failure as the Dutch boy sticking his finger in the dike. The electronic invasion of Europe was all but inexorable—notwithstanding all the talk about "cultural integrity."

"European television is entering an exciting period of turmoil that will run into the 21st century," said John Perris of Saatchi & Saatchi, quoted above, according to the same New York *Times* article.

According to one estimate, Europe was expected to add a minimum of a hundred new channels by 1992. American film vendors and television producers, in particular, were reaping a bonanza in the rush to sell programming to the new satellite broadcasters. While the intellectuals and politicians were worried about a cultural invasion from the U.S., the simple fact was that American shows—movies, television series, musical productions and other entertainment—were popular among European viewers, and they were less expensive to run than domestic programs with their high production costs.

"It's been fantastic for the American suppliers of programming," said Regina Dantas of Qintex Entertainment, an Australian media company, according to the March 16, 1989, New York *Times.*

Murdoch's Sky Television paid an undisclosed amount which was said to be a record for "Lonesome Dove," the mini-series based on Larry McMurtry's novel, and he announced a deal with the Walt Disney Company to buy some of its movies for Sky Television. However, he was not the only satellite broadcaster lining up U.S. programming. Before it even got rolling in the fall of 1989, British Satellite Broadcasting signed contracts with a number of U.S. film companies, including Columbia Pictures Entertainment, MGM/UA Communications, Warner Communications, the Cannon Group, Paramount Communications' Paramount Pictures and MCA's Universal Studios. The film companies were expected to reap revenues amounting to $300–400 million from the deals over the next five years.

Murdoch and his fellow pioneers were laying out staggering amounts of money to keep their ventures aloft, and the big question on everyone's mind was how long it would take before they begin to realize a profit. Capital Research's Gordon Crawford was somewhat less than optimistic about the outlook.

"I think [Murdoch is] liable to lose a bundle in his Sky Television over in the U.K.," he said in 1989. "Though again, nobody'll know that for two years."

John Perris of Saatchi & Saatchi was equally cautious.

"It will require deep pockets and time to sort out the winners from the losers," he said, according to the New York *Times* of March 16, 1989.

The fact that Murdoch had taken on yet another high-risk challenge, one that would require a heavy investment in money and energy during the next few years, was hardly news. What was amazing, however, was that he was doing it at a time when his empire was already $7 billion in debt and considerably over-leveraged even by the liberal Australian banking guidelines.

The battle for control of the European television market moved to Spain in May 1989. Rupert Murdoch's News International was among a group of international media investors bidding for licenses to run that nation's first three commercial stations in 1990, when the Spanish government gave up its television monopoly as part of its overall march toward democracy.

With economic liberalization already well entrenched, Spain enjoyed the highest growth rate on the continent during the previous three years. In January 1990 the revolution spread beyond the economic sphere into electronic media, following a similar move in print communications. For the first time, three commercial stations would be permitted to compete with two state-run channels. News International joined forces with a Spanish media conglomerate called Grupo Z in a joint bid for a license to operate one of the new stations. Italy's Silvio Berlusconi formed a similar arrangement with the Spanish publisher Anaya and a consortium of smaller investors, and Canal Plus of France had already taken a 25 percent stake in the mass market daily *El Pais* in a bid for the third station.

"The situation is still very fluid," an unidentified financial analyst said, according to the New York *Times* of May 29, 1989. "Some people are making a lot of money; others are losing heavily but gambling on the future. It's going to be a good while before things stabilize."

Was Murdoch erecting a monumental house of cards that could come crashing down at any moment? The newspapers at the time were filled with stories about how the Saatchi brothers of Great Britain may have done just that by pyramiding their advertising kingdom. Was Murdoch pursuing the same course in the media world? The final answers would not be clear for another few years, or longer.

Chapter
Twenty-Five

RUMORS THAT Murdoch would sell his shares in Reuters continued to circulate through the financial markets. Just how important was Reuters to a man with Murdoch's global media and communications interests? In order to answer that question, it helps to understand exactly what Reuters is.

Reuters Holdings P.L.C. is more than just a news wireservice like Associated Press. It is better described as a complete electronic information company, and one of its more innovative creations in 1989 was a system called Globex, which was designed to revolutionize the way commodities and other investment vehicles were traded across the globe.

Throughout history, buyers and sellers looking for bargains had haggled in bazaars over the prices of all kinds of commodities. This method of doing business—the open outcry system—prevailed on the floor of commodities exchanges until recently, even while international stock and bond markets conducted their own trading, for the most part, on computers. Globex was going to change all that by finally bringing the technological revolution to the commodities pits.

Traders resisted the move at first, but the impetus for change came from the U.S. federal government, which began investigating commodities market fraud in earnest in the aftermath of the Wall Street scandals. Computerized trading would serve the purpose of opening up the markets to the public, matching buyers and sellers more equitably with price quotes that were visible on a screen. Critics of the outcry system held the view that professional traders had gotten rich by denying the public the same access to information that they had.

"Those people who control the marketplaces, be they commodity exchanges or stock exchanges," said Junius Peake, a consultant specializing in trading technology, according to the Wall Street *Journal* of January 17, 1989, "benefit economically by having uniqueness of information. The fellows in the pit have information you and I in our offices could never have."

The value Globex technology had to Murdoch was its application to information and data transmission in general. We've already discussed his dream of publishing a U.S. version of the *Financial Times,* complete with up-to-the-minute financial data supplied by Reuters. We've also mentioned that TV Guide and the Daily Racing Form routinely gathered demographic data that could be marketed in various ways and transmitted by Reuters. Speaking of Reuters' Globex system, Peter Schwartz, who served on a government panel studying securities technology, told the Wall Street *Journal,* "The system has already gotten so complex that literally no one understands the interconnections."

William P. Frankenhoff, a portfolio manager for W.R.

Grace's pension plan, was asked by Kathryn M. Welling of *Barron's*, to explain what is unique about Reuters.

"News doesn't mean anything," Frankenhoff said. "That is not really what they do. They transmit information from financial market to financial market . . . their proprietary data that they are swinging between Tokyo and London— that's where the business is."

Because he understood Reuters' staggering potential, it appeared unlikely that Murdoch would divest himself completely of his stake in the company. For a clearer insight into the media lord's relationship with Reuters, I spoke to a high-level executive of the firm—a long-time friend of Murdoch— who asked not to be identified.

"Between you and me," he said, "Murdoch is a sensitive issue in Reuters. He has been a director for ten years now . . . Rupert has been a very good and very conscientious director. But, because of the nature of the shareholdings, he has a significant number of shares, which he has because Reuters is owned by the newspaper publishers of Australia, U.K. and New Zealand. And because of his extensive ownership of those institutions, he actually has access to the owners' shares both in the U.K., through his ownership of U.K. papers, and also in Australia. At the moment it's a particularly sensitive time because, in fact, as is public knowledge, there are a number of owner A shares which are likely to be converted into B shares."

That is precisely what did take place in April 1989. Reuters Holdings P.L.C. announced plans to convert the powerful A stock, which were voting shares, into B shares with fewer votes. The conversion succeeded in untangling the rather complicated three-tier capitalization of the company, and reduced the major owners' voting control of Reuters from 54 percent to 22 percent of the outstanding shares. The 97.3

million A shares—which were not traded publicly—carried four votes each. They were converted one-for-one into B shares with one vote each.

The conversion succeeded in weakening the directors' control of the company (including Murdoch's), but it was done primarily to allow Reuters to raise new capital by selling shares to the public and listing its stock on more overseas exchanges. It would also make it easier for Reuters to finance any new acquisitions it wanted to make. The price of doing that was considerable dilution of ownership, but the price was considered to be worth paying for the increased financial flexibility.

When I questioned Murdoch about his intentions regarding Reuters, he said, "We have a very close association. It's a company that I have a great feeling for. I'll continue to be a director for some time. I learn a lot from them."

Regarding the speculation that he might sell his shares at some point: "It's not a significant amount," he said. "We might sell it. We're of a size now where our investments should be where you have a cash flow."

Don Galletly of the News Corporation also confirmed this to me. "Reuters hasn't been sold yet," he said. "We now have twenty-six-and-a-half million shares, that's about 6.2 percent."

Whether or not they would be sold in the future was inside information that could not be discussed.

"We are listening to offers, and actually negotiating with interested parties for the hotel and travel publications," Galletly said, referring to the magazines the News Corporation bought from Ziff-Davis.

This was the first concrete information about Murdoch's plans for selling off various properties to meet the June 30, 1989, deadline for reducing his bank debt. Murdoch himself,

as mentioned earlier, had denied that he had any intentions
of unloading the travel publications.

"Part of those have already been sold," Galletly continued.
"The aviation magazines were sold eighteen months ago to
McGraw-Hill. So it's just the hotel and travel books."

Exactly how much debt was the News Corporation carrying in April 1989?

"In U.S. dollar terms it's over $7 billion at this point," Gal-
letly said. But, he added, that News Corporation's debt-to-
equity ratio would be "around one-to-one" by the June deadline.

What else was Murdoch doing to reduce the company's
debt load?

"We are in the process of trying to set up a new company,"
he said, "which will buy the book publishing interests from
News Corporation, and that will probably close some time in
June."

Galletly was talking about Murdoch's new proposal to raise
in the neighborhood of $1 billion in order to create a global
media colossus as part of an over-all restructuring plan.
Under the general terms of the plan, the investment banking
firm of First Boston Group would collect the money through
private placements. Once the money was raised, the new
entity would purchase News Corporations's book-publishing
properties, including Harper & Row and Collins. There
would be an exchange of shares between the News Corporation and the new media giant, giving each company equity in
the other. Part of the proceeds would be used to pay down the
$7 billion plus debt Galletly mentioned.

Murdoch said his intention was to "start a second News
Corporation," according to the Wall Street *Journal* of March
3, 1989. "The main purpose is not to be stopped from expand-

ing." If the plan succeeded, "it means we aren't tapped out . . . we can go on with everything."

The big question was whether or not First Boston could actually raise such an astronomical sum of money through a private placement. (Unlike a public offering, in which equity shares are offered directly to the investing public, a private placement is made to a limited group of people with relatively large amounts of discretionary capital.)

"It would be extraordinarily attractive for Rupert Murdoch to accomplish this," said Steven Rattner, a managing director of Morgan Stanley & Co., according to the Wall Street *Journal*, "but it's also extraordinarily ambitious to try and raise that kind of money," particularly in the private markets.

Stanley Shuman, Murdoch's banker at Allen & Co., was also quoted in the same article. The plan "allows Rupert to continue being as aggressive as ever without losing time," he said. "The media business is restructuring worldwide, and he doesn't want to be sitting on the sidelines while that is happening."

In April, 1989, Don Galletly discussed the private placement plan, which was still in the process of taking shape. "The final shape of it, I think, is still up in the air," he said. "But it will be big enough to absorb the book-publishing operations which, I suppose would be capital of several hundred million dollars."

Would stock in the new corporation be offered to the general public at some point?

"It probably will eventually be publicly traded, but not at this point."

Some Wall Streeters maintained that Murdoch had merely come up with an ingenious means of fobbing off a significant portion of his debt onto someone else. But Murdoch, while admitting that the new venture "will be highly leveraged," claimed that the new investors in his operation "will get a full return by the end," according to the same Wall Street *Journal* report. He denied that this style of financing was a typical leveraged buy-out (LBO), with all its negative connotations, that the public had been hearing so much about. An LBO usually involves the kind of junk bond financing popularized by Michael Milken, the indicted investment banker, during the past few years. Ordinarily, in an LBO the buyer does not put up any money of his own. The deal is financed by borrowing heavily against the assets of the target company.

"This is not a KKR," Murdoch said, referring to the firm Kohlberg Kravis Roberts & Co., which handled many high-ticket LBOs. "We aren't buying things to strip them down and sell."

His point was valid, since the News Corporations was not divesting itself of the book-publishing operations and using the cash simply to pay off its debt. Under the terms of the package, the parent company would retain a 20 percent interest in the new media firm and also retain management control.

"He is selling the business but taking a 20 percent ride on its future and continuing to manage it," said Frederic M. Seegal, head of media investment banking at Shearson Lehman Hutton, Inc., according to the March 3, 1989, Wall Street *Journal.* "It's as if Rupert is doing an internal leveraged buy-out."

"Something had to go, and it wasn't going to be Fox Film, or the Fox network, or the TV stations," said John Reidy, a Drexel Burnham Lambert analyst. "Clearly he is trading a significant interest in the book company to achieve his objective of having his cake and eating it, too."

All the speculation ended in May 1989 when the newspapers confirmed the information supplied to me by Don Galletly a month earlier. Murdoch announced the sale of his travel and hotel publications to Reed International P.L.C. of Great Britain for $825 million. With the sale, the total cash raised by Murdoch following his acquisition of Triangle Publications soared to $1.63 billion.

"This is a dramatic reducing of debt," said Drexel Burnham Lambert media analyst John Reidy, according to the Wall Street *Journal* of May 8, 1989. He stated that the reduction of interest costs would result in a rise in News Corporation's 1990 earnings.

The properties unloaded by Murdoch included the Hotel & Travel Index, the industry's main source of comprehensive hotel information in the United States; Travel Weekly; a number of directories serving the business-meeting and convention fields; and a recently developed electronic system that connected travel agents with on-line information from hotels and convention centers. Since Murdoch paid about $340 million for the Ziff-Davis properties in 1984 and subsequently invested about $50 million in them, his profit on the sale came to more than $400 million.

In a prepared statement, as reported in the May 8, 1989, issue of Advertising Age, Murdoch said, "We are very sorry to be leaving our group. But our own acquisitions over the last 12 months made it necessary to choose between trade and consumer publishing, even though we are confident of great growth in the travel and related industries."

Following the sale of the magazines, Murdoch's intentions regarding Reuters suddenly became much clearer. At the end of June 1989 Murdoch announced an ingenious way of hanging on to his interest in Reuters yet raising cash for his shares at the same time. He offered a cash exchange for a new issue of preferred stock tied to the price of Reuters shares. Buyers of the new preferred stock had a right to exchange the shares for cash, at a price based on the current level of Reuters stock. This provided Murdoch with the option of maintaining his interest in Reuters if the stock continued to rise in value, or of selling his Reuters shares if he chose to in order to pay off the preferred shareholders.

"This is a unique creation by one of the most astute financiers," said John Reidy, the Drexel Burnham analyst, according to the June 29, 1989, Wall Street *Journal*. "If Reuters shares hit the moon, it will mean Murdoch will have to pay more for the exchange, but he can then sell his Reuters shares to pay off the exchange."

Timothy Horking, another analyst with Bain Securities, was also quoted on the subject in the same article. "In a positive market for Reuters shares," he said, "investors aren't going to exchange their shares as they'll hold on for a higher price. This will mean Murdoch can also hold on to his Reuters stock."

In effect, Murdoch had hedged his bets with Reuters. He could either hold onto it for future profit, or use the stock to pay off the new shareholders. Meanwhile, he was raising cash through the preferred stock offering to finance new projects.

Despite the sale of the travel magazines, Murdoch had not lost interest in his print operations—not by a long shot. Even while he was selling off his travel magazines, he was expanding his magazine interests in other areas. Yet there was no question that electronic media, and their peripheral print publications, were now the focal point of his empire. And there was irony in this, too. In the spring of 1989, the former press baron turned media lord suddenly found himself in the somewhat unusual position of having his new electronic ventures funded largely by the print side of his empire. The *Sun* and the *News of the World* in England, and the Star in the United States, still remained the cash cows that paid to a great extent for everything else.

Chapter
Twenty-Six

FOX TELEVISION continued to lose money, but there were some signs in early 1989 that it was beginning to turn the corner.

"The American business is coming back a bit," First Boston analyst Richard J. MacDonald said. "It was in bad shape for a while."

Much of the credit for the turnaround belongs to 20th Century Fox chairman Barry Diller.

"The morning line on us was not good," Diller said, according to Betsy Sharkey writing in the April 24, 1989, issue of Adweek. "We went into a very hostile environment. But I felt it was more important to go into the business during a difficult phase—that we would learn to adapt in difficult waters."

The idea of beating the Big Three and creating a new network was just the kind of challenge Diller loved. And while Fox was not there yet, the numbers were starting to look better and better; the Nielson Television Index ratings in April 1989 showed NBC, CBS and ABC continuing to lose market share—down from 80 percent to a collective low of 67 percent—and Fox's share jumping by 50 percent in the past twelve months to 14 percent of the audience.

"When Rupert bought 20th Century Fox, he bought it with Barry Diller attached," an unidentified industry insider told Betsy Sharkey.

A former Diller associate, Jeff Katzenberg, who was chairman of Walt Disney Studios in 1989, added, "I wouldn't want to bet against Barry Diller."

The battle for market share among the viewing audience was fought largely in the arena of so-called tabloid television. The popularity of such programs as "The Morton Downey, Jr. Show" and "Geraldo" featuring Geraldo Rivera created a market for a televised version of the kind of journalism usually found in the National Enquirer and the Star. Not to be outdone in this field, Murdoch launched a tabloid show of his own on the Fox network—"A Current Affair," with Maury Povich.

Povich, who is married to television news anchor Connie Chung, had been in and around network television for more than twenty years when he got a phone call from Murdoch in 1986, shortly after the media lord bought his television stations from Metromedia. According to Maura Sheehy, writing in the April 1989 issue of Manhattan, Inc., Murdoch told Povich that he wanted to air a new program dealing with breaking news, and he wanted Povich to host it for him.

"We wanted to do emotional stories and people stories," Fox Television producer Peter Brennan told Sheehy, "and not screw around with language or try to save the world or be Dan Rather."

At the time, Povich was doing a regular news program for

Murdoch in Washington, but after Murdoch's summons he switched hats and was on the air with his new program within days.

"When Rupert asks you to do something," Povich said, "Well, you just do it."

"A Current Affair" appeared for the first time in July 1986 on Channel 5 in New York at 11:30 at night. A month later Murdoch moved the show to a prime-time slot at 7:30 P.M., and a year later he syndicated it nationally. The program was a hit, and so was its host. By April 1989 it was appearing on 146 stations in all markets across the country; it netted profits of approximately $20 million for the past year and was expected to earn two to two-and-a-half times that amount in 1990.

The team responsible for orchestrating most of what has been occurring on Fox Television has a distinctly Australian cast. It includes Ian Rae, who was quoted earlier and who edited the Star for seven years before becoming executive vice president of news; Peter Brennan, who serves as senior producer; Peter Faiman, another producer who earned his stripes as the director of *Crocodile Dundee* and the creator of "The Reporters"; Joachim Blunck, the art director; and Gerald Stone, an American who produced the Australian version of "60 Minutes."

Faiman credited the Australian attitude toward life with getting Fox Television off the ground. Americans tend to take things too seriously, he said, while Australians "are always ready to give things a boot up the ass. We're less concerned with structure and more concerned with results. If, in fact, we're ever concerned with anything at all."

Ian Rae, one of the men responsible for holding Fox together for Murdoch, is a bit more serious and less cavalier in style and tone. He is less the quintessential celluloid Australian and more the modern television executive with heavy responsibilities weighing on him. During an interview he gave to Electronic Media, published on January 23, 1989, he outlined his strategy for Fox.

His role, he said, was to bring together the news operations of the various Fox stations that air news. "That's Washington, New York, Chicago, Houston and Los Angeles," he said in the Electronic Media interview. "What's important to me is to quickly bring to Fox a solid news and information center that will be of great service to all of our stations."

How does Fox News interact with News Corporation's international operations?

According to Rae, bringing together the vast resources of News Corporation's television news operations was his job. That included the establishment of a 24-hour news channel in London. He was hopeful that he would be able to coordinate an exchange of news and information between Fox in the U.S. and the London operation.

Will Fox be selling any of its news and information gathering capabilities to other companies?

Rae said in the interview that he was talking to one of the networks in Australia to see if Fox could arrange a reciprocal agreement with them.

"But the immediate task is to take the facilities and resources and the talent that we have at all our Fox stations and . . . utilize them to the fullest potential," he continued.

Does Fox anticipate establishing a news division on a comparable scale to that of the three major networks?

If there was a demand, he said, and everything fell into place the way he liked, it could lead to the potential for a national news service.

How did Rae feel about Fox programs such as "A Current

Affair" and "The Reporters" being linked with tabloid or trash television?

"To label it 'trash TV' is nonsense and shows a complete lack of knowledge and understanding of the programs . . . ," he was quoted as saying in the Electronic Media interview.

He thought the word 'tabloid' was a term that had been turned into a dirty word for something that existed to differentiate between a broadsheet newspaper and a tabloid newspaper or magazine.

"If they're saying that 'tabloid' is enterprising," he continued, "at times a little cheeky, breaking new ground, breaking news stories, telling stories about all sorts of interesting people in all kinds of extraordinary circumstances, then it's 'tabloid.' "

Elaborating further on the subject—which has been blown into a major social and cultural issue of the age, with calls for censorship emanating from some circles—Rae said that he was a devoted fan of such programs as "Sixty Minutes" and did not mean to denigrate that type of journalism. But, he added, he considered "A Current Affair" to be quite simply an innovative news and current affairs program.

"What has happened is that all these copycat shows have rendered 'A Current Affair' the sort of doyen, the respectable father of this new genre of television. It's 'reality' television, is what you're talking about.

"We frankly are now appalled," Rae continued in the same interview with Electronic Media, "to get linked with the Morton Downeys and some of these other programs."

Like it or not, the association was made and continues in the minds of viewers to this day. Several of the so-called tabloid programs incited the wrath of some self-appointed custodians of national morality who called upon advertisers to boycott programs they found objectionable. One celebrated instance involved a Michigan housewife named Terry Rakolta who launched a one-woman campaign against the Fox Television series "Married . . . With Children."

Several fundamentalist ministers were quick to get in on the act, convincing everyone concerned about First Amendment freedoms in the United States that the Moral Majority was still alive and kicking. These included the Reverend Donald Windmon of Tupelo, Mississippi, leader of a group that beginning April 27, 1989, conducted a month-long period of monitoring television programming. Murdoch's "A Current Affair," Teletrib's "Geraldo" and NBC's "L.A. Law" were among the shows cited as objectionable—the latter for using the word "goddamn" in one of its episodes.

While many industry executives denied that this type of vitriolic neo-Puritanism would affect their programming, there were signs even before the Reverend Windmon's month-long period of monitoring got underway that the protests were having an impact. According to the New York *Times* of April 23, 1989, such major advertisers as Coca-Cola, McDonald's, Chrysler, General Mills, Campbell Soup, Ralston-Purina and Sears had cancelled commercials on some of the controversial shows.

"There are a lot of issues in the society that people are uneasy about," said Brandon Tartikoff, president of entertainment at NBC, who was under fire himself, according to the same *Times* article. "They look at television, see things on the news, drugs, violence, and say we can't have much impact on these issues as we'd like to have. But maybe we can on the programs we see on TV."

But he saw hypocrisy on the part of advertisers as well.

"I think some advertisers looking for a way to cut back on their budgets," he said, "to conserve money in the second quarter, are using this as an excuse."

No stranger to controversy himself, Barry Diller had a few strong opinions of his own on the subject. When informed during a weekly staff meeting in Los Angeles that General Mills didn't want Betty Crocker associated with another Fox program, "Cops," Diller was furious.

"Then they shouldn't advertise in it. Period!" he said as reported in the Wall Street *Journal* of May 25, 1989. "I'm sorry, I just get—when someone says Betty Crocker doesn't think 'Cops' is a great environment I just get angry. 'Cops' is as pro-social as the world gets, and beyond it. It's original, pro-social television."

But, with Fox capturing 23 percent of the eighteen-to-thirty-four-year-old viewing audience between 7:00 and 9:00 P.M. on Sunday against NBC's 19 percent, CBS's 16 percent and ABC's 12 percent, and with plans to challenge the major networks on other nights as well, there seemed little question but that Murdoch's string of independent stations would have to make some concessions to the tastes of advertisers.

"Life never gets easier, it gets harder," Diller said. "We no longer have to go through the pain of establishing ourselves. We have new pain to go through."

Murdoch himself is less involved with the editorial aspects of his television and movie operations than he is in the case of his various print publications. This is understandable since he cut his teeth on the newspaper business in Australia, and it is in this area that he feels most comfortable. He is content to let Barry Diller run the movie business and Ian Rae and company tend to the television part of his empire. But his eye is firmly fixed on the bottom line, his people tell me, and if an enterprise fails to show a profit within a reasonable period, he is quick to get involved.

"Rupert hires the people he thinks are right for the job," one of his associates said in 1989, "then stands aside and gives them room to work. But he always has a time frame in mind, and if they don't show results at the end of it, chances are he'll either find someone else to do it or pull the plug on the whole operation."

But not with the newspapers?

"No. Beneath it all he's still the old newspaperman who can't resist the urge to write headlines and sometimes even a story if he feels strongly about it."

"When Rupert travels around the globe," First Boston analyst Richard MacDonald wrote in an article published in the Winter 1989 issue of the Gannett Center Journal, "he takes about five newspapers with him and a pen, and he circles the headlines. He's always looking at headlines to see how they're written."

When I spoke to Murdoch in 1989, I got the distinct impression that, if there's one thing missing from his life today, it's the lack of time he has to spend on his daily newspapers because of all his other responsibilities. Newspaper work seems to give him the greatest pleasure of all.

Notwithstanding the hue and cry over the content of the various tabloid television shows, the popularity of "A Current Affair" and other Fox Television programs among the general public continued to grow. At the NATPE—National Association of Television Program Executives—convention in Houston during January 1989, "A Current Affair" was one of the leaders in sales to program buyers from local stations around the country. Media buyers were equally enthusiastic about other new programs scheduled by Fox.

"Fox's ratings continue to be low relative to the big networks," David Verklin, vice president and media director at Hal Riney & Partners in San Francisco, told me. "But the big story at Fox is the demographics. If you have to name the top seven or eight shows in terms of male members of the household, they're all Fox."

Referring to the competition in the industry, Bill O'Reilly, who replaced David Frost as host of "Inside Edition," was quoted in the February 21, 1989, Wall Street *Journal* as saying, "This is wild. It's a shoot-out. It's the OK Corral."

Fox Television producer Peter Brennan admitted as much when he said, according to the same article, that he still went drinking with his colleagues at other networks, "but we give wild misleads about what we're working on."

An ad that 20th Century Fox ran in the March 6, 1989, issue of Electronic Media compared its market share favorably against that of its prime-time rival "Inside Edition." According to the ad, "A Current Affair" was beating the competition in all major markets.

Fox continued to set the pace in the spring of 1989 with a move away from tabloid or "reality" shows, as those in the industry preferred to call them, toward a more traditional comedy, drama and news format.

"We've concentrated on fictional TV shows," Fox Entertainment president Peter Chernin was quoted as saying in the March 20, 1989, issue of Adweek. "We don't think there's a need for any more reality shows on Monday night. So our leading contenders are comedy and action."

The changes underway at Fox began to pay off in terms of advertising revenues and increased market share. Advertising Age of March 27, 1989, reported that the Fox Broadcasting Company had stolen the show from the major networks in selling advertising time for the new line-up of programs scheduled to be aired in the fall of 1989.

"The Fox development seemed the most interesting, with the most unique kinds of concepts," said Chuck Bachrach, president of syndication at Western International Media, according to the same Advertising Age article.

While network television was expected to remain the pre-eminent advertising medium, the heads of CBS, NBC and ABC all agreed that their share of the viewing audience would continue to decline in the years ahead. The network share had fallen from 80 percent to 67 percent during the past five years, according to the February 8, 1989, New York *Times,* and Robert C. Wright, chief executive of NBC, predicted that it might fall as low as 55 percent before leveling off.

He was lamenting the fact that the networks were losing viewers to the independent stations—including Fox Television—as well as to the cable stations and syndicated programming.

These statistics were confirmed to me in 1989 by Betsy Frank, senior vice president of Saatchi & Saatchi Advertising, who said, "Fox is doing extremely well with teens and young adults. Fox stations are a must-buy for any advertiser trying to reach a young audience."

After losing $90 million in its first full year of operation, Fox finally turned a profit during the six months ending December 25, 1988—attributable mostly to increased advertising revenues.

"There isn't a major debate anymore among advertisers about whether they should buy advertising on Fox," said Jamie Kellner, president of Fox Broadcasting, according to the February 28, 1989, Wall Street *Journal.* "It's just a matter of when and how much to spend."

One big advantage Murdoch has over the networks was that he was not required to spend a certain amount on news and public-interest programming, and could concentrate his resources on entertainment.

"The three networks are required by the Federal Communications Commission to program either news or children's programming from 7 to 8 P.M. on Sunday," said an unidentified industry analyst, according to the April 3, 1989, New York *Times.* "Fox had an advantage. It may call itself a network, but it is not bound by the FCC."

He was talking about just one of the requirements imposed on the networks that do not apply to the independents. With Fox becoming more and more competitive each month, however, it would appear to be only a question of time before the networks moved to have the same rules imposed on Fox.

The consensus in the industry was that Murdoch still had some distance to cover before fulfilling his dream of establishing Fox as a full-fledged fourth network. But there was little question that, by the early months of 1989, he was closer to it than anyone thought possible a few short years before. Close enough, in fact, that in May he commissioned Kenneth D. Laub & Co., a Manhattan real estate broker, to find a one-million-square-foot facility somewhere in the tristate area of New York, New Jersey and Connecticut to accommodate the burgeoning Fox operations.

Until this time, WNYW had been housed in an antiquated turn-of-the-century structure that was originally built as an opera house. An unidentified spokesman for the station said, according to the May 8, 1989, issue of Electronic Media, that "the building was never meant to be a broadcast facility, most television stations are housed on two floors, and we're scattered among seven."

Murdoch's various New York–based operations, as well as his 2,500 employees in the region, were scattered throughout a number of offices in midtown Manhattan and in Secaucus, New Jersey. His goal, according to WNYW vice president Carolyn Wall, was to gather them all under a single roof within the next couple of years. As this book went to press there was a report circulating that Murdoch was close to signing a lease for a million square feet of space in a new office tower on Broadway, just north of Times Square.

"It's going to be the biggest lease of the year," said an un-identified real estate executive, according to the Wall Street *Journal* of June 26, 1989. "It looks pretty solid . . . but I have seen a lot of these fall apart at the last minute."

Indeed, Kenneth Laub, Murdoch's broker, said the report was premature.

Chapter
Twenty-Seven

WHILE MURDOCH concentrated so much of his energy and resources on his burgeoning electronic empire, he did not neglect the lucrative print side. TV Guide and its overseas cousin were much on his mind, and he still maintained a strong interest in consumer magazines after selling Elle to Hachette.

Just when everyone thought there was no room for yet another publication in the women's fashion field, Murdoch announced plans for Mirabella magazine.

"It is basically an upscale fashion book for women who know who they are," said Grace Mirabella, the magazine's editor, according to the New York *Times* of November 25, 1988. "It's for women who are more than fashion groups. It's not about bubble gum and hula hoops."

Mirabella had taken the post after serving as editor-in-chief of Vogue.

"It's aimed at the reader Vogue abandoned 10 years ago," John Evans, president of Murdoch Magazines, said, according to the same article. "She's interested in substance, not glitter. She is 30 years old or more and has a household income that is high."

Despite the crowded field, some experts in the area believed that Mirabella had an excellent chance of succeeding. One of them, David Lehmkuhl, who is senior vice president and director of media services at the advertising agency Ammirati & Puris, Inc., said that the key is to "carve out a niche in the field. By concentrating on a particular segment of the market, Mirabella could succeed."

Another market observer, Sandra Rifkin, editor-in-chief of Marketing and Media Decisions, agreed.

"It's a good idea if it's packaged properly and well targeted," she said, according to the November 25, 1988, New York *Times*. "Grace Mirabella knows the field. Elle has indicated there's a healthy interest in fashion, and Lear's has shown there's advertiser interest in the older consumer."

"There is a market of 14 million women over 40 with household incomes of $40,000 or more," said Michelle Magazine, advertising director of Lear's. "And because the baby boomers are coming of age, that market will expand every year."

At a press conference held at Mirabella's spanking new office in February, 1989, publisher Julie Lewit-Nirenberg announced the first issue would appear in June 1989.

"We're not going up against Lear's," she said. "Our challenge is to position the magazine without age-specificity."

She was specifically referring to the fact that Lear's bills itself as the magazine for women over forty.

"I strongly believe that women do not dress or make love based on their age."

Grace Mirabella was upbeat about the magazine's prospects. She said it would devote nearly half its pages to substantive articles and the rest to fashion and style. She described Mirabella's typical reader as a woman who "can think about her suit and Solzhenitsyn at the same time."

The major challenge in the launching of any new publication is appealing to advertisers, and that task was growing increasingly difficult as more and more magazines competed for essentially the same advertising dollars. But Mirabella magazine seemed to be off to a good start. As Mirabella's public relations representative, Camille McDuffy, said "They've got a very impressive number of ad pages in the first issue, over a hundred and twenty. Their goal was eighty, so they far surpassed that. Advertisers are mainly fashion—Ann Klein, Donna Karens, Bill Blass—I mean you name the designer, they're in there. A lot of cosmetics, several cars, one or two liquor ads, travel . . . The response from advertisers was really very enthusiastic."

Murdoch expressed high hopes for the magazine and its editor at a prepublication party a week before the first issue reached the newsstands. Appearing at Grace Mirabella's side, he said he had great confidence that she would be able to make a success of the magazine. There was no question but that Murdoch was giving Grace Mirabella a free hand in the editorial content of the publication. This was her project and it would fail or succeed because of her efforts. It was another example of Murdoch acquiring a property he believed in, then hiring the person he thought most qualified to run it.

"This is a style magazine," Mirabella said at the party, according to the June 12, 1989, issue of Advertising Age. "It's not a magazine stridently trying to make women older, or free and independent in any way."

Mirabella's biggest competitor would be Vogue. And why not? Vogue was the magazine that had dismissed Mirabella a short time before.

Another new magazine launched by Murdoch in June 1989 was Sports Travel, which was tailored for people in the sports industry who select sites for various events, book travel arrangements and plan league conferences. The story of how the magazine came into existence is fascinating in that it sheds more light on how Murdoch operates when he believes in a project.

In April 1989 Edward J. McNeill, Sports Travel's publisher, recalled how he had approached Murdoch's people and explained his idea for a magazine.

"I'm twenty-nine years old, and they reviewed it and they came back and they made me a fantastic offer. They made me the publisher of the magazine and gave me the opportunity to fulfill a dream; they put me in business.

"[Murdoch] believes in his employees. I know he's got a lot of bad press in the past, but he's very entrepreneurial. He gives them the opportunity to realize their own personal growth, which gives a certain amount of allegiance."

Sports Travel was targeted for the "movers and shakers" in the sports industry—according to McNeill, "twenty-four thousand of the most influential people who can sign the dotted line to determine where an event's going to be, sporting conventions, or who may influence team travel decisions. So you're looking at a multi-billion dollar industry."

He cited people like Donald Trump who "generates a hundred million dollars worth of gross revenue" when he sponsors a major sporting event.

While Murdoch was preparing Mirabella and Sports Travel for their June 1989 launch dates, he experienced a moment of anxiety when trustees of Generoso Pope's estate put the Enquirer up for sale in December 1988.

Pope bought the Enquirer in 1952 for $20,000 and turned it into the nation's largest-selling weekly tabloid with a monopoly in the field until Murdoch brought the Star into existence. Now that the *Star* was a major profit center within the Murdoch empire, Murdoch was more than a little concerned about who the potential buyers of the rival publication might be, and what plans they envisioned for it.

Among the likely bidders were his old nemesis Robert Maxwell, who had already established a U.S. book-publishing presence, Hachette's Diamandis Communications, Inc. and Bauer Publishing of West Germany. Murdoch himself was not in a position to bid for the Enquirer since he was still in the process of selling assets to bring down his debt load. Obviously, the highly profitable Enquirer would be a plum for whoever acquired it.

"There are very few institutions in America today that reach such a wide audience," said Scott Marden, managing director of Bankers Trust Company, which represented another unidentified bidder, according to the April 3, 1989, issue of Advertising Age. "It's a property that reaches a large market. The potential buyers see a real opportunity based on the performance of the company."

That said, the Enquirer's performance had been slipping a notch or so recently. During the first six months of 1988, its paid circulation dipped 3.5 percent from a year earlier to just over 4.3 million, and it slipped another 2.2 percent in the next six months to 4.286 million. Still, there was no question of its clout in supermarkets across the nation.

"It's worth going after and having," said Hachette Publications' president, Didier Guerin, according to the same Advertising Age article. "The reason the publication sells millions of copies each week is because there is a real property there."

Speculation on who would win the bidding war ended a week later when Macfadden Holdings, Inc., a privately held publishing company, and the investment firm Boston Ventures, jointly won an auction to buy GP Group, Inc., publisher of the National Enquirer, for $412.5 million. Six other publishers had also put in bids, including Hachette Publications and Maxwell Communications.

Macfadden published a number of romance magazines—True Story, True Confessions, Modern Romances, Secrets and Teen Beat—as well as a couple of trade publications: Chief Executive and the Discount Merchandiser.

Boston Ventures owned Billboard magazine at one time, before selling it to Affiliated Publications. The investment firm bought the movie camera maker Panavision in 1985, and Motown Records in 1988.

The outcome of the bidding war shocked just about everyone else involved. A week earlier speculation about the eventual selling price centered around the $200–250 million range, and most observers dismissed a figure as high as $400 million as ridiculous.

"The $400 million being talked about is a crazy price," an unidentified overseas bidder was quoted in the April 3, 1989, issue of Advertising Age. "The real price will be closer to $200 million."

When it was all over, however, Diamandis's president, Peter G. Diamandis, said, "They're going to make it work. They certainly paid a full price. But for everybody that ever criticized the size of a media deal in the past ten years, somehow a few years later it looks cheap," according to the Wall Street Journal of April 14, 1989.

Robert Maxwell, who had been considered the favorite in the battle to buy the Enquirer, steamed off in his yacht in a major snit after losing out to the much smaller Macfadden. One imagines, however, that Murdoch lost little sleep over Maxwell's disappointment. He had a far better relationship with Macfadden than he did with Maxwell. Murdoch was a member of the advisory committee for Boston Ventures, and one of its original investors. First Boston, which arranged Macfadden's financing for the deal, was Murdoch's investment banker for his corporate restructuring program.

"From Murdoch's point of view," said an unidentified observer, according to the May 1, 1989, issue of Adweek, "having a player like Macfadden owning the *Enquirer* keeps it out of the hands of existing large publishers, like Hachette or Maxwell, who are more direct competitors." The same observer maintained that "once Murdoch gets his debt refinancing in order, he'll have easy access to the *Enquirer* if he's interested."

Others in the industry speculated that Murdoch might even attempt to team up with Macfadden to distribute the Enquirer through his own magazine distribution system. After the purchase of Triangle Publications with its TV Guide network and the subsequent demise of Select Magazines, Inc. in May, 1989, Murdoch Magazines distribution division suddenly emerged as a major force in the field, with 15 percent of total newsstand distribution in the United States.

The industry was now dominated by five companies that also published consumer magazines of their own, both in the U.S. and abroad. Besides Murdoch, other leaders in the field were Hachette Publications, Inc., which entered the industry through its acquisition of the Curtis Circulation Company, and now controlled 25 percent of the distribution; Warner Publisher Services with 28 percent, which would be joined with Time Distribution Services (8 percent) when the merger of the two companies was completed; ICD/The Hearst Corporation with 10 percent; and Kable News Company with 8 percent. A group of smaller outfits accounted for the remaining 6 percent.

The consolidation of consumer magazine distribution among a handful of publishing giants caused a considerable amount of concern among other publishers, but it was a move that reflected the trend toward megamergers throughout the publishing and communications world at large.

"If the national organizations don't get together," said Robert E. Alexander, vice president of the New York Times Magazine Company, according to the May 15, 1989, New York *Times,* "they will be played off against each other by publishers until there is no profit left for them."

The newspaper side of Murdoch's print empire was also facing revolutionary changes that threatened to affect the entire industry. As newspaper publishers met in Chicago in April 1989 for their annual convention, they discussed the possibility that the current year would be critical in determining the role newspapers would play in the future.

"It's very scary," said Arthur Ochs Sulzberger, chairman of the American Newspaper Publishers Association and publisher of the New York *Times,* according to the New York *Times* of April 24, 1989.

What worried Sulzberger and other publishers attending the convention was the increasing competition from electronic publishing and from the phone companies which were invading the news distribution industry. As the newspaper publishers met, the Congress of the United States considered a bill that would permit the seven regional telephone companies to compete with newspapers in the generation of information. AT&T had already expressed its own intention of entering the field, and NYNEX introduced a service on April 25th that would enable its customers to receive a broad range of information on their personal computers.

The type of data that would be made available included financial news, stock and commodity quotes, real estate information, home shopping services, job listings, restaurant reviews, food recipes, horoscopes, celebrity gossip, gardening advice, government and political news, sports news and scores, travel information and the ability to make reservations, health tips, weather reports and numerous other information people have traditionally obtained from daily newspapers.

"It is the most hopeful sign we've seen in years," said Richard Adler, a consultant at the Institute for the Future, according to the New York *Times* of April 26, 1989, "and it brings a new group of players to the table. They're very serious about this and they bring a lot of resources . . . The question is, will they be flexible enough to respond to the feedback they get in the market."

The debate over whether new technology would eventually replace print is as old as the advent of radio and television, and will continue with each generation of technology that comes along. Television was supposed to replace books years ago, but it never happened. People simply watch it in addition to reading more and more books each year. But the dissemination of information is different from reading for enlightenment and pleasure, and many in the industry expect that newspaper publishers will be under a lot of pressure to respond to the new challenge in coming years. The ones that do will prosper; those that don't will likely fade into oblivion.

If any newspaper publisher in the world is positioned to

exploit the new environment and turn it to his own advantage, it's Rupert Murdoch. Reuters, Citicorp, Dow Jones & Company and Dun & Bradstreet—along with the telephone companies—are among the major electronic publishers in the world today. Murdoch, with his satellite television and cable stations in Europe, his film and television companies in the United States and his growing ability to transmit data and information electronically throughout the world, is at the very cutting edge of the new technological revolution.

"You can be sure Rupert's not going to get left behind in all this," one of his associates said. "He'll be right up there with the giants."

The international media giants were slugging it out in 1989 as never before in their struggle for supremacy. No longer was it a question of who owned the most profitable newspapers or magazines, who made the best films or most popular television shows, who published the biggest-selling books. The major portion of the market would belong to the media giant who did *all* those things better than everyone else. A real revolution was taking place, and the spoils of victory had never been greater.

Chapter
Twenty-Eight

IN MARCH 1989, Time, Inc. and Warner Communications, Inc. announced plans to merge their print and movie empires, and create the largest media conglomerate in the world. Time was a major publisher of books and magazines, including Time, and Warner, of course, was the movie giant that Rupert Murdoch had sought control of a few years before. If the merger was permitted to stand, it would put Time-Warner ahead of Bertelsmann A.G. and Murdoch's News Corporation in terms of total assets, market capitalization and annual revenues.

Moreover, Time-Warner would become the largest media conglomerate in the world, with annual sales of about $8.7 billion, ahead of Bertelsmann A.G., Capital Cities, the News Corporation and Hachette.

When I discussed the situation with Murdoch in June 1989, he said, "Time-Warner changes things for all of us." He thought the combined assets and capabilities of the proposed new entity would put pressure on everyone to expand their own operations.

The deal as it was first presented would involve an exchange of stock with no cash changing hands, and would enable the new media conglomerate to play a leading role as one of a handful of global media companies able to produce and distribute information in every conceivable medium.

Just when it appeared as though the proposed merger would go through, however, Paramount Communications (formerly Gulf & Western) complicated matters by launching a separate tender offer for Time that would make Paramount-Time the largest communications giant in the world if the bid succeeded. But the dispute was finally resolved in court in favor of Time which was given the green light to acquire Warner; it was now increasingly apparent that continued growth and consolidation within the industry was all but inevitable.

"Only strong American companies will survive after the formation of a unified European market in 1992," said Warner's chairman Stephen J. Ross, according to the March 5, 1989, New York *Times*.

"What you've got," Drexel Burnham Lambert analyst John Reidy said of a Time-Warner merger in the same article, "is a company that will be the largest magazine publisher in the country, the world's most profitable record company, a cable television entity with more than 5.5 million cable subscribers, one of the world's largest book publishing operations and the country's largest supplier of pay cable programming."

Besides Time magazine, Time, Inc. owned People, Money, Fortune, Sports Illustrated, Time-Life Books, Little, Brown & Company, the Book-of-the-Month Club, Home Box Office (HBO) and more. Warner Communications was the parent company of Warner Bros., Warner Books, Warner Records, Lorimar Telepictures and several cable systems.

"We have a large treasury and a strong balance sheet," said Time's chairman J. Richard Munro, as quoted in the New York *Times* of March 5, 1989, "and we have plans."

He was not specific about those plans, but analysts speculated that they had to include acquisitions in the growing electronic publishing field (discussed in the preceding chapter) to allow the new conglomerate to compete directly with Murdoch's News Corporation. As J. Kendrick Noble, the Paine Webber media analyst, said, "Time in particular has always had the ability to bring resources and talent together from different media fields to create synergies they never had before. The new company's going to be totally integrated."

Others, however, said that it would not be easy for any conglomerate to compete successfully with Rupert Murdoch in the international arena. Murdoch's advantage was that he still ran his huge empire as though it were a family enterprise. He—not a committee—made the decisions, then hired others to carry them out.

"It will take innovative, visionary management to compete with foreign media giants such as Rupert Murdoch's News Corp.," Laura Landro wrote in the Wall Street *Journal* of March 6, 1989. In her article, she quoted J. Richard Munro of Time: "We have a shared vision of our industries facing a global battle. We see Robert Maxwell and Rupert Murdoch and Bertelsmann and Sony coming into our market and raising hell, and we see this as an opportunity for an American company to get competitive."

One of the big stumbling blocks Munro saw for the Time-Warner conglomerate was the relationship that would develop between Munro and the more free-wheeling Steve Ross.

"The co-chief executive structure is an unwieldy one that rarely works for long in U.S. companies," Landro wrote.

In a later piece that appeared in the March 21, 1989, issue of the Wall Street *Journal,* she speculated that "few people who know Mr. Ross expected him to take a secondary role at Time Warner. If anything, Mr. Ross . . . has positioned himself to be the guiding force at Time Warner for the next five years, some associates say."

As the battle for media dominance heated up in the early months of 1989, it appeared as though these were the companies that would determine much of what we read, saw on television and in the movies, and the kind of information that was transmitted back and forth across the globe well into the future.

Bertelsmann came into existence in 1853 as a publisher of hymnals. It catapulted into the major leagues of media in 1986 with the purchase of RCA/Ariola Records from General Electric, and the book publisher Doubleday & Co. Bertelsmann extended its reach further into Europe by acquiring a mail-order book club and a variety of television and women's magazines. It established a big presence in television when it won the rights to televise German soccer matches beginning in 1990, and acquired a 50 percent interest in a European pay-Television channel. In 1989 Bertelsmann was highly profitable, and it was the largest communications company in the world prior to the Time-Warner merger.

Murdoch's News Corporation was considered to be the international role model for the rest of the competition. Murdoch's mix of media properties was the envy of the industry; his record of innovation and aggressiveness was described as "brilliant" by Time, Inc. president N.J. Nicholas, according to the March 7, 1989, Wall Street *Journal.* One of News Corporation's great strengths was its history of not only gobbling up media properties, but—with few exceptions—turning them into even more profitable enterprises than they were before.

Total assets under News Corporation's control in 1989 were close to $12 billion. And, since Rupert Murdoch and his family owned 48 percent of the empire, he remained the single most influential media owner in the world.

Capital Cities/ABC was a massive media conglomerate itself, but not without substantial problems, the biggest one being the ABC television network which continued to limp along a distant third behind CBS and NBC. In addition to its eight television stations, Cap Cities owned twenty-one radio stations, 80 percent of cable sports channel ESPN, Women's Wear *Daily,* Hog Farm Management, an assortment of shopping guides, and it had recently made a foray into Europe by buying a stake in a West German television producer and distributor, as well as an all-European satellite sports service. But, while Capital Cities/ABC's annual sales were slightly higher than News Corporation's in 1989, the company lacked the overall international clout of the Murdoch empire.

Hachette S.A., the French company to whom Murdoch sold his half-interest in Elle, was founded in 1826 as a producer of school books. It was ranked fourth in the world in 1988 in terms of annual sales—$4.1 billion—and was regarded as a major international player since more than half of Hachette's revenue came from outside its own country. Hachette bought Grolier, Inc. and Diamandis Communications, Inc., two American publishers, in 1988, and it was well positioned for a long knock-down, drag-out fight internationally with the other media giants. It forged a partnership with Time, Inc. in February 1989 to publish magazines in Japan. It is only a question of time before Hachette acquires a stake in the burgeoning European television market.

Further down the ladder in terms of assets controlled and annual sales, but still forces to be reckoned with, were Sony Corp., Paramount Communications, Maxwell Communications, Walt Disney Co., MCA, Inc. and, of course, the two major U.S. television networks, CBS and NBC.

Sony, once strictly a manufacturer of consumer items, has been gradually diversifying into the communications industry. It was already the world's largest music producer in 1989 after its purchase of CBS Records. Sony attempted to buy MGM/UA Communications, Inc. in 1988; the talks broke down, but the company's interest in acquiring a major movie studio lingered on. And Sony now sells entertainment software to run on the hardware it has been selling for years past to consumers all over the world.

Paramount Communications owned the largest book publisher in the U.S., Simon & Schuster, as well as the country's most profitable movie studio in 1988, Paramount Pictures Corp. The company had also established a presence in broadcasting with the purchase of TVX Broadcast Group, Inc., owner of independent television stations.

Murdoch's old rival Robert Maxwell remained a threat in the international arena, but he was forced to consolidate his resources somewhat following a major buying binge. Maxwell Communications bought the book publisher Macmillan, Inc. for $2.51 billion in November 1988, a month after he purchased Dun & Bradstreet Corporation's Official Airlines Guides for $750 million. Maxwell was still looking for new properties the next year—most notably his failed bid for the National Enquirer—but he was considered to be over-leveraged and needed to spin off some holdings to pare down his debt. His annual sales for 1988 amounted to $1.4 billion, less than a third of Murdoch's News Corporation.

MCA, Inc. expanded its own media horizons beyond films and music with the acquisition of book publisher G.P. Putnam's Sons and a major independent television station. In 1989 the company was in the process of building a $500 million studio and theme park in Florida, but it was still a long way from seriously challenging the media giants in the international arena.

A newly rejuvenated Walt Disney Co., following a period of retrenchment, extended its interest beyond theme parks when it purchased some broadcast properties, including an independent television station in Los Angeles. The company's new management under CEO Michael Eisner was said to be aggressively interested in establishing a presence in European broadcasting, and was also well positioned to market its own entertainment products to much of its competition.

Among the two major American television networks, NBC—which is a division of General Electric—was in a better position than CBS to grow beyond its own broadcast operations. In 1989 NBC signed an agreement with Cablevision Systems, Inc. to jointly develop a broad variety of cable programs and services. At the same time, CBS remained bogged down with continuing problems in its own broadcasting network and was forced to concentrate primarily on them before entertaining any serious notions of expansion.

Rivalry between two of the giants became litigious in May 1989 when Murdoch's Sky Television sued Walt Disney Co. for $1.5 billion, charging it with violating a joint venture agreement to provide satellite programming in the U.K. The previous November, both companies agreed to own and operate two pay television channels in Great Britain—Sky Movies, which was a general entertainment channel, and the Disney Channel, featuring films and cartoons as well as other family programs.

According to the terms of the contract, each company was to contribute $75 million toward the venture, plus additional funds to acquire the films of other studios. In its suit, Sky Television claimed that Disney devised an elaborate scheme to back out of the deal in an attempt to renegotiate more favorable terms. A spokesman for Disney claimed that Sky Television had proceeded too quickly, without fully consulting with its partner.

"We have great regard for Mr. Murdoch and the accomplishments of his organizations," an unidentified spokesman said, according to the Wall Street *Journal* of May 16, 1989, "but we are surprised at his suit, which has no merit."

With the Americans and Europeans battling for dominance, a Canadian family suddenly tossed its own hat into the ring. The Thomson family controlled two large organizations: Thomson Newspapers Ltd. and the International Thomson Organization. In March 1989 the family proposed a merger of the two that would create a single media conglomerate with combined 1988 earnings of $472.5 million and total sales of $4.76 billion.

The Thomsons were best known for their strong presence in the Canadian and British newspaper industries, but less known was the fact that the two companies also derived a substantial portion of their revenues from magazines, electronic information services, travel and leisure operations, and books, including Jane's Fighting Ships, Medical Economics and Ward's Automotive Handbook. Combined assets under Thomson control at the time of the announced merger amounted to $5.3 billion.

While all this jockeying for position among the media giants was taking place in the early months of 1989, a new contender entered the arena from out of the blue, as it were. The new would-be media lord hailed from the country of Murdoch's birth, in the person of a brash 40-year-old Australian named Christopher Skase, the self-made son of a radio announcer. Young Skase made a quantum leap onto the fast track in the media world with his purchase of MGM/UA from financier Kirk Kirkorian.

One can't help thinking that Murdoch had to be looking over his shoulder with some degree of admiration, if not concern. Perhaps he remembered those heady days of over thirty years ago when another young Australian took over a failing newspaper that his recently deceased father had left him, and parlayed it over time into a $12 billion empire.

When Skase was twenty-five, just two years older than Murdoch was when he ventured into the newspaper business for the first time, he invested $15,000 Australian currency in a small investment company. The company later evolved into Qintex, a publicly traded firm that invested in diverse areas, including television stations, timberlands, real estate and an automobile distributorship.

In 1987 Qintex expanded into media in a big way with the purchase of several television stations from their owner at the time, John Fairfax Ltd. Skase turned the stations into the Channel 7 network, which became Australia's third commercial television network. Like Murdoch before him, Skase ventured northward into the United States when he acquired control of the Hal Roach Studios, Inc. and Robert Halmi, Inc., America's largest producer of television miniseries (the enormously successful "Lonesome Dove" was one of the company's productions).

By 1988, Christopher Skase had ascended to the ranks of Australia's 200 richest citizens, with an estimated net worth upwards of $65 million dollars Australian. A year later, following his acquisition of MGM/UA Communications for about $600 million U.S., the total assets under Qintex's control amounted to approximately $3.2 billion—or roughly 25 percent of those controlled by the News Corporation. Like Murdoch, Skase also believed in keeping his growing empire under his own control, with 51 percent of the shares under his direct ownership.

The purchase of MGM/UA amounted to "a quantum leap" for Skase, said one Australian stockbroker who was quoted in the Wall Street *Journal* of April 3, 1989. "If it works it is obviously a tremendous coup to go from where he came from to being one of the big players" in the United States.

"Our vision for UA," said Skase, according to the April 17, 1989, issue of Electronic Media, "is to bring it into a new era of superior film making that reflects contemporary issues, broad appeal, family values, and that has international implications."

A spokesman for Skase, Steven Mills, described his boss as a "visionary. He knows how to get where he wants to be and he's not going to be deterred."

Others close to the new Australian challenger in the world of international media suggested that Skase was likely to add a commercial U.S. television network to his empire within the next few years.

Visionary. A man who would not be deterred. Someone who knows exactly where he is going.

All these descriptions, and more, suited Rupert Murdoch as he forged his way to the top—and they still do today. The battle for influence and power, as well as for hundreds of millions of dollars in profits, in the world of media and communications can only grow more intense in the years ahead. It will be a war fought by visionaries and risk takers, modern-day warriors and empire builders whose weapons are genius, determination and courage instead of high-tech tools of destruction.

One thing remains certain: If anyone succeeds finally in knocking Rupert Murdoch from his throne, it will not be without a long and bitterly contested fight.

Chapter
Twenty-Nine

WHILE MURDOCH'S corporate headquarters remained in Sydney, Australia, his base of operations continued to be centered in New York, and his triplex apartment overlooking Fifth Avenue and Central Park remained his primary residence.

In 1989, Rupert and Anna Murdoch began to spend more time traveling back and forth between New York City and the huge Beverly Hills villa they bought from the estate of MCA founder Jules Stein, complete with its 18th-century antique furnishings, some of which Stein had purchased himself from William Randolph Hearst's legendary estate at San Simeon. Home to the Murdochs was also a ski house in the mountains of Aspen, Colorado, a flat in London and an estate outside Canberra, Australia.

The Murdochs' growing family was a visual reminder that time stopped for no one, not even the most powerful media lord on earth and his novelist wife. Their daughter Elisabeth, the oldest of their three children, was well along in college. Lachlan, the older of the two boys, would soon be ready to attend. And James, the youngest, attended the Horace Mann School in the Riverdale section of the Bronx and enjoyed going off on long bicycle rides with his friends. Prudence, Rupert's daughter from his first marriage, married an insurance broker named Crispin Odey in St. Michael's Church in London in 1985. She was twenty-six at the time.

Anna Murdoch's second novel, *Family Business,* dealing with the travails and successes of a woman media tycoon, was published by William Morrow & Co. in 1988 to a generally favorable critical reception. She discussed the novel with Cynthia Cotts of The Illustrated London News, who reported on the interview in August, 1988. Anna Murdoch insisted that the novel was not a roman-à-clef, despite the main character's similarity to her husband.

"I didn't want to write one of those," she said. "It would be too easy. And besides, Rupert or I might write an autobiography one day."

Anna maintained that she and Rupert both like to lead a low-profile social life because "a certain shabbiness and a certain quietness are important to us."

Nonetheless, Anna, who is a devout Roman Catholic, unlike her Presbyterian husband, is active in several church-related social causes that reflect her generally conservative views.

Good taste is important to both Anna and Rupert. Their Fifth Avenue triplex is done up in Chippendale, a baby grand piano and other elegant furnishings. The view of the Central Park reservoir from their slate terrace is befitting a man of his accomplishments and an attractive, successful novelist.

Love birds and canaries lend a chorus of birdsong in the background.

Thomas Kiernan reported on some marital strife between Rupert and Anna in his earlier biography, but quotes attributed to a couple of gossip columnists in Cynthia Cott's article paint a different picture.

"I've never heard of him fooling around," said one.

"I like to think they're the one happy couple left in New York," said another.

Now that Murdoch's debt-to-equity ratio was back down to a level that the banks found acceptable, he was able to continue his plans for expansion. In late May 1989 News Publishers Ltd. acquired world rights to Quickscan, an electronic publishing system that would enable TV Guide to be transmitted to viewers on videocassette recorders. Using the scanning function on a VCR, subscribers would be able to scroll up the contents of TV Guide if they chose, instead of reading it in print.

The inventor of the system was George Van Valkenburg, who operated Quickscan Systems Ltd. in Beverly Hills, California. Speaking of its benefits to Murdoch's organization, Van Valkenburg said, according to the May 29, 1989, issue of Electronic Media, "They recognize it as something that could possibly improve or substitute for a printed *TV Guide.*"

In June 1989 Murdoch's News America Publishing, Inc. said it planned to acquire a magazine called Soap Opera Digest from the Network Publishing Corporation. The biweekly publication chronicled the activities on daytime soaps and had a circulation of 1.2 million. Leslie Hinton, executive vice president of Murdoch Magazines, thought

Soap Opera Digest could dovetail nicely with TV Guide. "They have a lot in common," he said, according to the New York *Times* of June 6, 1989.

"We saw a magazine that went from 400,000 to 500,000 single-copy sales to 800,000 to 900,000 over the past four years. We think there is a lot of growth left, possibly as a weekly."

June 1, 1989 was a hot, muggy day in New York City. Rupert Murdoch was dressed in shirtsleeves and a loosened tie as he sat in his third-floor office above the Avenue of the Americas. He appeared to be in a reflective mood as he spoke about the past, as well as his plans for the future.

"How's the refinancing going?" I asked, referring to the private placement that First Boston was working on.

"It's going all right. Not as quickly as I'd hoped, but we'll come up with the minimum at least."

What would that be?

"A billion, but I was hoping it would be much bigger. We're going to wait and see about that."

Was it near completion?

"No, it's a couple of months away I think."

Would Murdoch shed any light on his plans for the future?

"Print media is still enormously influential," he said. "I enjoy that as much as ever. But, I think running a big public company driven by all the normal forces that exist out there in the business world takes us more and more towards the electronic industry.

"Technology's taken you a long way. And life style. And they're intermingled. There's no doubt that people are reading newspapers less than they used to. In some ways the newspapers are not as good as they used to be. At least, there's no choice of newspapers—which has partly something to do with the fact that fewer people read them and you don't have newspapers catering to different tastes. They can be very bland. They try to please everybody.

"I think the journalists in newspapers are losing a lot by not having a competitive situation. The economics of the game have moved. The popular press, not all the press, used to be a lot sharper. The writing, the urgency, they were much more important and evoked lovely skills there. You have to learn those skills today to compete with television news services. Some of those skills are the same, some aren't. I believe that the skills that came from writing and polishing words and editing words came about competitively, and are still of paramount importance if we take them into other branches of the media."

What are the major differences between newspaper and television news coverage today?

"If you watched CNN from the square in Beijing. People acutely interested in public affairs are one of the great events in history. They saw it happening. Now, the masses who watched that, they know enough to know what it's about. If you're highly educated, acutely interested in international affairs, you might actually buy an extra newspaper to read all about it. To get better depth to it. But it does change the nature of the game. You don't pick up your newspaper the next morning and read it for the first time, because you already know it.

"And that's made it very hard for newspapers," Murdoch continued. "There's more interpretation. There's more opinion. And very often more boredom, too, in the sense that you know a lot of it already. And there's more pontificating about it rather than bringing you that exciting news for the first time. That's a real difficulty. The cutting edge of news gathering and news telling has moved to the electronic area. No doubt about it."

I asked Murdoch if he found any time in his hectic schedule for leisure and relaxation.

"Yeah, I just had a pretty lazy weekend in Los Angeles," he said. "I work seven days a week. I'm doing something, take home work, I'm on the telephone. But I unwind a bit on weekends. I have a bit of tennis, skiing at Christmas. I'm not particularly athletic. I like spending time with Ann and time with the children. It's a normal existence, except that it's a bit more frenetic now that I'm here."

Has Rupert Murdoch changed his philosophy of doing business? Would he advise others starting out today to follow the same path he has over the years? Apparently so.

"We borrow, we don't pay dividends or we pay very few dividends relative to any other company," Murdoch said. "We put back the money always into the company. And the assets usually increase in value. We revalue them occasionally so we can borrow more to get the next asset. Very occasionally you sell some off. Either they've matured or you have to for some reason or another."

"It seems to have worked well for you," I said.

Rupert Murdoch looked at me and smiled. It was the smile of a man who had long ago grown accustomed to gambling—and winning.

Chapter
Thirty

"THE THINGS dissidents in the Iron Curtain countries are trying to move toward," Murdoch said in an interview just before Christmas, 1989, "free speech, free elections, free markets, are all things that the U.S. has had, more or less, for over two hundred years. And this leads us to a great truth, which being an immigrant perhaps I can see more objectively: modernization is Americanization. It is the American way of organizing society that is prevailing in the world."

I asked him why he seemed so bullish on America at a time when the rest of the world seemed to believe we had entered a stage of irreversible decline.

"The U.S. has been extremely lucky in its continental size, its natural resources, its hard-working population, its diversity," Murdoch said. "But the ultimate American resource is more intangible."

He quoted the Economist in a survey of Japan it had published a month or so before. The Japanese people, according to the Economist, were increasingly pessimistic about their country's chances of maintaining their widening economic gap over the United States. Eventually, the United States would reassert its dominance because of America's natural resources, the resilience of the people, and its ability to keep attracting the best and brightest talent from various countries.

"The twentieth century was the American century," Murdoch said, "and the twenty-first century will be the American century. Whatever the human race is going to achieve will probably be achieved here first. And this will continue as American institutions remain supple, which means that American policy makers have to respect open communications."

Murdoch ended our conversation on a philosophical note, paraphrasing Voltaire's statement that, in the eighteenth century, every man had two countries: his own and France.

"Today that's true of the U.S.," Murdoch said. "I exemplify this in my own family. My mother, now eighty, is Australian. One of my daughters lives in Britain. My other daughter will soon graduate from Vassar. And of course my wife and I are American citizens and we live in New York with our boys."

On a more mundane level, Murdoch's Fox Broadcasting Company seemed to have a better feel than his competitors did for what the youth of America wanted to see on television. As 1989 rolled to a close, 77 percent of Fox's viewers ranged in age from eighteen to forty-nine; by contrast, ABC's share of viewers in that age group was 63 percent, NBC's 59 percent, and CBS's 50 percent.

The youth market was particularly important since the lion's share of advertising dollars was targeted for the eighteen to forty-nine viewing audience. Fox's success in appealing to this market allowed the company to turn a $90 million loss in the 1988 season into a profit the following year.

Jamie Kellner, the president and chief executive of Fox, told the author that Fox had implemented its "youth strategy as a matter of survival. Younger people are much more likely to sample any new product," he said, "and they're more willing to scan the UHF dial of their TV set to find a program they like."

Murdoch was less successful, however, in launching his satellite television operation in the United Kingdom. The entire industry was facing gigantic production and financing troubles in 1989, and a poll conducted by Kensington Research of London revealed that less than 5 percent of Britons intended to buy a satellite receiving dish. As a result, Murdoch's Sky Television continued to reach the majority of its audience via the more expensive route of cable. Murdoch actually gave away over 10,000 free dishes early in 1989 in an attempt to get viewers accustomed to using the service, according to the July 10, 1989 issue of Advertising Age, but the gesture failed initially to achieve its intended goal. If anything, there was some speculation that it might have backfired since people tend to resist paying for a service they once got free of charge.

As far as the rest of the continent was concerned, the competition for viewers had turned into a "battle between Babel and the British Way"—between sending signals in many tongues or in the English language across the continent, according to Randall Rothenberg, writing in the August 15, 1989 New York *Times*. Murdoch's Sky Television, which originally intended to blanket Europe with programming in different languages, was forced to scale back to an English-language service because of enormous operating losses in its first year. Super Channel, a cable competitor of Murdoch, opted to go with a multilanguage strategy after losing money for two years on English-only broadcasts.

"There are two ways of looking at Pan-European television," said Derek W. Bowden, media director of Saatchi & Saatchi Advertising International in London, according to the same *Times* report. "One is thematic and the other is by language. Murdoch is adopting the thematic approach, while Super Channel is opting for the other side of the coin."

At the time, both approaches appeared to be light years away from anything approaching profitability.

The print side of Murdoch's empire in the United States was also beginning to show signs of strain in the closing days of 1989. In the struggle to boost both circulation and advertising pages at TV Guide, Murdoch launched a $10 million advertising campaign—an enormous amount by magazine standards. Rather than publishing one fall preview, as it had done in years past, TV Guide published five issues covering the lineup of new fall programs.

"The effort was an attempt to get some excitement back into TV Guide," according to Joseph Cece, president of the magazine. "We needed to send out a big message."

Murdoch had been criticized for sensationalizing the publication after he bought it. One issue contained a cover photograph of Oprah Winfrey's face superimposed on Ann-Margaret's body, something for which the editors apologized later. Other issues tended toward the tabloid in tone and content.

"The quality of the magazine and its covers has deteriorated noticably," said Cable Neuhaus, editor of TV Entertainment, a monthly cable magazine that competed with Murdoch's publication. "It's clear Murdoch will use the magazine as he likes. They are feeling pretty severe pressure to get their circulation back up so they are reaching for the lowest common denominator."

Neuhaus, of course, was not a nonpartisan observer, and his comments were refuted by TV Guide's president, Joseph Cece, who told me that the cover idea had come from Van Gordon Sauter, former president of CBS News. "You put things on the cover to sell the magazine," Cece said.

While TV Guide's circulation had declined 3.5 percent from a year earlier, it was still the most widely read weekly magazine with a paid circulation of over 16 million for the first six months of 1989. The publication's major problem was the same one endemic to the entire industry: declining advertising revenues. Ad pages in TV Guide dropped 7.6 percent to 1,607 pages for the same period, but magazines across the spectrum were all experiencing the same phenomenon.

With it all, Murdoch made it crystal clear that his primary emphasis in the future was going to be on the electronic side of his empire—films and television in the United States, and satellite television in Europe. He had been criticized more and more for using print revenues to subsidize the struggling electronic operations he had already launched. At a cultural festival in Edinburgh, Scotland in September 1989, Murdoch delivered a spirited defense of this strategy.

Sky Television, he said, was not merely a business venture; it was an answer to the ills of British television, which was controlled by a narrow elite that had contributed to Britain's postwar economic problems.

"The socially mobile are portrayed as uncaring," Murdoch was quoted as saying in the September 11, 1989 New York Times, "businessmen as crooks; money-making is to be despised. British television has been an integral part of the British disease."

These were fighting words, to be sure, and in speaking them Murdoch sounded more like a man on a geopolitical mission than like a businessman looking to turn a profit. He described Sky Television as "market led" rather than elite-driven, and responsive to viewer demands rather than entrenched cultural snobbishness. Murdoch's comments created as big a storm in the United Kingdom as had his earlier attacks on the anachronistic unions and their stranglehold over the British newspaper industry.

"Our critics cannot make up their minds," Murdoch said, "if Sky Television is a threat to the existing broadcasters or destined to be seen by fewer people than [have seen] the Loch Ness monster."

Murdoch had always believed that most attacks against him were politically motivated, and that if his views were more "socially acceptable" in Great Britain his critics would not be so alarmed by his presence. Commenting on this charge, one of Murdoch's spokesmen, Sky Television's corporate affairs director Jonathan Miller, pointed out that a typical day of programming might include coverage of the Bulgarian women's volleyball tournament, a talk show offering advice on marriage and family life, and an old movie starring Robert Mitchum and Jane Russell.

"So there it is," Miller said a bit sardonically, "the dreaded right-wing, down-market face of Murdochian television."

Murdoch was not merely interested in beaming American-style television programming into the United Kingdom and Europe. He regarded the fall of the Berlin Wall and the push for democratic reforms in the Soviet Union and Eastern and Central Europe as nothing short of revolutionary. With communications markets opening up behind what had once been known as the Iron Curtain, Murdoch was determined to be among the first to establish a presence there. In the fall of 1989 his News Corporation acquired 50 percent shares of two Hungarian newspapers, *Reform* and *Mai Nap.* Around the same time he also bought a 25 percent interest in Grupo Zeta, a leading Spanish magazine and newspaper publisher.

Chapter
Thirty-One

M URDOCH'S AMBITIOUS program of expansion suffered
something of a setback in the early days of 1990. His style
of doing business, of increasing the size of his empire by
borrowing against assets and leveraging himself to the hilt,
had served him and many other successful businessmen well
throughout the 1970s and 1980s.

Donald Trump had created a real estate and gambling kingdom by utilizing essentially the same techniques. Robert
Campeau of Canada and Australians Alan Bond and Christopher Skase had amassed fortunes of their own by borrowing,
acquiring, and growing.

Then, suddenly, as the new decade began, the old rules no
longer seemed to be working. Campeau, Skase and Bond filed
for bankruptcy, and Trump skated dangerously close to it,
saved only at the eleventh hour by some bank refinancing.

The art of leveraging works as long as the assets acquired
keep appreciating and cash flow is sufficient to service all the

interest payments. This had been the case with all the titans, Murdoch included, for a couple of decades. Buy low with borrowed money, watch your investment grow in value, then borrow against it to buy something else. On a smaller scale, many homeowners had done precisely that by mortgaging their homes, which kept on rising in value, and using the proceeds from the sale to buy second and third homes and other investment real estate.

No sooner had the decade of the nineties gotten started when the unthinkable took place. The economy slowed, not just in the United States, but in Europe and other areas as well. People lost their jobs, and their incomes dried up. Their houses stopped appreciating, and in some cases, actually depreciated, and they could no longer meet their mortgage obligations. The financial giants of the era were not exempt from the economic sluggishness. Revenues from their varied and assorted operations fell off, and they had trouble paying the interest on their loans. The assets they owned—real estate, gambling casinos, newspapers, TV stations, film studios— were worth less and less as profits declined, and the equity in those investments began to shrivel.

By the spring of 1990, Murdoch felt the financial pinch along with all the others. He was still over $7 billion in debt, Sky Television was losing somewhere around $3.2 million a week and the losses were expected to reach almost $200 million by the end of the year, News Corporation's overall earnings were off 67 percent in the first half of the most recent fiscal year, interest rates were rising again, the pilots at Ansett Airlines were on strike, and it was clear that something had to go.

Murdoch shocked the financial community in March when he announced that he was selling his big money-making tabloid, the Star, to the owners of the rival National Enquirer for

$400 million in cash and stock. Most analysts did not expect that he would let go of the lucrative Star, and believed he would strip off other assets instead. The fact that he did agree to let go of the weekly tabloid was indicative of just how serious his financial crunch was.

"We're in shock," Barry Levine, the Star's Hollywood bureau chief, told the author. "Up until this moment, we and the Enquirer have been bitter enemies."

Jim Brady, former Star editor, columnist and author, wondered only half-jokingly whether Murdoch might be able to regain control of the publication since he took half of the selling price in stock. "Is that possible, or have I spent too much time drinking with Australians in Tim Costello's bar?"

Knowing the way Murdoch operated, nothing was too far-fetched, which is what I told him in a phone conversation in April, 1990.

Without admitting that he was in trouble, Murdoch did say that he would concentrate more on improving earnings at News Corporation in the future and less on making new acquisitions.

"We are not going to purchase anything major," he said. "We are sorting out our portfolio of media assets. Our main concentration is going to be on developing our earnings."

Publicly, Murdoch continued to insist that he was not under financial pressure to sell off assets and raise cash, but by April 1990, losses at Sky Television had already climbed to more than $400 million, and by his own admission he anticipated losses totaling $600 million before Sky Television began to turn a profit by the end of 1991.

Most analysts thought even that assessment was overly optimistic.

"We're going to grow organically," Murdoch was quoted as saying in the April 12, 1990 issue of the Wall Street *Journal*.

"We've got to restore and increase our profits before we can look at any major purchases."

Murdoch's ambitious plan to raise $1 billion through a private placement, which I had discussed with him a year earlier, had not been successful. Less than half that amount had been lined up and the deal was jettisoned. "We failed to make the thing fly," Murdoch said. Consequently, News Corporation had been unable to pay off a significant portion of its debt, and that debt load had actually risen when Harper & Collins's obligations had to be taken back on the parent company's balance sheet.

While many of Murdoch's traditional enemies were waiting for him finally to take a great fall, some analysts were encouraged by his sale of the Star and expected him to turn things around.

"Murdoch has been able to start numerous businesses such as the Fox network from scratch," said Karen Firestone, a money manager at Fidelity Management and Research Corporation in Boston, according to the same issue of the Wall Street *Journal.* "If he just works on what he's got without starting another venture somewhere, maybe the market will begin to respond."

The great challenge for Murdoch, it seemed, would be to stem the flow of red ink at Sky Television before it bankrupted his entire empire. News Corporation's profits for the first nine months of the fiscal year ending June 30, 1990 plunged 74 percent from the same period a year earlier. Heavy cash drain at Sky Television, plus the seven-month-long pilots' strike at Ansett, were primarily responsible for the decline.

The true measure of Murdoch's problems was apparent in May 1990, when he sold J.B. Lippincott, a medical publishing division of HarperCollins, to a Dutch scientific and technical publisher for $250 million. The sale to Wolters Kluwer N.V. was completed after a vigorous auction involving a number of publishing giants.

"We think we paid a fair price," said Bruce Lenz, the senior vice president of the acquiring company's U.S. unit, as reported in the New York *Times* of May 22, 1990. "Although it was at the higher end of presale estimates. We aim to develop the international side of Lippincott's business."

At the same time, Advertising Age published a story that Murdoch was also shopping around TV Guide for a prospective buyer because of difficulties at that publication, but Murdoch rigorously denied that it was true. He went so far as to threaten a lawsuit, and he said he would pay Rance Crain, president of the company that owned Ad Age, $1 million if he could identify anyone who had held discussions with News Corporation about the sale of TV Guide. Crain responded in a column he wrote himself, entitled "Rupert, thanks but no bet," appearing in the May 28, 1990 issue of his magazine. Crain ended his piece with the speculation that, by publicizing the situation with the threat of a lawsuit and the offer of $1 million, Murdoch "was calling more attention to the story than it normally would have gotten."

"Could it be," Crain wrote, "that Mr. Murdoch, in his own unique style, was trying to drum up buyers for TV Guide after his earlier, lower-key efforts had failed?"

"We're definitely regrouping. You shorten sail when the barometer drops," said John Evans, president of Murdoch Magazines and an avid sailor. "Murdoch has always been able to handle down markets and we're definitely not withdrawing, but rather consolidating our operations."

Other Murdoch observers believed that the media baron

would weather the financial storm, but with some degree of difficulty. "The question is, did he start being careful soon enough?" an analyst who requested anonymity said. "Thank God he didn't go ahead and buy MGM/UA. That really would have strained him to the limits. The banks are more nervous now than ever, so it's going to be more and more difficult to get money out of them."

No more borrowing? If so, that would definitely put a crimp in Murdoch's style of doing business in the years ahead, but perhaps the inability to borrow at will would be the tonic that could save him in the longer term. It might force him to sell off assets and raise cash before he acquired other assets, and adopt a more conservative financial posture. During the spring and early summer of 1990, Murdoch had let go of approximately $880 million worth of assets, including the Star, real estate and book publishing operations in Australia, and his equity in the South China *Morning Post*. At the same time, he had been careful to minimize his need to liquidate properties so as not to depress the prices he could fetch for other assets he might need to sell in the future. It was a delicate balancing act, but one he had been performing deftly so far.

Murdoch's ability to turn things around in the end depended to a great extent on the success of Sky Television. All along, he had maintained that his enormous television operation in the United Kingdom and on the continent would become profitable by the end of 1991. Many observers thought this scenario was a shade too optimistic but, in any case, Murdoch was prepared, he said, to support Sky Television until 1994 if he had to. It was a big gamble; if Sky Television went under, it would be a symbolic as well as a financial failure for Murdoch.

News Corporation's profits plunged significantly in fiscal

year 1990, but not as severely as some analysts had been expecting. Earnings came in at $282.3 million Australian against $496.5 million Australian the year before (at the time the Australian dollar was worth about 80 cents American). "This is above my estimate," said Carla Bakker, a media analyst at Morgan Stanley, according to the August 24, 1990 New York *Times*. "My sense is they have reached the bottom of the curve."

Perhaps. Despite its sale of assets, however, the company's overall debt remained forbiddingly high at about $7.5 billion U.S. currency. Taking advantage of Australia's accounting rules, Murdoch used the opportunity to revalue his company's assets upward by about $3 billion Australian (U.S. $2.4 billion), thus bringing his debt–equity ratio down to 0.9 to 1. But this was merely an accounting tactic designed to dress up the balance sheet. The bottom line in the end for Murdoch would be his ability to continue covering his debt service with cash-flow revenues. If inflow continued to surpass outflow, he would survive and prosper, as he had in the past.

Therein lay the risk. There were some signs that Sky Television was beginning to catch on in the United Kingdom. Installation of satellite dishes was rising, and Murdoch's service reached 1.6 million British homes in the summer of 1990. But the jury was still out. Risk, of course, was nothing new to Murdoch. This was only the latest in a series of risks that had elevated him to the heights of the communications industry. And he would live or die on the outcome—until the next opportunity came along.

Postscript

IN AN article he wrote for the Winter 1989 issue of the Gannett Center Journal, First Boston media analyst Richard J. MacDonald discussed the differences between what he called the "monster" entrepreneurs and the "builder" entrepreneurs. A monster entrepreneur, according to MacDonald, is in it strictly for the money. He or she is motivated by greed and is only concerned with the question: How fast can I get the cash out?

The builders, on the other hand, acquire a property, invest heavily in it, sometimes for years before it begins to show a profit, and in the end the acquired property is stronger and healthier than it was before the acquisition.

Among the builder entrepreneurs in the field of media, MacDonald states, "Rupert Murdoch is the one most in the mold of the old publishing barons. Murdoch is very much a publisher. The TV Guide deal was classic Murdoch. He spent

$3 billion, which is probably rather too much; but . . . it generates over $200 million in pretax profit, so Murdoch is not quite going to cover his interest at 10 percent. But asset sales will reduce his debt. [At some point his] revenues will go up, his costs will stay the same, and he will cover the interest expense without even thinking about it."

In a single paragraph, MacDonald presents perhaps the best argument against those who have sought to link Murdoch with the so-called greenmail specialists whose names have been adorning the headlines of our daily newspapers for years past. Like him or not, Rupert Murdoch builds things—newspapers, magazines, television networks and more; he does not strip them down and dispose of assets simply to turn a profit.

Murdoch, according to MacDonald, is "always trying to build readership. Over the past three years, his revenues worldwide have gone from about $900 million to more than $3 billion—$4 billion with TV Guide. His annual cash flow has gone from about $200 million to more than $800 million."

There are other media lords, to be sure, who are working to create and expand upon their own empires, to utilize the new technology and blend it with the world of print in the communications revolution that is rapidly changing life on earth in dramatic and startling ways. We've talked about most of them in the course of this book; others, following in the footsteps of those who led the way, are certain to burst upon the scene in the years ahead.

But Rupert Murdoch—and it is for the reader to decide whether it is for better or worse—was one of the pioneers. Today he is perhaps the most successful pioneer of all, and he is certainly the most influential and powerful single individual in the world of media and communications. Some have argued that he is simply adept at making grand acquisitions, the ultimate gambler who enjoys risk and has been fortunate enough to have luck and timing on his side which enabled him to pyramid his holdings into an empire. Others say no one's luck lasts that long, that Murdoch—like most successful people—makes his own luck through hard work and effort, by hiring the right people to do a job and replacing them quickly when they fail.

After interviewing Murdoch myself, plus dozens of his colleagues, associates, business partners, writers, editors and others who have dealt with him in one capacity or another over the years, I've arrived at some conclusions of my own.

First, Murdoch is driven by forces I don't think he himself fully understands. When I asked him what drives him, he seemed a bit perplexed, as though he didn't quite know what to make of the question. He simply does what he does because he has to; it's in his nature to work and plan and strive and achieve, and I don't believe he's taken a lot of time to analyze what's behind it all. He doesn't strike me as a terribly introspective man. He's careful with people, guarded, concerned about his public image. He's received a lot of bad press over the years, and I think it bothers him more than he cares to admit to himself.

Second, he's a prototypical workaholic. If the word didn't exist, it would have to have been coined to fit him. He can't stop. His average day is crammed full with meetings, telephone calls to and from editors, bankers, executives, managers, lawyers, politicians and other dignitaries. There's barely a second of his time that's unaccounted for. He emanates a kind of raw energy, an intelligent force that's akin to and interrelated with power. He is said to get along on four hours sleep a night, and you find yourself surprised that he has any time to sleep at all.

POSTSCRIPT

Third, Murdoch is very much what has come to be called a hands-on CEO. He delegates much authority and responsibility to his executives, but he is intimately involved with what is going on in every corner of his empire. In the old days, when he was a newspaperman first and a businessman second, he truly enjoyed writing headlines and sub-heads, laying out pages, dirtying his hands with ink and putting his personal stamp on the printed pages. Today, as film and television and electronic communications have shunted print more and more into the background, he is less closely involved with the actual production of his products, and more dependent on the talents of those he has handpicked to run those enterprises.

Fourth, I think this bothers him more than just a little. Newspapers are his area of total competence; the world of electronic communications is too sprawling and many sided for any single individual to understand fully. Thus, Murdoch needs to hire more and more outside experts, and that leads to a kind of dependency on them which does not sit comfortably on his shoulders.

Fifth, Murdoch's great strength is his genius in understanding—instinctively, it seems—exactly what must be done to turn a losing property into a successful one. He has done this time and time again, not only with failing newspapers, but more recently with Fox Television. It is too glib to say that he accomplishes this by pandering to public tastes with his own brand of tabloid journalism. For better or worse, the demand is there and Murdoch has demonstrated a unique capability of beating out his competition in the race to meet it. Murdoch has never denied that he manufactures mass market products; they pay the bills for his quality publications, and this has been a fact of economic life throughout human history. It affects every industry.

Sixth, Murdoch is a tough negotiator, a rough-and-tumble competitor in a highly competitive field. He is smart, calculating, shrewd. He can be a bit rough on those who have crossed him, but even his detractors admit that he is enormously generous to those who have been loyal to him. He is an innovator. To a great extent, he has set the pace for much of what has been happening in the world of media and communications today. One of the definitions of the word *revolutionary* is someone who changes the existing order "fundamentally or completely."

No one will question that the existing order in the way we receive information, conduct business, perform routine tasks such as shopping and enjoy our entertainment is undergoing fundamental and maybe even complete change. In that sense, Murdoch—ironically, a man who by his own admission is singularly conservative in style and opinion—stands as one of the preeminent revolutionists of the era.

Perhaps, in the end, the final word should belong to Murdoch himself. When William H. Meyers of the New York *Times* asked Murdoch how he evaluated William Randolph Hearst, a man to whom Murdoch has frequently been compared, the media lord replied, "Hearst had great gifts . . . But he was a spoiled boy, self-indulgent. I'm more Presbyterian, Calvinistic, more Scottish."

Were there other role models in his life? What about his own father?

"I'm my own man," said Rupert Murdoch.

No one will argue with that.

Appendix

In 1989 Murdoch controlled approximately $12 billion in assets worldwide. As of this writing, Murdoch's current assets are approximately $6.7 billion because of sales and depreciation.

MAJOR HOLDINGS WORLDWIDE

United States

NEWSPAPERS

The Boston Herald   San Antonio Express-News

MAGAZINES

New York   New Woman
TV Guide   Sportswear International
Seventeen   Mirabella
Daily Racing Form   Sports Travel
Premiere (50%)   In Fashion
Automobile

APPENDIX

BOOK PUBLISHING

HarperCollins
Zondervan

Salem House

TELEVISION AND FILMS

20th Century Fox Film
  Corporation
Fox Broadcasting Company
DeLuxe Laboratories
Fox Television Stations:
  KDAF—Dallas;

KRIV—Houston; KTTV—Los
Angeles; WFLD—Chicago;
WNYW—New York;
WTTG—Washington, D.C.;
WFXT—Boston (held in
trust)

COMMERCIAL PRINTING

World Printing

MAGAZINE DISTRIBUTION

Murdoch Magazines

Australia and the Pacific Basin

NEWSPAPERS

The Australian
The Courier Mail and the
  Sunday Mail (46%)
Quest Media Group (46%),
  includes 11 titles in Brisbane
  and suburbs
Gold Coast Bulletin (46%)
Daily Mirror
The Daily Telegraph and
  Sunday Telegraph
Sportsman
Cumberland Newspaper

Group, includes 21 titles in
  and around Sydney
Cairns Post
FNQ Sunday
Tablelands Advertiser
North Queensland Newspaper
  Group
Townsville Bulletin
The Herald
The Sun News-Pictorial
The Weekly Times
Sporting Globe

APPENDIX

Bendigo Advertiser
Geelong Advertiser
Leader Media Group, includes
  28 titles in Melbourne and
  suburbs
Wimmera Mail Times (67%)
The Mercury
The Sunday Tasmanian
Tasmanian Country
The Treasure Islander
Derwent Valley Gazette
The Advertiser
Messenger Press Group,
  includes 12 titles in Adelaide
  and suburbs

Sunday Mail (South Australia)
Sunday Times (Western
  Australia)
Northern Territory News
Sunday Territorian
Centralian Advocate
Sunday Morning Post (Hong
  Kong)
The Fiji Times
The Sunday Times (Fiji)
Nai Lalakai (Fiji language)
Shanti Dut (Hindi language,
  Fiji)
Post Courier (63%) in Papua
  New Guinea

MAGAZINES

New Idea
TV Week (50%)
Australasian Post
Epicurean
Home Beautiful

Family Circle
Better Homes & Gardens (50%)
Your Garden
Pacific Islands Monthly

COMMERCIAL PRINTING

Progress Press
Norman Keppell (46%)
Brownhall Printing
Spectron Print
Wilke Directories
Wilke Color
Leader Westernport Printing
West Web Printers
Griffin Press
Multiform Business Systems

Giganticolor
Computer Graphics
Prestige Litho
Queensland Tourist
  Publications
Willmetts Printers
Mercury Walch
Prestige Colorprint (46%)
National Paper Vuepak

APPENDIX

OTHER OPERATIONS

Ansett Transport
  Industries (50%)
East West Airlines (50%)
Australian Newsprint Mills
  (50%)
Computer Power (26%)

Festival Records
F.S. Falkiner & Sons
Gordon & Gotch
Independent Newspapers (40%)
Lanray Industries
Sunshine Plantation (46%)

United Kingdom

NEWSPAPERS

The Times
The Sunday Times
The Sun

The News of the World
Today

BOOK PUBLISHING

William Collins
Times Books
Robert Nicholson Publications

John Bartholomew & Son
Geographia Ltd.

MAGAZINES

Sky (50%)
The Times Educational
  Supplement
The Times Higher Education
  Supplement

The Times Literary
  Supplement
Trader

COMMERCIAL PRINTING

Eric Bemrose

TELEVISION

Sky Television

Sky Channel

APPENDIX

OTHER OPERATIONS

Pearson P.L.C. (20%)

Reuters P.L.C. (8%)

Convoys Group

The Times Network for
   Schools

Reform and *Mai Nap*
   (Hungarian newspapers)
   (50%)

Townsend Hook & Co.

Utell

Martins (30%)

Circle K (U.K.) (50%)

News Datacom (60%)

Grupo Zeta (25%)

It is worth noting that Ansett, which is 50 percent owned by Murdoch, is one of the two major domestic airlines in Australia. Through Ansett, Murdoch also owns Ansett New Zealand, Ansett Fair Freight, 25 percent of the Chilean airline Ladeco, 20 percent of America West based in Phoenix. Ansett also manages Polynesian Airways for the Western Samoan government, and Cook Islands International, which operates between Rarotonga and Sydney, and it operates Sydney-Vanuatu Services under license to Australia's big international carrier Qantas.

Remuneration of Directors and Executives

Directors

Aggregate of income received or due and
receivable by Directors of The News
Corporation Limited

$10,895 $16,535 $10,895 $16,535 $10,895 $16,535 $10,895 $16,535

The number of holding company Directors is
shown in their relevant income bands:

$	1988	1987
20,001 – 30,000	1	
50,001 – 60,000		1
60,001 – 70,000		2
70,001 – 80,000	1	
100,001 – 110,000	1	
130,001 – 140,000		1
160,001 – 170,000	1	

$	1988	1987
300,001 – 310,000	1	
360,001 – 370,000		1
440,001 – 450,000		1
480,001 – 490,000	2	
630,001 – 640,000		1
660,001 – 670,000	1	
670,001 – 680,000	1	

Remuneration band	Number
180,001 – 190,000	1
190,001 – 200,000	1
200,001 – 210,000	1
210,001 – 220,000	1
250,001 – 260,000	1
280,001 – 290,000	1

Remuneration band	Number
780,001 – 790,000	1
1,060,001 – 1,070,000	1
1,330,001 – 1,340,000	1
1,720,001 – 1,730,000	1
1,830,001 – 1,840,000	1
4,190,001 – 4,200,000	1
10,180,001 – 10,190,000	1

Total remuneration received, including salaries and other benefits as employees, or due and receivable by Directors of subsidiary companies in the Group and Directors of the holding company from respective corporations and related corporations was $34,597,000. The inclusion of figures following the acquisition of subsidiaries during 1988 does not permit meaningful comparison with 1987. At 30 June 1988 outstanding loans to Directors of subsidiaries amounted to $4,548,000 (1987 $4,080,000) and loans to Directors of the holding company amounted to $2,941,000 (1987 $3,373,000).

Aggregate amount paid to persons in a prescribed office or to a prescribed superannuation fund in connection with the retirement of those persons from the prescribed office was $625,000. The Directors consider that having regard to the number of Directors to whom payments relate and the nature of the payments the provision of full particulars would be unreasonable. Comparative figures for 1987 have not been presented as that information cannot be specified without unreasonable expense or delay.

Executives

Aggregate of income received or due and
receivable by the executive officers including
executive Directors

	$110,078	$113,071	$110,078	$113,071	$10,655	$16,275

The number of executive officers of the Group whose income was at least $85,000 is shown in their relevant income bands:

$	1988	1987	$	1988	1987	$	1988	1987
85,000 – 94,999	128	121	325,000 – 334,999	1	1	665,000 – 674,999	1	
95,000 – 104,999	88	91	335,000 – 344,999	1	1	675,000 – 684,999	1	1
105,000 – 114,999	81	55	345,000 – 354,999	3	3	705,000 – 714,999		3
115,000 – 124,999	46	51	355,000 – 364,999	2	5	735,000 – 744,999	1	1
125,000 – 134,999	39	32	365,000 – 374,999	1	4	745,000 – 754,999	1	1
135,000 – 144,999	43	39	375,000 – 384,999	1	1	755,000 – 764,999		
145,000 – 154,999	34	25	385,000 – 394,999	4	3	765,000 – 774,999	1	1
155,000 – 164,999	30	20	395,000 – 404,999	2	1	775,000 – 784,999		1
165,000 – 174,999	31	14	425,000 – 434,999	1	1	785,000 – 794,999		
175,000 – 184,999	27	17	435,000 – 444,999	1		845,000 – 854,999	1	1
185,000 – 194,999	13	19	445,000 – 454,999		2	855,000 – 864,999		
195,000 – 204,999	10	10	455,000 – 464,999	1		865,000 – 874,999	1	1
205,000 – 214,999	11	10	465,000 – 474,999	1		895,000 – 904,999	1	
215,000 – 224,999	3	4	475,000 – 484,999		1	1,005,000 – 1,014,999	1	1
225,000 – 234,999	10	9	485,000 – 494,999	3	1	1,065,000 – 1,074,999	1	1

Number of executives in each income band — The News Corporation Limited and its subsidiaries (world wide)

Income band ($A)		
235,000 – 244,999	3	7
245,000 – 254,999	2	7
255,000 – 264,999	6	4
265,000 – 274,999	4	3
275,000 – 284,999	5	7
285,000 – 294,999	5	3
295,000 – 304,999	4	3
305,000 – 314,999		2
315,000 – 324,999	2	3
495,000 – 504,999	1	
505,000 – 514,999		1
525,000 – 534,999	1	1
545,000 – 554,999	1	
565,000 – 574,999		1
575,000 – 584,999		1
595,000 – 604,999	1	
625,000 – 634,999		1
635,000 – 644,999		1
1,155,000 – 1,164,999	1	
1,325,000 – 1,334,999	1	
1,485,000 – 1,494,999	1	1
1,725,000 – 1,734,999	1	1
1,835,000 – 1,844,999	1	
1,845,000 – 1,854,999	1	1
1,945,000 – 1,954,999	1	
2,045,000 – 2,054,999		1
4,185,000 – 4,194,999	1	1
10,175,000 – 10,184,999	1	1

The number of executive officers of the holding company whose income was at least $85,000 is shown in their relevant income bands:

Income band ($A)	Number
105,000 – 114,999	1
135,000 – 144,999	1
185,000 – 194,999	1
195,000 – 204,999	1
205,000 – 214,999	1
215,000 – 224,999	1
255,000 – 264,999	1
285,000 – 294,999	1
295,000 – 304,999	1
365,000 – 374,999	1
445,000 – 454,999	1
485,000 – 494,999	2
635,000 – 644,999	1
665,000 – 674,999	1
675,000 – 684,999	1
785,000 – 794,999	1
1,065,000 – 1,074,999	1
1,325,000 – 1,334,999	1
1,725,000 – 1,734,999	1
1,835,000 – 1,844,999	1
4,185,000 – 4,194,999	1
10,175,000 – 10,184,999	1

The above tables cover executives of The News Corporation Limited and its subsidiaries on a world wide basis and include salaries, performance bonuses and other benefits translated to Australian dollars.

SHAREHOLDER INFORMATION
At 8 August, 1988

Corporate Ownership

Number of shareholders	13,626

Distribution of shareholding	
1 — 1,000	8,037
1,001 — 5,000	3,840
5,001 — 10,000	861
10,001 and over	888
	13,626

The company's register of substantial shareholders shows that the Cruden Investments Pty. Limited group holds 116,133,648 ordinary shares. The twenty largest shareholders held 199,554,291 ordinary shares equal to 75.00% of issued ordinary shares.

Top twenty shareholders as at 8 August, 1988.

Cruden Investments Pty Limited and subsidiary companies	116,133,648
National Nominees Limited	19,384,125
I.S.I.T. Nominees Pty. Limited	10,611,890
A N Z Nominees Limited	8,198,721
Corcarr Nominees Pty. Limited	6,435,510
Bank of New South Wales Nominees Pty. Limited	5,836,698
The Colonial Mutual Life Assurance Society Limited	5,061,520
Pendal Nominees Pty. Limited	4,690,176
Indosuez Nominees Pty. Limited	4,181,673
News Nominees Pty Limited	4,159,424
Australian Mutual Provident Society	2,363,140
Superannuation Fund Investment Trust	2,145,540
MLC Life Limited	2,116,050
The National Mutual Life Assoc of A/Asia Limited	1,751,140
Capita Financial Group Limited	1,191,400
ICIANZ Pension Fund Securities Pty. Limited	1,100,160
Stephenson & Watt Pty. Limited	1,085,200
Wardley Australia Nominees Pty. Limited	1,068,406
Government Insurance Office of N.S.W.	1,043,950
News Corporation Nominees Pty. Limited	995,920
	199,554,291

Index

295

INDEX

INDEX

INDEX

INDEX

INDEX

Rees-Mogg, Sir William 28, 81–83, 188–89
Reidy, John 222–24, 249
Reinking, Ann 90
"Reporters, The" 228, 230
Reuters Holdings P.L.C. 203, 216–19, 223–24, 247; Globex, 216–17
Rich, Marc 26, 132
Rifkin, Sandra 239
Ritch, Herald 172, 174
Robert Halmi, Inc. 256
Robinowitz, Joe 101
Rogers, Kenny 133
Rohatyn, Felix 52, 60–61
Rolling Stone (magazine) 58–59
Ross, Steve 118, 120, 249–51
Rothermere, Lord 159
Royko, Mike 112–13
Rubenstein, Howard J. 50, 135
Russell, Barbara 115, 117

Saatchi & Saatchi, P.L.C. 25, 39, 212–15, 235
Safire, William 95
St. Regis Corporation 123–28
Salem House 147, 176
Sarazen, Richard A. 123, 199–200
Satellite Business Systems (SBS) 103–104
Schanberg, Sydney H. 93
Schein, Harvey L. 104
Schiff, Dorothy 50–52, 68–69
Schwartz, Peter 217
Securities & Exchange Commission 115
Seegal, Frederic M. 222
Select Magazines, Inc. 244
Senate Committee on Banking, Housing & Urban Affairs 6, 77
Senate Commerce Committee 135
Seventeen 199–201
Shapiro, Geri 21
Sharkey, Betsy 226–27
Shea, Michael 110
Sheehy, Gail 50, 53, 57–59, 61
Sheehy, Maura 227
Shuman, Stanley S. 50, 61, 73–74, 90, 103, 123, 221
Sigler, Andrew C. 127–28
Silha, Otto A. 96
Simon & Schuster 173, 253

Singerman, Martin 199–200
"60 Minutes" 228, 230
Skase, Christopher 255–57
Sky Channel 208
Sky Movies 254
Sky Television 86, 205, 207–213, 254–55, 267, 269–270, 272–73, 277
Skyband, Inc. 104, 109
Slattery, Bill 170
Smith, Adam 210
Snyder, Richard E. 173
Soap Opera Digest 261–62
Sony Corporation 250, 252–53
South China Morning Post 18, 163, 276
Sports Travel 241–42
Squadron, Howard 21, 50, 78, 91
Squires, Jim 113
Star, The (weekly) 48–450, 53, 61, 101, 199, 225, 227–28, 242, 272–73; RM launches, 48–49
Stark, Howard E. 136
Stark, Kathleen ("Koo") 109–10
Stein, Jules 259
Stern, Leonard 140
Stigwood, Robert 89–90
Stone, Gerald 228
Straus, Roger 174
Strauss, Robert 78
Styles, Jim 208
Sulzberger, Arthur Ochs 245
Sunday Times (London) 42–43, 51, 81–86, 181; RM acquires, 81–82
Sydney (Australia) Daily Telegraph 15–16, 37–39; RM acquires, 37–38
Sydney Mirror 15–17, 19–20, 37

tabloid television 30, 227, 330–32, 234
Talese, Gay 58
Tartikoff, Brandon 231
TCF Holding Company, Inc. 132
telecommunications companies 146, 145–46; AT&T, 146, 246; ITT, 146; MCI, 146; NYNEX, 246; Sprint, 146; Telecom USA, 146
television: advertising on, 231–35; network, decline in, 231–35; KNBN-TV (Dallas-Ft. Worth), 136; KRIV-TV (Houston), 136; KTTV (Los Angeles), 136–37; WCVB-TV (Boston), 135; WFLD-TV

INDEX